Heather Muell

MW00472840

Testimonials

"It has been said that success or failure is usually determined on the drawing board. David's insight is a great guide for any company executive or entrepreneur to apply original thinking before taking their business initiatives forward."

- Christopher A. Marlett, CEO, MDB Capital Group

"Wanetick's analysis of business models is multi-dimensional and unique. Jam packed with practical advice."

- Reid Drescher, Chief Investment Officer, Cape One Advisors

"Business Model Validation distills over two decades of conducting painstaking company and industry research down to a readable book filled with valuable insights unavailable anywhere else."

- David Sterman, Market Strategist, StreetAuthority.com

"David Wanetick provides an exhaustive but easy to read review of the key metrics needed to assess business models. Business Model Validation is packed with hundreds of examples from a wide variety of industries. This work is a wise investment for all analysts, investors, bankers and entrepreneurs looking for an edge."

- David T. Foster, Partner, 1624 Capital LLC

"Brilliant. No one tackles the subject of evaluating business models with as much rigor as David Wanetick in Business Model Validation."

- Steven Dresner, Founder & CEO, Dealflow.com

"David Wanetick synthesizes over twenty years of industry and company analysis into a very readable and enjoyable book. Business Model Validation is ideal for anyone that wants to sharpen their analytical skills. Decision-makers and investors at all levels will learn powerful lessons from these pages."

- Jeffrey Kadlic, Co-Founder & Managing Partner, Evolution Capital Partners

"In an era of evolving business models, David delivers to us a beacon and a guide post as to what works and what doesn't in both established and emerging industries. If your company operates in a dynamic environment, this is a must read for your executive team."

- Andrew J. Sherman, Partner, Jones Day, Author of *Harvesting Intangible Assets* and 20+ related titles on business growth and strategy

Business Model Validation

What Makes Business Models Work?

David Wanetick
Chief Executive Officer
Business Model Validation &
Certified Emerging Company Analyst

ISBN: 978-0-692-36956-2 (hc)
ISBN: 978-1-4834-2692-1 (e)

Library of Congress Control Number: 2015903398

Because of the dynamic nature of the Internet, any web addresses or links contained in this book may have changed since publication and may no longer be valid. The views expressed in this work are solely those of the author and do not necessarily reflect the views of the publisher, and the publisher hereby disclaims any responsibility for them.

Business Development Academy rev. date: 2/27/2015

Dedication

נעמי היקרה,

עד הסוף, יחד.

בשמחה.

To my children ~

Daniel, Zoe and Zachary

Never be afraid to ask questions.

Never go to sleep until you learn something.

Contents

Business Model Analysis

Analysis of Emerging Business Models

Analysis of Selected Traditional Business Models

Selected Company-Specific Business Model Analysis

Final Analytical Considerations

Conclusion

Introduction

Who Should Read This Book

This book was written for both investors and business professionals. While reading these pages, I hope that individual and professional investors will gain more perspectives and greater dimensionality for assessing investment opportunities. This book is also intended to help business development executives, mergers and acquisitions professionals, corporate directors and other executive decision-makers add additional scrutiny and rigor to their evaluation of business initiatives.

A Note on the Examples Provided in This Book

It takes a long time to write a book and get it into readers' hands. There is no way for me to know when you will actually read the pages that follow as you may not have time to peruse this book immediately upon purchase. Thus, companies and business models referred to in this book are for illustration purposes only and should not be misconstrued as investment advice. Further, the companies mentioned in this book may modify, pivot or completely reinvent their business models by the time you read these pages. Rather, the purpose of this book is to help you think critically and to formulate penetrating questions to pose to company managers and other industry authorities.

Objectives of This Book

Soldiers are required to perform daily calisthenics, but not because they will be expected to do jumping jacks in the heat of battle. Rather, soldiers practice jumping jacks to render their bodies more limber. So it is the objective of this book to render the reader's mind more limber. This book deliberately tackles a range of subjects in order to draw links between them. By going through the mental gymnastics of reviewing a wide array of business model considerations from a multitude of industries, the reader should become more adroit in evaluating, critiquing and formulating more durable and promising business models.

In the years ahead, businesses will come and go. Industries will fall in and out of favor. Various business models will be heralded while others will be the subject of severe ridicule. You will probably pivot the business initiatives under your authority many times over your career. By having a broader spectrum of ideas to draw from, you will be better able to navigate ever-changing business and investment landscapes.

The Generalists Advantage

Too many people mistakenly believe that having a generalist's perspective is a liability, or at least a deficiency compared to those with a purported expertise in one industry or another.[1] I would like to take a moment to explain why generalists are commonly and mistakenly undervalued and underappreciated.

---

[1] For purposes of clarity, allow me to illustrate the differences between generalists and specialists. In the world of investing, a specialist would be a biotech analyst whereas a generalist would be small cap money manager. In the legal realm, a law firm could have an expertise in negotiating water rights whereas a general practice law firm would have much broader capabilities. In the medical sphere, a cardiologist would be the specialist whereas a general practitioner would be the generalist.

In an age where businesses constantly profess to search for "outside-of-the-box thinking" it is peculiar that they too often seek the counsel of experts whose knowledge is contained in a box. On the other hand, generalists have a much easier time providing out-of-the-box advice because they often do not know what the box looks like or where it is located.

Among the reasons that subject matter experts often do not render the most insightful advice are:

- Specialists believe that the course of action is obvious and therefore not worthy of extended contemplation. As Abraham Maslow said, "If you only have a hammer, you tend to see every problem as a nail." People with deep subject matter expertise tend to rapidly formulate conclusions and spend the remainder of their review looking for data that confirms their viewpoints. Specialists tend to give short-shrift to ideas that do not conform to their pre-conceived notions. Admitting that the solution lies elsewhere would effectively repudiate one's decade's worth of investment in developing such expertise. Specialists tend to congregate among themselves and this insularity results in a rigidity of thinking as to where solutions to problems lie.

  A very successful private equity investor made a fine point when he said, "When you work for a corporation and you buy a firm you think is in your core business or fits with your core business, you assume you know what you are buying. By contrast, private equity investors have to rediscover everything. Their due diligence is more rigorous and their line of questioning is more penetrating than corporate acquisition professionals whose focus is limited to one industry. There can be a certain arrogance in corporations which causes them to make silly mistakes."

- Specialists often are quick to want to demonstrate their expertise, often to impress (potential) clients. Frequently, they have a vested interest in encouraging clients to accept their advice because they have ongoing consulting services to sell.

- The advice of specialists is often disconnected from the situation on the ground. When such advice is prescribed from above by "experts" it is less likely to be implemented by rank-and-file employees. Generalists are more likely to provide common sense recommendations which are more likely to be implemented.

- Wall Street research analysts that have a focus on one particular industry usually feel compelled to issue "Buy" ratings on some of the companies they follow. However, when the entire segment is out of favor, these recommendations are really just the least bad alternatives proffered by a poorly positioned sector.

- Generalists can communicate better than subject matter experts with diverse constituencies. If an oil services engineer writes a report it will likely be filled with industry jargon, indeterminable acronyms and frames of reference that are foreign to many readers. This is why many American presidents, such as Ronald Reagan, have insisted that their speechwriters be generalists. If a speechwriter was a decorated military veteran with 40 years of service under his belt and was an expert in nuclear weapons systems, no one would understand his use of military terms, nuclear physics or theoretical strategic constructs. However, if the speechwriter was a generalist he would be compelled to write the speech in the same vernacular that the listeners would understand.

- One of the most important benefits that a generalist has is that he can bring new ideas to the table. I was once interviewed to write a report on the valuation of patents related to the cement industry and was asked by the prospective client about my expertise of the Southeast Asian cement industry. I responded by saying that I did not have any such expertise whatsoever. However, I continued by saying, "There are advantages to hiring a generalist. A cement expert is not going to be able to tell you anything that you do not already know, so there is no value in hiring a cement expert. However, I can bring a wealth of experience to the table as well as new ideas and best practices from the medical device, Internet router, oil services, personal hygiene and many other industries."

I believe that the Heisenberg Principle supports my contention that generalists can add a great deal of perspective in assessing the potential of a company. The Heisenberg Principle holds that the more accurately we know the position of a particle, the less accurately will we know its momentum, and vice versa. In other words, the more we know about where a particle currently lies, the less we know about where it is going. The analogy in analyzing business models is that the more we study a specific company to the exclusion of exogenous factors, the less we know about how such factors will impact that company in the near future.[2]

Examples of importing best practices from seemingly unrelated businesses include:

- When Southwest Airlines wanted to reduce the time its planes idled on the tarmac, management of that company did not benchmark against other airline operators. Rather, Southwest took notes from NASCAR, where no efforts are spared to reduce milliseconds off the time that cars spend in the pits.

- Before Tim Cook became the CEO of Apple Computer, he ran that company's logistics. At that time he was quoted as saying, "You want to manage inventory like you are in the dairy business. If it gets past its freshness date, you have a problem."

- In a similar vein, the winners of Kaggle competitions—the online platform for facilitating collaboration on big-data projects—are typically new to the sector in which they produce successful results. According to Kaggle's chief executive Anthony Goldbloom, a British physicist developed winning algorithms to predict insurance claims and identify defective used cars. Meanwhile, statisticians at Microsoft's machine-translation group often say that translation accuracies increase whenever a linguist leaves the team. Similarly, many inventors derive their flashes of genius by connecting disparate observations. For instance, John Fabel's inspiration for designing the Ecotrek backpack hailed from suspension bridges

---

[2] For example, if we were to lock ourselves in at a store for three months, we would have a keen understanding of that retailer's revenues, costs, customers, and inventory management systems. While all of our observational powers would be focused on daily transactions, we would not be terribly in-tune with how macroeconomic factors are poised to impact such retailers. Also, while reporters embedded with troops have first-hand insight into the plight of soldiers, such reporters do not have much time to assess how geopolitical factors, or the political dynamics in the enemy's country, may affect the fighting that lies ahead.

while Georges de Mestral developed Velcro when he noticed how burrs stuck to his dog's fur.

- Finally, in many cases, the half-life of subject matter expertise is extremely abbreviated. There probably is not a lot of demand for typewriter or pay phone experts nowadays. In situations where industries converge, expertise limited to one industry is clearly deficient. We see this happening with smart phones morphing into medical devices, televisions taking on some of the functions of computers, and farmers becoming active in monetizing their real estate through land sales and development. In other cases, companies are reclassifying themselves. For instance, Windstream Holdings (a regional telephone, Internet and television provider) is reclassifying itself as a Real Estate Investment Trust in order to reduce its federal income taxes by millions of dollars annually. In these and many other similar situations, whose expertise should be brought to bear? I would argue that a generalist can bring value-added insight to these messy scenarios.

Business Models in Context

"Success has a thousand fathers. Failure is an orphan."

- President John F. Kennedy

The point of this book is to engender critical thinking, even about the premise of this book.

Business models are important. I would not have written a book that revolves around business models if I did not think this was true. However, business models are not the only determinant of a company's success. The prevailing economic environment, execution, a large cash position, and serendipity are major contributors to a business's success. Similarly, the reverse of President Kennedy's words are also true: there often are multiple contributors to a company's failure.

The economy plays a role in determining which business models will be successful. When the economy is in the doldrums, people generally have more time than money. Discovery-based retailers (those offering compelling deals in return for customers investing time to locate them) are more appealing in lackluster economies. Thus, operators of flash sales such as QVC, Fab.com, the Gilt Groupe or One Kings Lane may thrive. So too might Zulily and eBay. However, when the economy is buoyant, consumers generally have more money than time. Thus, they gravitate to retailers such as Amazon that offer them the assurance of locating what they want without steering them into what often results as time-wasting scavenger hunts.

At one of the investor conferences I developed many years ago, Monroe Millstein, founder of Burlington Coat Factory, spoke about a few episodes where serendipity played a key role in that company's success. In one episode, Mr. Millstein promised his son who was then living in Israel that if he returned to New Jersey, the elder Mr. Millstein would give the younger Mr. Millstein a store to manage. This offer was sufficient to entice the younger

Mr. Millstein to return to New Jersey. In those days, retailers were required to remain closed on Sundays. However, the Millsteins were a Jewish family whose day of Sabbath is Saturday. So the Millsteins went to a judge and requested that their store remain closed on Saturday in return for permission to open on Sunday. This petition was granted. As a result of not having any competition on Sunday, the store was such a phenomenal success that an employee had to count how many people were in the store on Sundays in order not to violate local fire codes.

In another story, Mr. Millstein said that he wanted to remove a wall in one of his Burlington Coat Factory stores. The estimate from the contractor was $10,000; this was in the 1970s or 1980s. Mr. Millstein thought that perhaps $10,000 for building a wall was reasonable, but not to simply tear down a wall, so he did not authorize the work. A few days later, Mr. Millstein saw a construction crew working on a road nearby. When it started to rain, he offered to let the construction crew come into his building to avoid getting drenched. Once inside, Mr. Millstein struck a deal with them: they would remove the wall in return for two cases of beer. Thus, Mr. Millstein saved $10,000. He said that such fortuitous events occurred during pivotal points in Burlington Coat Factory's history and were a key ingredient in his company's success.

Another instance of serendipity comes from LinkedIn. One of that company's largest profit generators is its professional placement service. This service, not envisioned during LinkedIn's formative years, consists of licensing out seats to corporate recruiters. With this tool, recruiters can mine all of the extremely granular details about LinkedIn members when they are trying to fill open positions. If a recruiter is looking to fill a position for an outgoing (as demonstrated by lots of LinkedIn connections), Ivy-league educated, senior tax accountant with between seven and ten years of relevant experience, such searches can be conducted in a few minutes. Last I heard, seats for this tool cost $7,500 a year. This is a bargain considering that the tool is available for a year and that commissions payable to recruiters for one placement could be four to six times this annual fee.

A large cash position can bail out a floundering business model. At the time of this writing it is not clear to me what Zynga's business model is. If Zynga finds a growth elixir, its large cash position deserves a great deal of credit for giving that company's management team the time to arrive at a workable business model.

Why Business Models are Important

Are business models really important? After all, one could argue that the integrity of a business model should be reflected in a company's financial performance. You may believe it is sufficient to review a company's historic financial performance, current financial ratios and comparable metrics. While traditional financial analysis is indeed important, it is not sufficient.

The problems with limiting your analysis to numbers are two-fold. First, in many cases, the numbers do not exist. This is almost always the case with start-up companies. Numbers deprivation also occurs when assessing a family-owned business or a foreign privately-held company. In some cases, such as with firms that serve the defense establishment, companies will not reveal much about their financial performance because they are bound by confidentiality requirements. Further, the electronics outsourcing companies to which Apple Computer subcontracts the manufacturing of its products are prohibited from disclosing how much of their business comes from Apple. When writing a valuation report for a company involved in applying biometric technologies to handguns, I learned that the Bureau of Alcohol, Tobacco and Firearms (ATF) has imposed an embargo on disclosing the number of guns manufactured in the United States.

The second problem with relying solely on numbers in your review of companies is that you might come to the wrong conclusions. Many financial reports do not meet the highest standards for reliability; roughly a third of earnings results reported by publicly-traded companies are restated. Even the most professionally and ethically prepared financial reports cannot capture the subtle undercurrents that will enormously affect the subject company going forward. In many cases, reported numbers are merely a blurry reflection of past performance.

Here are two examples where relying on traditional financial analysis could have led to the wrong conclusions:

First let's look at Crumbs Bake Shop. Crumbs—which boasts Marcus Lemonis of The Profit as a key investor—was America's largest chain of cupcake outlets. Some financial analysts criticized Crumbs for having extremely high costs of goods sold and thus very low gross profit margins. These critics pointed out that Crumbs' gross margins were much lower than those of companies such as Krispy Kreme. Those critics were right: Krispy Kreme reported lower costs of goods sold, and higher gross profit margins, than Crumbs. Crumbs' critics were also wrong because they did not take into account how divergent the two business models were.

Krispy Kreme produces each donut it sells at its stores. Thus, its costs of goods sold are limited to the ingredients needed to bake its donuts. Crumbs, on the other hand, does not produce its cupcakes at its stores. Rather, Crumbs contracts with several bakers to prepare its cupcakes and have them delivered to the Crumbs outlets. Do you see the difference? When it purchases cupcakes from its bakers, all of the costs for ingredients, labor, electricity, rent for baking facilities, and related overhead necessary to produce cupcakes are baked into Crumbs' cost of goods sold. Certainly, these costs are much more onerous than just the ingredients that constitute Krispy Kreme's costs of goods sold. It is not that Krispy Kreme is relieved of expending money on the labor, electricity and rent associated with producing its products; it just does not report those costs as costs of goods sold, but rather as operating expenses.

The second example of how honing in on numbers can lead to misdiagnosis comes from Nova Measuring Instruments. Nova is an innovator and a key provider of optical metrology solutions for advanced process control used in semiconductor manufacturing.

Nova's critics have expressed great concern that Nova's days' sales outstanding metric was significantly more extended that that of its peers. (Days' sales outstanding is a measure of how long it takes a company to collect its accounts receivables.) It was true that Nova's days' sales outstanding number was long in the tooth. The problem with the critics' analysis is that they considered this to be a cause of concern rather than a reflection of strength. Yes, we want to invest in companies that promptly collect their accounts receivable. No question about that. However, in the case of Nova, its accounts receivables were extended because of that company's extremely strong cash position. Here is my thinking: it is not just me who can look at Nova's balance sheet and discover its extremely strong cash position. Nova's customers must surely do the same cursory analysis. When customers discover that Nova can afford to allow them to delay payment, the customers will take advantage of that fact and demand longer payment periods in return for booking orders with Nova. Thus, looking at just the numbers would present a warped view of Nova's financial strength.

The Crucial Elements of a Business Model

A business model should be as simple as "a man and a dog" business; so easy to operate that you just need a man and a dog. You need the man to feed the dog and the dog to bite the man if he does anything else. On the other hand you should avoid investment and business opportunities where a great deal of luck is required to earn paltry returns. You would not want to cross five lanes of traffic to pick up a nickel.

As many scandals have erupted because of the opacity of business models—witness Enron, Worldcom, Parmalat, Ahold and Lernout & Hauspie—you should avoid business models that are difficult to decode. Be wary of management teams that imply that their superior intelligence overcompensates for the complexity of their business models. Too often such management teams—such as those led by Bernard Madoff—erect a façade of intelligence. The sophisticated energy trading that Enron was supposedly conducting was a sham. When analysts visited Enron in Houston, a group of that company's employees were acting as though they were busy trading energy futures when the reality was that they were just staring at computer screens. Similarly, United Kingdom software company, Autonomy, was said to be performing spectacularly under its brilliant management team. The key to Autonomy's success was supposed to lie in a secret room that no one could enter. In reality, this room was just a closet.

Opaque business models are often an invitation to a scandal or shareholder lawsuit. If you can't explain your business model in a few sentences in simple terms in your native language, you don't have a business model. However, if you can determine how revenues are generated and what the costs of generating such revenues are, you have already performed 80% of a business model validation.

Another reason that a simple business model is crucial is that the employees will not understand the mission of a company that has a convoluted business model. And if employees don't know what it is that the company is supposed to strive to achieve, then there is no chance that the nebulous objectives will be attained.

Evaluating Business Models

The best way to identify promising business models is to review a large number of business models. It is easy to become enamored with any particular company, technology or business model. Limiting your review of business models will cause you to settle for the business model that you found rather than motivate you to continue searching for the most promising business models.

The first step in searching for a successful business model is to carefully define "success". The fact that a company has successfully raised several rounds of venture capital does not necessarily mean that its business model has been validated. While having a large cash cushion enables a company to survive until the cash is exhausted, it does not mean that whatever direction such company takes is sound.

It is more impressive when a company is capturing revenues and customers through the reinvestment of its cash flow than when it is gaining customers and revenues through the deployment of its raised funds. The former is recurring while the latter capital source is episodic and expensive in terms of dilution.

In determining how much precedential value should be attached to a particular business model, the analyst should determine the strength of the economy during the time of benchmarking. This is because a strong economy can enable a company with a bad business model to prosper and a weak economy can sink companies with very sound business models. It is more impressive to cite a business model of a start-up company that has a 2009 vintage (when a great deal of discretion was applied to funding such businesses) than a business model that has a 1999 vintage (when very little, if any, discretion was applied to funding such businesses).

When you believe that you have found a promising business model, you should make an effort to determine to what extent the success of that business was a function of its business model versus external factors.

For instance, at the beginning of my career, a bottled water company called Clearly Canadian was all the rage. Customers seemed to buy Clearly Canadian water just as fast as retailers could restock their shelves. However, one of the drivers of this company's success was the fact that during this time there was a recall of Perrier water, Clearly Canadian's arch rival. Bottles of Perrier were literally being removed from retailers' shelves. Thus, a good bit of Clearly Canadian's success was due to the setback experienced by Perrier.

The Four Ps of Business Models

A business model should incorporate the four Ps—pain, passion, perfection and profit.

Pain While some businesses are very successful by selling elective or even irrelevant products, most business models should resolve pain points. Instead of sizing a target market by a generic marker, size the market by those who have the greatest pain. For instance, if you are selling a teeth whitener, you could say that the addressable market in the United States is 310 million customers. The rationale would be that this is the size of the American population and just about everyone could benefit from having teeth that are at least a little bit whiter. However, suppose that your research shows that the most likely buyers are women that are about to get married. Thus, a better sizing of the teeth whitener market would be the number of women that get married every year.

Passion This is less of a business model issue but it is critical for the founders and employees to have a passion to create superior products or services. The differences between an ingenious business plan and an insane business plan—and the difference between commercial success and failure—are razor thin. Passion is needed to surmount the skepticism and setbacks that every business will inevitably face.

Perfection As customers are increasingly able to source their purchases worldwide it is critical that a company's products are of world class quality. Today, businesses that deliver defective products or unresponsive service are at risk of being subjected to immediate and worldwide scorn via social media.

Profit   Before I discuss the importance of profits, allow me to digress. When Albert Einstein was a young man he struggled to find teaching positions at universities across Europe. He became so desperate to join a faculty that he pioneered the idea of sending pre-paid postage envelopes with his applications so as to increase his chances of receiving responses to his requests for employment.

The point that I want to bring up with respect to Einstein is that if you are struggling to find a job, that fact does not mean that you will be the next Einstein. So too, if your company is failing to generate revenues and is hemorrhaging money, that fact pattern does not mean that your company will be the next Twitter, LinkedIn, or Instagram.

It seems obvious that companies with valid business models will—at least strive to—generate profits. This common sense notion is often lost at companies that are successful in raising capital as excess cash on their balance sheets becomes cause for complacency. Other times, cash rich companies delude themselves into thinking that eyeballs, "Likes," and clicks are substitutes for generating old-fashioned cash flow. While it is hard to think of any family with more sizzle than the Kardashians, the sizzle associated with their name was neither sufficient to profitably sell their labels at Bebe or Sears nor to ensure the success of their own retail ventures (Dash and ShoeDazzle). Companies that are not at least on a short path to producing profits will lose the confidence of their investors, employees, vendors and customers. These constituents will not want to peg their futures to companies that have no clear means of sustaining themselves.

> **Caveat**   As far as I can tell, there has never been a company with 50 million or more users that failed to figure out a way to monetize such a robust user base.

The Most Important Skills for Assessing Business Models

I believe the most critical skills an analyst or business development professional can have are:

- The ability to ask penetrating, revealing and insightful questions. The renowned anthropologist Claude Levi-Strauss once concluded: "The learned man is not the man who provides the correct responses, rather he is the man who poses the right questions." Whatever you know now will become obsolete in a few years. The most expedient way to keep abreast of changes occurring at companies and within industries is to pose questions to well-informed people.

Oftentimes, when meeting with the management team of an emerging company, you are not even presented with a business plan to assess. Rather you are bombarded with a flurry of disjointed ideas spouted off by an overly energetic entrepreneur. Or, you may be presented with a hail of unfiltered brain spams from a discombobulated inventor. The ability to ask incisive questions cuts through and crystalizes an otherwise cloudy jumble of ideas in need of coalescing into a cogent business model.

> **Gedankenexperiment** Suppose you were employed by Wrigley China and were responsible for selling that company's chewing gum to young Chinese women. What issues would be on your mind? Here are some ideas: Given that there is so much garlic in Chinese food, will chewing gum be looked at as a way to freshen breath after eating?

Will chewing gum build up jaw muscles and make young women look fat? Or, will chewing gum reduce appetite and help girls stay slim? We don't need to grapple with these questions here but I hope to impress upon you that asking probing questions gets you a long way in refining and validating business models.

Often, the most effective research method is to conduct interviews with company management, industry authorities, subject matter experts, and people directly and tangentially involved with the subject business. All of these people will have limited time to spend with you. Thus, you, the analyst, must be able to quickly hone in on the most critical issues.

- Perhaps, the second most important analytical skill is the ability to ask probing follow-up questions. Your interviewees will sometimes ignore or try to evade your questions; they may not wish to comment. They may claim that your question is out-of-bounds or reflects ignorance. To overcome these evasions, you must be able to articulate follow-up questions, sometimes in a circuitous, non-linear manner.

Too often professional investors behave like dogs watching television. They do not understand a company presentation but continue to bob their heads as if they do. Never be ashamed to ask seemingly elementary questions. For instance, if you are listening to a presentation by a life sciences company and observe that the size of the pills appear to be abnormally big, you can ask if the pills are too large to swallow. If you are conducting business with a foreign company, seemingly basic questions are crucial, such as, "Where is the money right now that you are going to wire me?" (Due to currency controls, it can be extremely difficult to wire money out of some countries. Thus, you would feel more comfortable if the money was sitting in a bank account in your country.)

- Yogi Berra once remarked, "You can observe a lot just by watching." Developing a keen sense of observation is indeed important in conducting due diligence. If you were at a cocktail party, would you know how to spot a virtuoso violinist, a champion fencer, or a speaker of

!Xóõ, a language native to Botswana? (To do so, you should look for brown marks on necks, asymmetrical buttocks, and lumps on larynxes, respectively.) Starbucks CEO Howard Schultz disliked how the smell of cheese overpowered coffee aroma, leading the chain to temporarily halt sales of breakfast sandwiches.[3] Traders on the floors of stock exchanges can divine the direction of stocks just by listening to the overall pitch. (Higher pitches indicate that more selling is taking place while lower pitches indicate that more buying is taking place.) The loudness of Frito-Lay's SunChip's bags—which registered 100 decibels (louder than a lawnmower at 90 decibels)—resulted in diminishing potato chip sales and then the removal of those bags ten months after the bags' debut. Again, the point that I am trying to make here is that another crucial analytical skill is the ability to detect subtle nuances. To this end, New York City detectives and New York University medical students are taken to art museums for purposes of honing their perception skills.

The ability to detect such subtleties can only come from conducting first-hand research. Walt Disney refused to air-condition the Anaheim, California offices because he wanted his people out in the amusement park, learning about the operation firsthand rather than being cool and comfortable but out of touch. Thomson Reuters made enormous investments in developing a terminal to compete with Bloomberg machines. One subtle reason this effort failed is that the Thomson Reuters machines had no chat feature which stock brokers likely relished so as to convey their lewd jokes. Also, if first-hand research is not conducted, the intensity of customers' relationships with products and companies cannot be understood. A distant analyst might realize that sales at Apple and Whole Foods are rising but without direct interaction (or at least observation of) with customers, the analyst will miss the passion and loyalty that customers have for brands such as these.

A powerful story about detecting subtleties whilst conducting first-hand research comes from Bill George. When Mr. George became the CEO of Medtronic, that company was functioning abysmally and its products were unreliable. Rather than relying on reading reports

---

[3] Similarly, Starbucks' employees are prohibited from wearing perfumes or colognes so as not to mask the coffee aroma.

prepared by his staff or outside consultants, Mr. George insisted on going to the operating rooms where Medtronic's medical devices were used in surgeries. To his horror, Mr. George saw that Medtronic's fluoroscopes were breaking. He learned the intensity of the surgeons' ire when surgeries were delayed because Medtronic's instruments were malfunctioning. During one operation in which Medtronic's products failed, a surgeon threw a catheter at Mr. George.

By being in the theater in which the subject products are used, you can observe how the products are performing—not only with your ears—but with all of your senses. Conducting first-hand research with a product enables you to see, hear, feel, smell and taste a product. Better yet, you can activate all of these senses much faster than it will take someone to write a report on the product. Thus, first-hand research will give you a time advantage over reading second-hand research reports.

A further advantage of first-hand research over second-hand research is that second-hand research is often filtered. For instance, if Mr. George ordered his deputies to prepare a report on the quality of Medtronic's medical devices, chances are, that report would not only take at least six-months to prepare but it would also be sanitized. Instead of writing that surgeons were absolutely ballistic over malfunctioning catheters during surgeries, the report would probably have stated some watered-down, politically-correct mumbo jumbo such as, "While our research is not conclusive—certainly our sample size of observations is not statistically significant—it does appear that there is a bit of dissatisfaction on the part of some surgeons who use Medtronic catheters." It would have been very possible that the writers of such report would have allowed office politics to enter into their analysis. Maybe they would not want to rankle the feathers of the manufacturing director by stating that the devices were poorly made or maybe they would not want the report to leak out from the company and cause the salesforce to lose prospective clients.

Another benefit of honing one's senses is that you will be better able to detect when someone is lying to you. Meredith Whitney, a very astute and successful banking analyst, knew that there were potentially fatal problems at Bear Stearns when she detected that one of her sources was lying by listening to his intonation and fluency of speech. Upon hearing these lies, no further probing or analysis was required; Ms. Whitney knew that Bear Stearns was doomed.

- Another crucial success factor in assessing business models is the willingness to approach research with unbridled rigor. When reviewing emerging businesses, it is often the degree of rigor that is brought to bear—not the methodology through which such research is processed—that is the most important success factor. Understanding an emerging business is akin to detective work: the analyst must collect disparate pieces of evidence to try to put together the puzzle. The pieces of collected evidence should be observed at different angles and at different times. For instance, if you were considering buying an apartment, you should visit the neighborhood with a member of the opposite sex at different times of the day. The neighborhood might appear to be serene at 10:30 am but sketchy at 9:30 pm. And all politically correct gibberish aside, men and women observe the same things differently.[4]

- Business model evaluators should have a high—but not excessive—level of intelligence. There is no substitute for sheer intelligence. Fortunately, one does not need to have enormous intelligence because assessing business models is really quite simple. Warren Buffett once said, "If I had an IQ of 160, I would sell 40 points." Sometimes, overly intelligent people infer conclusions based on extrapolating patterns that do not exist. Other times, analysts make bad calls because they peer too far into the future. As Edgar Bronfman once said about one of his unsuccessful initiatives, "We were very, very early. And that is the same as being wrong." He was right.

---

[4] One example of how men and women see the same things differently comes from former President Calvin Coolidge and First Lady, Grace Coolidge. The First Couple toured a chicken farm in the 1920s. During the tour, Mrs. Coolidge observed two chickens making quite a ruckus. She was told that one of the roosters was busy mating and that it was common for roosters to do so dozens of times a day. Mrs. Coolidge told her guide, "Tell that to the president." When the message was conveyed, President Coolidge inquired whether the rooster mated with the same hen. The guide answered in the negative and went on to explain that roosters preferred a variety of partners. President Coolidge responded, "Tell that to Mrs. Coolidge."

Political Correctness

Another element of business model assessment is a complete and unapologetic disdain for political correctness. Everyone has a choice to make. You can either be an analyst or you can be myopic beacon of political correctness. You cannot be both. Analysis entails making decisions, rendering judgments and applying discretion. An analyst will declare that one sales team is more impressive than another, that one group of customers is more appealing than another group of customers, and, that one company's executives are more intelligent and capable than another company's. Analysts must be able to rate one company's marketers, researchers, and legal team higher than those of other companies.

By contrast, an adherent to political correctness is too pusillanimous to make any judgments or to apply discretion. Political correctness is a form of analytical sloth and reeks of anticipatory intellectual surrender. In the netherworld of the politically correct, no management team is any better or worse than any other and no customer base is any more or less attractive than any other. To those hyper-sensitive souls sinking in the intellectual quagmire of political correctness, it is unacceptable to state that one company's executives, pricing strategy or balance sheet are better than those of another company because it could hurt the tender feelings of an inferior management team. The cancer of political correctness would have investors make bad investment decisions and lose money rather than apply judgment. In the world of the politically correct, avoiding hurting anyone's feelings is sacrosanct and judgment is offensive. In the world of analysts and executive decision makers, judgment is the *sin qua non*.

Assessing Founders

Let's say that you are an angel investor who is going to spend the day listening to 20 roadshow presentations. Each of these very early-stage companies will have 15 minutes to present. The only thing that any of these companies have is a business plan and a management team. Let's further suppose that all of the business plans are equally promising. Thus, the only thing you need to do is assess the quality of the management team. How would you go about making such assessments? If the management teams consisted of middle-aged or older entrepreneurs, they should have a career record for you to assess. You would be able to review their career histories and determine if they had relevant experience and how impressive their careers were.

However, if the founding teams of entrepreneurs consisted solely of 23-year-olds, they would not have career histories to review. So how would you assess each team? This is where political correctness can separate you from your money. Those who recite politically correct gibberish like "I don't want to judge anyone," or "All entrepreneurs are special in their own special way," should be culpable of analytical malpractice.

Hygiene is a Risk Determinant at Start-Up Companies

The risk of having a few key people out of commission at the same time due to lapses in hygiene and cleanliness at a start-up is very real. I have seen several situations where the flu has knocked-out several key people at start-up companies. Sometimes their incapacity coincides with a critical event such as a product launch.

Companies located in cramped facilities, common for start-ups, are at more risk than companies located in sprawling offices. Also, it is common for people at start-ups to eat lunch together, use the same office equipment and spend time hovering over one another's computers. In start-ups predominated by young people, there is a lot of personal contact such as hugging, high-fiving, etc.

Anyway, here is what I would look for during the procession of 15-minute presentations. First, I would consider the number of founders. I prefer founding teams that consist of two or three people. Four or more founders risk presenting too many ideas and opinions which clouds the laser focus that an emerging company must possess. One founder is not enough to do all of the work necessary to get a start-up company off of the ground. Entrepreneurs need fellow entrepreneurs as a support system. (According to one study, solo rock stars are much more likely to commit suicide than rock stars that are members of bands.[5] One reason is that being a rock star is a solitary life and full of ups and downs. The same is true for founders of companies.) A lot of all-nighters are pulled and weekends are sacrificed for companies. One minute you get a request for an interview with the leading trade publication and the next minute the mailman drops off a bill that you can't pay. One day you arrange a pitch with a leading venture capital firm and the next day your prospective licensing deal falls apart. These trials and tribulations are much easier to deal with when you have a support system.

Another problem with start-ups that have one founder is that they have not been able to convince anyone to join their venture. On the other hand, it is a very encouraging sign when the initial entrepreneur has been able to lure one or two more partners to join the fledgling concern. Start-ups are especially promising when the second and third founders have known the first founder for many years since this is an indication that the follow-on founders believe that the initial founder possesses intelligence, persistency and integrity. It is also encouraging when the follow-on founders have made a sacrifice to join the start-up. These sacrifices can include moving across the country or giving up a good job. In fact, Arash Ferdowsi, Dropbox's second employee, was so impressed with Drew Houston's idea for Dropbox that he dropped out of the Massachusetts Institute of Technology with only one semester left before graduating. It is my understanding that the second gentleman to join at Zynga gave up $1 million in AOL stock options to become Zynga's second employee.

When founders have known each other for many years, there are usually high levels of trust among the team members. High levels of trust are critical in enabling management teams to make decisions quickly. Suppose that the two founders of a firm came together as a result of their venture capitalist making a shotgun wedding. If one of those founders was going to meet with a lawyer about allocating equity between the founders, one founder would not trust the other to negotiate in his best interest, so the second founder would want to join the meeting. However, this would represent a waste of valuable founder time since neither founder would stay back at the office and continue developing the business. But, if these founders were brothers, then there would more likely be sufficient trust for one founder to discuss the allocation of equity with the lawyers and for the second founder to continue working.

---

[5] Source: http://www.salon.com/2012/12/21/study_solo_rock_stars_die_young/

This brings me to the next point, one that guardians of political correctness may not want to read, which is that the founders should be as similar as possible in terms of age, gender and ethnic background. (Remember, the context for this discussion is that you are listening to twenty 15-minute company pitches in one day.) It would be most comforting to me if the founders were brothers. However, other family relationships, especially parents and children, would be a concern because most parents will make decisions based on what is best for their children rather than what is best for the company.

As for the closeness of age among the founders, I have simply never seen a situation where two founders, ages 23 and 53 are working in a tiny office for upwards of 16 hours a day, six or seven days a week. I just can't image such a scenario working. These tensions would be further exacerbated if different genders were involved. How many of you middle-aged readers could tell your spouse that your co-founders—with whom you will share the same shadow throughout the day and into the late night and with whom you will share meals and travel itineraries—are two 23-year-olds of the opposite sex? Even if these readers' spouses would allow them to commence the venture, tensions would arise at home which would affect the *esprit de corps* at the office.

Now, why would I say that I would be more inclined to invest in one of the presenting management teams that appeared to be very close in terms of ethnicity? Because not understanding others' ethnicities or religions represents a friction point in a company that I would rather didn't exist. Let's say that your partner is Chinese and you are not. You might commit to your investors that you will launch your product on February 15. In the weeks prior to the launch date, you are working 20 hours a day to meet the deadline. However, you were unaware of the importance that the Chinese attach to the Chinese New Year and are caught off guard that your partner is celebrating two work-free weeks in early February. It is less likely that all of these fracture points can be foreseen when different ethnicities and religions are in play.

Let's say that one of the presenting companies' management teams consists of three students who met at the local university. One of the students/ entrepreneurs is from Greece, one is from Korea and one is from Poland. In my experience, a surprising number of foreign students that attend universities in English speaking countries do not speak English 100% fluently. Thus, I would be very concerned that these students could not completely express themselves to one another. It is a critical and fundamental problem when founders do not share one vision, a laser focus and speak with one voice. Thus, the diverse ethnic composition of this company would be of concern to me. On the other hand, I would feel much more confident in the cohesiveness of a management team that consisted of either three Greeks, three Koreans, or three Poles.[6]

> **Analytical Consideration** It is crucial that non-citizen students have permission to reside in the country in which they plan to grow their businesses after they complete their studies. It is tragic for all involved to see an enterprising foreign student launch a business, raise capital and then be forced to leave the country.

Finally, I would be impressed if at least one of the founders had military experience. Being responsible for the lives of fellow soldiers and equipment worth tens of millions of dollars has a tendency to imbue tremendous maturity in an individual. Best yet, the investor is getting an entrepreneur with the maturity of a 40-year-old and the energy of a 23-year-old.

---

[6] I am not saying that it is impossible for a company founded by nationals of three different countries to succeed but rather that it is less likely. For instance, SanDisk is a successful company that was founded by immigrants from Israel, Taiwan and India. However, even this rare example breaks with the storyline set above: the founders were much older than 23 and had quite a few years of work history to review. Investors and business professionals should deploy capital based on what is probable, not what is possible. (After all, anything is possible.)

Industry Sizing

Industry Sizing

Many analysts make the mistake of assuming that their product can secure at least one percent of a very large addressable market. This is called the Myth of One Percent. There are several problems with this assumption. First, the analyst usually chooses the largest possible addressable market against which the 1% is multiplied. It is tempting to state that if our tooth-paste can capture just 1% of the Chinese market our company will make a fortune. A more accurate addressable market would focus on the segment of the market that is experiencing high levels of pain for which your product is a solution. The second manifestation of the Myth of One Percent is that 1% is the minimum market share that a company can command. This is not true. Your company may only capture 0.5% of the market, yielding a 1% market share forecast doubly overstated. Your product may not be able to enter the market at all. Further, implicit in the Myth of One Percent is another fallacy that holds that some markets are so lucrative that merely participating in them is sufficient to build a great business.

Analytical Consideration Analysts are supposed to challenge what passes as common knowledge, especially when that common knowledge is propagated by the same government that represses investigative journalism to a point of it being a simulacrum. It is often said that China's population stands at 1.5 billion; China's population is undoubtedly enormous. However, after walking down Nanjing Road (Shanghai's equivalent to Rodeo Drive in Beverly Hills) during mid-day and not seeing many people at all, I began to question whether China's population can really be 1.5 billion. If the German rate of childbirth is more than one (but below the replacement rate of roughly 2.1 births per woman) and China had until very recently a strict policy of one child per family (its more recent attempts to loosen such policy have been ineffective in spurring childbirths), why is China's population rising while Germany's population is falling? I do not understand why the math behind population replacement rates works so differently in China than in Europe.

I haven't heard any explanation for why there are so many ghost buildings—even entire ghost towns—in China, especially in view of China supposedly bursting at the seams with humanity. Somehow, we are to believe that the absence of people is evidence of an overwhelmingly large population.

Having a huge population is a source of great pride for the Chinese. On a recent trip to Shanghai, during breakfast, my hosts told me that the population of Shanghai was 20 million. That same day, at lunchtime, my hosts told me that the population of Shanghai was 40 million. (How can any city's population double in a few hours?) Maybe China's reported population is the result of sandbagging by its regional authorities who try to outdo one another in terms of reporting regional growth. (These leaders' advancement is based on their regions' growth.)

Maybe the Chinese government feels it must report a population that exceeds India's 1.25 billion people in much the same way it feels it must report economic growth rates in excess of those of Taiwan. Maybe China's population statistics are a governmental corollary to vaporware: China's military wants to project its power and the Chinese economy stands to benefit by luring investors into China. The enticement being, that yes, foreign businesses that enter China will lose money for a long time, but these losses are well worth it since the Chinese market is nearly infinite.

One method of forecasting a company's revenues is to estimate the size of the addressable market and then determine the share of the market that the subject company is expected to capture. Let's say that you are hired by a company that produces teeth whitener to forecast its revenues. You could spend a great deal of time and money estimating the size of the market for teeth whitener. You could also get a fairly good estimate in just a matter of minutes.

Your analysis might be something like this:

Q. What is the geographic scope of the addressable market?
A. The market potential is limited to sales within the United States.

Q. What is the population in the United States?
A. There are approximately 310 million Americans.

Q. Which group of Americans is most likely to purchase teeth whiteners?
A. The most fertile target market is women about to be married.

Q. How many American women get married each year?
A. There are roughly 2.1 million weddings a year in the United States.

Q. What percent of these brides are likely to purchase teeth whiteners?
A. Let's say 10%.

Q. What is the second demographic most likely to purchase teeth whiteners?
A. Smokers.

Q. How many smokers are there in the United States?
A. There are roughly 42.1 million smokers in the United States.

Q. What percent of smokers are likely to wish to purchase teeth whiteners?
A. Let's say 5%.

Q. What percent of these smokers have the means to purchase teeth whiteners?
A. Let's say 70%.

Q. What is a realistic uptake rate of other Americans (aside from brides and smokers)?
A. Let's say 1%, but we have to exclude the roughly 40 million children and elderly that we know will not be consumers of teeth whiteners.

Q. How much is the average spend per year on teeth whitening solutions?
A. Let's say $35.

Thus, the addressable market for teeth whiteners in the United States is $137 million. I rounded down by about $1 million to take into account that some brides are also smokers.

Q. How much market share can our company realistically capture?

A. Well, our company does have a superior product. However, the two market leaders each control about 35% of the market. They have much larger advertising and slotting fee budgets. I think our company can capture half of the remaining market share so my estimate is 15%.

Thus, we would expect our company to generate $20 million in annual revenues. (We should round our estimates down to be conservative.)

Population in the United States		310,000,000
Number of Weddings in the United States Annually		2,100,000
Number of American Women Getting Married Annually		2,100,000
Percent Likely to Purchase Teeth Whiteners		10%
Number of Brides Likely to Purchase Teeth Whiteners Annually		210,000
Number of American Smokers		42,100,000
Percent Likely to Purchase Teeth Whiteners		5%
Percent of Smokers Likely to Purchase Teeth Whiteners with Means	70%	3.5%
Number of Smokers Likely to Purchase Teeth Whiteners Annually		1,473,500
Gross Addressable Americans for Teeth Whiteners		265,800,000
Minus Young Children and the Elderly		40,000,000
Net Addressable Americans for Teeth Whiteners		225,800,000
Percent Likely to Purchase Teeth Whiteners		1%
Number of Other Americans Likely to Purchase Teeth Whiteners Annually		2,258,000
Total Number of Potential Customers for Teeth Whitener		3,941,500
Average Spend per Year on Teeth Whitener		$35
Total Industry Wide Revenue Opportunity		**$137,952,500**
Adjustment for Some Brides Being Smokers		$137,000,000
Estimated Market Share of Our Company		15%
Estimated Annual Revenue of Our Company		**$20,550,000**

While a quick analysis like the one above should provide a reasonably accurate estimate of market potential, you could expand on this analysis by modeling in answers to questions such as those below:

- To what extent will photoshopping of wedding pictures reduce the demand for teeth whiteners?
- For which ethnicities is it of particular importance to preserve memories of weddings with pictures?
- What percent of weddings cost more than, let's say, $50,000?
- Are couples that pay for their own marriages more or less likely to splurge for teeth whiteners?
- Are couples that marry earlier or later in life more likely to purchase teeth whiteners?
- Are couples that remarry more or less likely to purchase teeth whiteners?
- Are dentists inclined to encourage or discourage their patients from using teeth whiteners?
- Are e-cigarettes more or less likely to darken and stain teeth?
- Compared to traditional weddings, are same-sex weddings more or less likely to result in greater demand for teeth whiteners?

Analytical Consideration If you were in the business of selling natural gas pipeline, you might be emboldened to hear that, say, 40% of the one million miles of existing pipeline infrastructure is not in sufficient condition to accommodate maximum allowable pressure. You might think that your addressable market is 400,000 miles of replacement pipeline. (Maybe a little more, taking into account demand for pipelines in virgin territories.) However, your addressable market could be far less because the current pipeline owners can simply de-rate them, which means reducing the maximum pressure allowed from, say, 1,600 pounds per square inch to 1,200 pounds per square inch.

The Seduction of Extrapolation

Extrapolation—making forecasts about the future success of one product or market by applying what you know about the success of another similar product or market—is a natural starting point for making estimates. (Thus, when Shai Agassi of Better Place projected that his company's battery-operated autos would quickly capture at least 50% of the Israeli market, his forecast was delusional since it took the Prius about 10 years to capture 1.5% of the American market and the Prius was a hit.[7]) This is true not only in terms of making financial projections but in many other areas of life. For instance, when snipers estimate the distance to their target they are taught to apply familiar frames of reference. So a sniper might estimate that the target is 350 yards away because that distance seems similar to the length of three and a half football fields.

While extrapolation is often a sound starting point for making projections, it should neither be reflexively nor formulaically applied. It would be a mistake to believe that the demand for yoga classes is a function of the number of women wearing yoga pants from the likes of Lululemon.

One problem with extrapolation occurs when an analyst projects that past performance will persist into the future without considering how changes in the industry, customers, regulation, demographics or other factors will cause the demand curve to shift. At a minimum, one cannot expect soaring sales to continue ad infinitum, especially when such sales are the result of pent-up demand. A new nightclub that has throngs of patrons waiting for admittance on opening night will usually lose much of its customer base when the novelty wears off or another, hipper club opens up down the street. With a great deal of pre-release marketing, digital

---

[7] Better Place was an emerging purveyor of battery-operated cars and battery-switching services for electric vehicles. Better Place raised nearly $1 billion in venture capital in the late 2000s but has since dissolved and disbanded.

entertainment can enjoy enormous sales within a few days of release. But it would be irresponsible to project that initial sales levels will be sustainable for the long-term. For instance, some 50% of first-year sales of Take-Two Interactive Software's Grand Theft Auto V came in the first three days of its release.

Another misapplication of extrapolation is to allow high demand for one feature to cause you to believe that there will be strong demand for an entire product line. Early in the release of Apple's 5C iPhone there was very strong demand for the gold-colored model. Apple may have mistakenly ramped up production on its entire line of the 5C model based on this color preference.

Over the long-term, seemingly logical ratios may break down due to demographic shifts. It might seem reasonable to project automobile sales based on population. You could come up with ratios such as "x new auto sales for every million people in the country" or "y used car sales for every 1000 people that turn 16 in a given year." However, over the long-term, the perceived merits of owning a car can shift, perhaps due to it becoming more accepted to work from home and as reliance of public transportation and car sharing schemes becomes more common. Interestingly, there seems to some evidence of these societal changes occurring as:

- In 1995, 87% of the U.S. population aged 20 to 24 had a driver's license, according to the Federal Highway Administration. By 2011 that had fallen to 80%.

- In 2012, according to an analysis of census data by the University of Michigan's Transportation Research Institute, 9.2% of U.S. households did not have a car, up from 8.7% in 2007.

Analytical Trap It is tempting to believe that the presence of antique automobiles or growing numbers of mopeds in developing countries are signs of rising economic fortunes. These are not always safe assumptions to make. For instance, Cuba's fleet of 1950s-era automobiles is not a result of wealthy Cuban classic car aficionados investing in antique cars, but rather a consequence of the difficult economic climate forcing Cubans to preserve very old vehicles. The growing number of motorbikes in Cambodia is more likely a fore

It is easy to understand how an analyst might forecast changes in the size of the population to participation in youth sports. One might project that participation in youth sports is proportionate to the changes in the birth rate some ten years earlier. However, such shoddy analysis would fail to factor in societal changes such as the increasing costs of enrolling children in these activities and the related costs for equipment, parents having less time to chauffeur their children to these activities, excessive pressure on kids to perform at high levels in youth sports, cuts in school physical-education programs, children spending more time playing video games, and the fear of children suffering concussions when playing contact sports.

Demand for a product can deteriorate even if the number of people that will require it increases over time. Even funeral homes in countries with steadily growing populations are likely to face dramatically diminishing revenues. As the costs of burials soar and as Americans' religiosity continues to wane, Americans are more likely to cremate instead of bury their loved ones. In 1960 fewer than 4% of Americans chose cremation; now it is 43%. In London it is 70% and in Tokyo there is no alternative to cremation. (Of course, cremation services are priced much lower than burial services.) As families are more dispersed, they are less likely to visit their loved ones' graves anyway. Instead, they may opt to take urns with them or to run electronic memorials for the departed.

Analytical Insight As an aside, the developments occurring at funeral homes illustrate how a company's revenues may decline precipitously while its profitability surges. Less revenue is collected for cremating corpses but less work is entailed. With cremation there is no need to prepare corpses for viewing (the problem of which is exacerbated by it being increasingly difficult to recruit morticians), the constraints of land availability are removed from the equation, no gravediggers need be hired, the issue of expensive landscaping at cemeteries is eliminated, and less real estate needs to be set aside for parking.

The Dangers of Extrapolating Internationally

On the face of it, it would seem reasonable to extrapolate the spending habits of the citizens of one country onto the spending patterns of citizens of another similarly situated country. Hence, one could project American spending habits onto Germans. However, this would be a mistake since Germans are much more frugal than Americans. Largely because it is less common for German mothers to work outside the home, shopping hours in Germany are much more restricted than in the United States. Most German shops close by 8 p.m. on weekdays and even earlier on Saturdays. With few exceptions, shops are closed on Sundays and bank holidays. There is much less stigma associated with using second-hand items in Germany: it is not uncommon for Germans to completely furnish their homes with used furniture.

The Germans' extreme frugality, in part, is due to their aversion to debt (especially among the older generations). Only about 30% of Germans have credit cards whereas about 70% of Americans have credit cards. Most purchases in Germany are still made in cash. (Germans are fearful that information transmitted via electronic payment is not safe.) Germany is the only country I know that has the same word—*schulden*—for debt and guilt. It had long been a tradition for German banks to celebrate World Saving's Day, a day in which children would bring their savings to the banks and receive toys, balloons or face-painting in return.

The spending proclivities of other nations can mislead those relying on extrapolation to predict future spending activities. It would be a mistake to assume that just because many seemingly wealthy Russians buy high-end fashionable products, that they have the means and appetite to buy as much as Americans. In Russia, people are so eager to show off their bling-bling (e.g. iPhones) that such purchases are made at the price of several generations living crammed into one or two rooms or by refusing to see a doctor when they are sick.

It would be a mistake to prepare a correlation analysis between time spent shopping and consumer expenditures of one nation to that of another nation. The nearly ten hours per week that the average Chinese citizen dedicates to shopping does not translate into Western levels of consumption. Part of the reason for the large blocks of time devoted to shopping in China is a function of the less efficient shopping process such as challenging public transportation and difficulty in making price comparisons. Also, the novelty of being able to browse a wide selection of merchandise in China means that window shopping is a form of entertainment.

The hospitality industry should not expect Chinese tourists' spending levels to parallel those of western tourists. Knowing the price sensitivity of the Chinese, Chinese travel agents scour the Internet for the cheapest tickets and plan their itinerary according to where the cheapest routes lie. They demand discounts on their bulk airline tickets purchases and then negotiate mercilessly for bargain basement hotel rates in distant suburbs. Many Chinese tours to Europe primarily consist of hopscotching from Chinatown to Chinatown in each city throughout the itinerary.

In some cases, extrapolation would underestimate demand. Companies like Priceline made robust profits in Europe because Europe was dominated by small hotels with little to no web presence that were eager for referrals from increasingly Internet-savvy travelers. Travel-sites such as Kayak and Expedia also earned healthy profits by serving Europeans, who enjoy more travel time than Americans.

Now that we have seen how culture affects how money is spent in various countries, let's take a look at how culture affects the portability of consumer goods. We will focus on consumables.

One could fail to appreciate how divergent eating habits are between Americans and the French. One difference is the number of times that these two peoples eat. The French are extremely disciplined about not eating between meals while Americans tend to graze all day long. This difference in eating habits proved problematic when Euro Disney first opened outside of Paris. Disney, believing that the French would exhibit eating behavior similar to the Americans, scattered concession stands all over Euro Disney. (Heaven forbid that food be beyond arm's reach!) Euro Disney also erected fewer dedicated eating establishments which were inadequately staffed during lunch time. The result was that the concession stands were seldom frequented while the overwhelmed restaurants were incapable of serving the thongs of patrons that converged on those facilities during lunchtime.

There are a few other interesting things to note about how the consumption of food differs from one country to another. For instance, the

French display much more patience for waiting for their food. In France, the lunch crowd can wait up to an hour to get a made-to-order burger from a food truck. (In the United States, fisticuffs and lawsuits would start flying if Americans had to wait that long.) There are a variety of reasons why not all American foods translate well in France. The French are extremely selective about procuring the right ingredients which in some cases are just not available in France. Pastrami is not available and some variations of potatoes are not available all year round in France. Corn is inedible in France because it is not made for human consumption, but rather for farm animals.

Below are other examples of how extrapolation, sans cultural synthesis, can lead to the wrong conclusions.

- The toy company Mattel opened a six-story Barbie megastore in downtown Shanghai—with a spa and a cocktail bar—only to discover that Chinese parents did not approve of Barbie's study habits.

- The appeal of do-it-yourself in the context of home improvement does not translate well among the nouveau riche of countries as far-flung as China and Chile. Home Depot found that the last thing the sons and daughters of farmers and laborers wanted to do was perform manual labor in their homes during their spare time.

- One reason—that does not translate the world over—that Avon's door-to-door salesladies are still performing relatively well in Latin America is that the machismo of Latin American men means that they do not want their women going out of the house.

- The size of a retailer's parking lot is of great significance for retailers in Guatemala. This is because Guatemalan men are obsessed with their cars. (It is not uncommon for them to wash their cars twice a day.) They prefer to patronize stores that have large parking lots so they can show off their cars by driving around the lots once or twice before parking.

- Email marketing campaigns are less successful in Japan because the Japanese consider email too invasive. Thus, companies such as Groupon may have difficulty expanding into Japan.

Revenue Analysis

Revenue Analysis

Revenue is the lifeblood of every company. Without it companies cannot pay their bills and will wither away. Thus, it is important to determine if the company's goods and services provide enough of an economic benefit for a sufficient number of customers to pay for those goods and services. A company's goods and services should prove their utility by meeting at least one of the criteria below:

- The service makes the pre-purchase review of a product or service more convenient. For instance, travel sites such as Expedia and Hotels. com provide voluminous reviews of hotels and resorts as well as make booking hotels and airline tickets a breeze. Angie's List provides easily searchable and rich reviews for contractors in much the same way that SitterCity.com does for babysitters or as Yelp does for restaurants. Ultimately, these services reduce risk for customers.

- The service makes the process of purchasing a product or service less risky, more convenient or more rewarding. Traditional credit cards offer all of these attributes. So too do a slew of new gifting companies such as Plastic Jungle, Giftango, and Wrapp.[8]

---

[8] A counter-example regarding the ease or difficulty of purchasing a product or service comes from Better Place. Better Place bought sedans from Renault and refitted them with electric batteries and electric motors. Thus, it was not clear if the customers were buying an electric Renault or buying a Better Place vehicle. After this cloud of uncertainty was removed, customers were confronted with an arduous purchasing process. First, customers needed to seek approval from Better Place which required proving that they lived close enough to a Better Place battery swapping station and a commitment from the customer that they would adhere to predictable driving routes. The second obstacle was that customers had to sign up for a fueling subscription in order to recharge their cars. Only then could Better Place customers begin learning the new behavior of stopping to swap out battery packs at dedicated stations.

- The service reduces the upfront costs of purchasing the product. Many manufacturers of machines, white goods (kitchen appliances) and automobiles have their own financing units which allow customers to pay for their purchases through installments. In fact, one of the reasons that General Motors outpaced Ford Motors in market share during the early days of automobile manufacturing was that GM created a finance unit that made it easy for people to pay for their cars over time. (Henry Ford's decision to pay his workers $5 a day so that they could afford to buy cars still required those workers to save for a long time before they could accumulate enough money to purchase a new car.) Also, textbook publishers have become even more aggressive in terms of their pricing as more university students roll their textbook purchases into their student loans.

Conversely, revenue growth may be more restrained than one anticipates in situations where the cost of a product represents only a fraction of the cost of implementing it. For instance, the cost of robots to be placed on factory floors are only about one-third of the entire cost of implementing robotics as safety cages must be built, employees need to be trained to interact with the robots, severance payments might be due, insurance premiums may rise and reserves should be made for software upgrades.

Analytical Consideration While subsidizing sales of a product can stimulate demand, removing those subsidies can dramatically diminish demand. U.S. wireless carriers have long subsidized the sales of expensive mobile phones by bundling the cost of the phone together with long-term contracts. This eliminated sticker shock on the part of handset customers. Apple, with its very expensive phones, was a primary beneficiary of this phenomenon. Now, phone carriers are moving towards unbundling handset sales from phone service. To gauge how much a handset's sales might be impacted by the removal of subsidies we can consider the percent of phones sold by carriers with and without subsidies and the trends related thereto. If only a

- The service makes the installation of a product more convenient. Best Buy's Geek Squad is a good example of a service that makes the installation of home entertainment as well as computers and related peripherals effortless on the part of the customer. Apple's stores also do a good job of getting their products ready for customer use.

- The product enables customers to make more money. Any piece of equipment—commonly research equipment—that enables the buyer to receive disproportionate tax breaks meets this criterion. Bloomberg terminals used by equities, bond, currency, futures and options traders are a great example of expenditures that offer high returns. According to surveys that I have seen, most Bloomberg terminal users would rather take a cut in salary than lose their Bloomberg machines. Another example comes from GrainSense which is producing a handheld device that detects various properties and characteristics of grain seeds. The benefit of GrainSense to farmers is that now farmers can be sure they are receiving the right prices for the quality of grains they are selling. Finally, a primary consideration of homeowners buying appliances such as refrigerators and washing machines is not how long those appliances will last but how much of a selling point the appliance will be when they go to sell their homes. Thus, the perception of the value of buying an appliance to the customer has somewhat shifted from the near-term utility of the appliance to the leverage that the appliance will deliver in terms of raising a home's selling price.

Actually, the opposite phenomenon can surface in terms of solar panels. While solar panels demonstrate utility by enabling homeowners to reduce their monthly electricity bills, the appraisals banks use for determining the mortgages they underwrite do not always reflect the full value of the solar paneling. Interestingly, there is even value in faux returns on investment: studies have shown that the music and sounds that slot machines make cause people to overestimate how much they are actually winning by as much as 24 percent.

- The product enables customers to save money. Examples of this include sensors that turn off lights when no movement is detected for a given number of minutes, smart windows that change their tint to become increasingly dark when the sun shines the strongest, and photovoltaic-piezoelectric fibers woven into carpet so that when that carpet is walked on, the fibers collect the kinetic energy to convert it into usable electricity.

- The product enables businesses to lose less money. Minibar monitors from companies such as Dometic alert hotel managers when items have been removed from minibars so that they can be restocked and charged to guests' bills.

- The product or service intimidates adversaries. Military weaponry and law firms that have developed a reputation for never settling cases before verdict meet such criteria.

- The product saves customers time and enhances customer convenience. For instance, DocuSign reduces the time, clutter and confusion associated with signing contracts. A company called Fast Customer eliminates annoying wait times that callers typically experience when calling large companies. Instead of calling a company's customer service number, anyone can call 855-DONT-HOLD and arrange for a company they want to speak with to return their call.

- The product reduces risk for the customer. Property and casualty insurance and litigation finance providers meet such criteria.

- The product enhances the customer's image. Branded consumer goods such as apparel, prime office space, upscale hotels and luxury cars fit the bill here.

- The products or services remove stigmas. Most people do not like going to pawn shops because of the associated stigma and because they are quite often located in seedy parts of town. However, pawn operators such as Pawnup that put their shops on the Internet remove the stigma and danger associated with transacting with bricks-and-mortar pawn shops.

- The product extends the life—and enhances the functionality—of a previously purchased product. Service contracts, premium support contracts, agreements for scheduled or preemptive maintenance, and warranties exemplify the notion. Microelectromechanical systems (or sensors) that are affixed to things as diverse as airplane wings and bridges are programed to send alerts when maintenance is required.

Similarly, packaging can extend the shelf life and enhance product quality. For instance, since there is no chance of breakage associated with aluminum beer cans, they provide added shelf-life compared to glass bottles. Also, aluminum beer cans offer airtight seals devoid of oxygen as well as complete protection against ultraviolet light, both of which affect the taste and quality of beer. Further, retailers not only save on shipping and recycling costs associated with lighter aluminum, but they are able to stack more products in their coolers.

- The service renders the disposal of a previously purchased product less risky, more convenient and maybe even enhances the image of the disposer. Examples include:

  o Peer-to-peer lending sites, such as The Lending Club, that offer secondary markets where lenders can sell their non-accruing loans, reduce lenders' risks.

  o Darling International provides recycling services for food processing companies. For instance, it collects inedible waste from bakeries and converts it into a corn-replacement product for animal feed. These products are primarily sold to the agricultural, pet food, leather and biodiesel industries.

  o BrightStar and uSell.com are leaders in facilitating the buying back and trading-in of mobile devices.

  o Gessner AG's Dualcycle invention enables the inexpensive separation of different substrates of textiles so that the various textile layers can be optimally recycled and reused.

- o Flash sale sites such Gilt Groupe, Rue La La and One Kings Lane enable upscale fashion-oriented designers to sell their out-of-season inventory or overstocked merchandise.

- New uses for existing products are discovered. Titanium shavings ground off an airplane jet engine part can be repurposed for fireworks material. Coal tar can be used to produce saccharin while broken tea leaves and cocoa waste can be processed into caffeine. In view of coffee grounds being a natural deodorant, a company called the Ministry of Supply is blending coffee grounds with polyester to create blazers that absorb body odor. Coffee Flour is turning the cherry pulp that accompanies coffee beans, traditionally discarded into rivers, into gluten-free, high-fiber flour that enjoys a range of high-end culinary applications. Companies such as Kentucky Bioprocessing, Mapp Biopharmaceutical and Caliper Biotherapeutics are in the process of developing serums cultivated from tobacco leaves that will combat the Ebola virus.

Cetologists are using facial recognition technology to identify whales and to placate animal rights activists who oppose tagging marine animals. Ultrasound technology can be used to view the uterus of sturgeon so that its roe (more commonly known as caviar) can be harvested in a timely manner, sometimes by inducing labor so as to spare the sturgeon. Missile defense technology can be placed in the ceilings above basketball courts so as to help players react to passes and shots based on the balls' trajectories, velocities, arching, drag, and the like.

Replaceability

Aside from the utility of a product, demand can be engineered, at least to some extent. A variety of businesses have interesting methods for spurring replacement sales. For instance, some printing companies trigger warnings to users that "ink is low" when there is still 40% more ink available in the cartridge. Manufacturers of over-the-counter pharmaceuticals have been known to place pre-mature expiration dates on their medicine bottles. When consumers see these dates, they are more likely to discard the medicine.

Apple Computer stimulates the replacement of its laptops by making it nearly impossible to upgrade its laptop computers. The ultra-thin MacBook Air's sleek profile means that its components—memory chips, solid state drive, and processor—are packed so tightly in the case that there's no room for upgrades. Customers are further dissuaded from trying to upgrade these machines by the unusual screws used to hold the case together, thus making home repair even more difficult. This engineering is designed to spur demand for new machines.

The Merits of Encouraging Unethical Behavior

I have noticed that some customers are more likely to buy if they believe they are cheating the company. There is a men's clothing store that I have purchased from for many years. This store is owned by two brothers who are now of advanced age. Over the years, they have perfected a charade that lets the customer believe he is basically stealing a suit. The game works like this:

Brother Frank pretends that he is hard of hearing. When a customer is interested in a suit he yells across the room to Brother Henry, "Henry, how much is this suit?"

Henry: "Six-hundred dollars."

Frank: "Four-hundred dollars. Is that what you said?"

Henry: "I said, six-hundred dollars."

Frank to the customer: "Four-hundred dollars it is."

The customer, of course, hears this dialogue and readily closes the sale believing that he is cheating the store to the tune of $200. But, the revenues the brothers wished to receive was really $400.

There is an interesting story about an enterprising man who made lots of money selling watches in Brooklyn back in the 1950s. This clever businessman bought watches at a very low price, let's say $10 apiece. His pitch to customers was for them to purchase the watches for four installments of $20 each. He said, "Pay me $20 now and walk away with the watch. For the balance, just send me $20 a month for the next three months." The entrepreneur knew that while there were lots of takers (who relished in believing they were cheating the watch seller out of money) almost no one would remit the installments. But he still made a tidy profit on the initial payment.

When I was developing industry conferences in a partnership that I had with The New York Society of Securities Analysts, I heard Roland Schaefer, founder of Claire's Stores, say that he did not want shrinkage to fall to extremely low levels.[9] This was because if the merchandise was too difficult to access, fewer girls would try on or inspect the merchandise and sales would also diminish.

---

[9] Claire's is a retailer of accessories and jewelry to girls and young women.

Revenue Trajectories

How fast will a new product or technology diffuse? How fast will a company's revenues grow? To answer these kinds of questions, I would like to introduce you to the Diffusion of Innovations Theory which was advanced by the late Professor Everett Rogers. The first five considerations below are from Professor Rogers' research; the rest are my ideas.

Consideration	Sample Questions	Analysis
Relative Advantage	How much better is the innovation than alternatives already in use?	Innovations that offer huge advantages are more likely to spur action than those that offer slight ones. The iPad—which saves users the inconvenience of carrying around 500 books—offers a huge convenience advantage.
Visibility	How readily can reluctant consumers see early adopters using the innovation?	If you were the first one to bring an iPad into your office, lots of your colleagues would want to take a look at it. On the other hand, there is not much visibility associated with a catalytic converter that is buried in an auto engine, under the hood of a car. As far as specialty desserts go, there is more visibility and virality associated with cupcakes than frozen yogurt since customers more often take pictures of cupcakes and post them on Pinterest and Facebook. Not so with frozen yogurt.

Consideration	Sample Questions	Analysis
Trialability	Can a potential adopter try the product without sacrificing much time, effort and money?	Can I borrow your iPad over the weekend? Or to get my hands on a product do I have to submit to a credit check, supply references, and take a drug test?
Simplicity	Is the function and use of the innovation obvious?	Are iPads intuitive to use? Or to use the product, do I have to take a three-week training course and then submit to an exam in order to achieve certification?
Compatibility	Does the innovation require adopters to change other elements of their lives, or can the innovation be adopted as a single, independent action?	Can anyone use an iPad? Are they interoperable or systems agnostic? Or are iPads only for Apple users?
Degree of Conformist Culture	How much does the relevant society value conformity versus individualism?	Since the Japanese society is more conformist than the individualist American society, trends are more likely to spread faster and more thoroughly in Japan than in the United States.
Industry Culture	What is the average age of decision makers in the industry? How much regulation exists in the industry?	New technologies are more likely to be embraced by the mobile advertising industry than in the reinsurance industry. Since regulation slows down decision making, technologies diffuse slower in industries that are more heavily regulated.

I would like to make a few additional points with respect to projecting the adaption of new products and technologies. First, let's look a little deeper at what can trigger faster uptake of a new product or technology. More people recommending or even mentioning your product will fuel uptake. Twitter and Facebook benefit from a whole slew of other companies, television programs and entertainers promoting Twitter and Facebook.

It is now common for television news anchors and pop singers to invite their viewers and fans to join them on Twitter and Facebook. One of the primary reasons that Hotmail achieved a $400 million exit in 1997 when it was sold to Microsoft was that its default email postscript—"Get your free email at Hotmail.com"—catalyzed growth. LinkedIn's ability to crawl through your email inboxes and invite everyone you have ever contacted to join your LinkedIn network is one of the primary contributors to that company's explosive growth. A similar phenomenon is at play with electronic payment services such as PayPal and Venmo: every time someone makes a payment via PayPal or Venmo, they naturally invite more and more people into the network.

Analytical Considerations One idea for measuring the virality of your product is the Net Promoter Score which is the percentage of your customers that recommend your product to their friends and colleagues. This is a very telling measure of your customers' satisfaction with your product, since when they recommend your product to their network they are putting their own reputations on the line. Separately, one confirmatory signal that a market is evolving from selling products that appeal to early-adapters, to products that appeal to the mass markets, occurs when there is an evolution in measurement. An example of this phenomena occurred during the birth of the consumer Internet, when pricing for online services evolved from price-per-hour to price-per-kilobit.

While referenceable customers help a company recruit more customers, not all customers are referenceable. Suppose you sell diamond drill bits to an oil exploration firm for purposes of probing ore deposits in central Africa and then sell identical diamond drill bits for similar purposes to a natural gas exploration firm in Oklahoma. Since the geologists of these two companies have no reasonable basis for communicating with each other, then you are dealing in two different markets. Similarly, if you sell diamond drill bits to an exploration firm in Oklahoma and then go across the street and sell the same product to a construction engineer who wishes to use the diamond drill bits to drill holes in concrete, you are also dealing in two different markets. In both cases, the reason you have separate markets is that the customers would not reference each other. As companies are limited in the salesforces that they can retain and in the resources they can dedicate to marketing, companies that wish to achieve rapid revenue growth must have earned positive word-of-mouth marketing and this word-of-mouth marketing is most likely to diffuse when customers speak to each other.

Second, it is important not to overweight the enthusiasm that some technical people employed by a targeted customer might have towards your disruptive innovation. Technical tinkers have a passion for evaluating new technologies and may have a budget for purchasing samples of each of the new relevant technologies that are brought to their attention. However, these people will typically not have the authority to make division- or company-wide purchasing decisions. The people with real purchasing power are usually only receptive to technologies that can improve existing processes. This is especially true in industries with tremendous fixed costs. Quite a few entrepreneurs have been shocked to learn that large companies do not want to abandon billions of dollars of fixed costs in order to adopt a supposedly breakthrough technology that has not yet even proven that it is compatible with other of the large company's processes. That new technology may not have even demonstrated that it is bug-free.

Theory is all well and good. But a review of leading indicators can help an analyst determine how strong sales will be in a given industry. For instance, if there is a surge in people submitting to background checks to purchase firearms, then it is reasonable to expect that there will soon be a surge in gun sales. The performance of sourcing agents (which act as middlemen between factories and retailers) such as Li & Fung provides insight into the direction of sales in the retail industry. A rise in mortgage applications is a precursor to mortgage origination fees, home sales and increased business activity at real estate agencies as well as at home improvement stores.

Value of Revenue

As George Orwell might have said, "A dollar of revenue is equal to any other dollar of revenue. But some dollars of revenue are more equal than others." More equal revenue has the following characteristics:

- It is predictable and consistent. Examples include the revenues that are collected annually for the use of domain names by web registrars like Web.com Group and GoDaddy, monthly premiums collected by insurance companies, monthly service charges for utilities and telecom usage, and subscriptions for newspapers and magazines.

- It derives from sales of products that require a high reorder velocity. For instance, toner cartridges are reordered frequently. One way to spur demand for products with high reorder rates is to sell the razor-type product at compelling prices while selling the razor-blade type product at relatively high prices. Other examples of razor, razor blade business models include iPods (the razors) and iTunes and Apple's App Store (the razor blades) as well as video games (the razor blades) and video game consoles such as Xbox and PlayStation (the razors).

Some appliances such as refrigerators that historically enjoyed long-lives are now becoming more disposable: the more electronics embedded in refrigerators, the faster they break down. (Even momentary electrical surges can irreparably damage digitally-driven refrigerators.) Undergarments directed at the incontinence market are an example of how a reusable product becomes disposable. On the other hand, many readers might guess that robots used for bomb detection would be disposable. However, soldiers actually grow attached to robots that detect improvised explosive devices and therefore make great efforts to reuse their intrepid robots. Finally, during periods when dressing down is the norm, t-shirts, jeans, and khakis do not go out of style as quickly as dresses and suits. During these times, people do not feel compelled to shop for clothes so often, cancelling out the built-in obsolescence that keeps clothing retailers' cash registers ringing.

- It comes from marquee and referenceable clients. It is easier to sell deeper into an industry once your product has been embraced by the leading companies in that industry. (Interestingly and conversely, some of the top consulting firms are forbidden to divulge the names of their clients because those clients do not want it known that they are confronted with managerial or strategic problems. So too are drone manufacturers reluctant to disclose the names of their U.S. clients because the use of drones in the U.S. at the time of this writing is illegal.)

- It comes from customers that are not price sensitive. For instance, if you run an accounting firm, you might be better off not taking on a client that is extremely price sensitive. You won't make much money providing service to him in the current year and next year the client will shop for an even less expensive accounting firm. Also, I have found that the degree of price sensitivity a customer has is related to the professionalization of the purchasing decision. If you are selling office supplies to a small company, the CEO will want to dispatch with those pesky issues as soon as possible. He won't have much time to quibble about pricing. However, if you are trying to sell office supplies to a large company with a procurement division, those procurement specialists will try to squeeze the last penny of profit out of you.

> **Analytical Consideration** Similar to revenue not being fungible, investment funds are not fungible. Thus, it is not correct to say that receiving a $1 million investment from one investor is the equivalent of receiving a $1 million investment from another investor. Having Sequoia Ventures

A few industries benefit from being relatively immune from pricing pressure. Take jewelry. Jewelry is desired because it is expensive. Even if it could be bought at discounted prices, customers would be unlikely to rave about those finds and such jewelry would largely be unsuitable for most gifts. How many brides and grooms do you think would gloat about how cheap their wedding rings were? It is interesting to note that Amazon has largely been unsuccessful in selling jewelry. In addition to the issue I just raised here, jewelry makers do not want to upset the jewelry stores by making the same products available for discounted prices via Amazon. Due to their compact sizes and high values, jewelry is at risk of being pilfered in fulfillment centers. Finally, the intricacy of upscale jewelry is difficult to display in full detail online.

Another virtue of charging extremely aggressive prices is that customers are less likely to complain about any perceived shortcomings with the product or service. For instance, if you are the CEO of a company that has been paying McKinsey $15 million a year (or maybe a month if we are talking about a conglomerate), would you really let it be known (to your board members) that this money was ill-spent? Probably not. Instead, you might be inclined to sing your consulting firm's praises.

In a similar vein, extremely high fees can be the reason that some service providers are successful. There is a corporate arbitrator that charges $25,000 a day for his services. He is successful but not because of any magic that he performs in terms of ideas for dispute resolution. Rather he is successful because the disputants realize that they damn well better find a solution or else they will pay another $25,000 tomorrow. Similarly, it is the extremely high fees that some top-tier law firms charge that dissuade their clients' adversaries from pursuing litigated remedies to commercial disputes.

- It is collected quickly. The earlier revenues are collected, the better. For instance, newspaper and insurance companies collect their subscriptions and premiums in advance of delivering their services. Priceline collects its revenues at the time of its bookings but pays hotels at the time the stay occurs. Also, funeral companies such as Carriage Services and Service Corporation International have very sizable backlogs of future revenues in the form of prepaid funeral fees.

> **Analytical Questions** To what extent are the benefits of prepaid funeral expenses to the funeral home operator offset by lower prices locked in by the customer? What is the revenue breakdown in terms of revenues from burials and cremations versus profits from investing the prepaid funeral expenses? Is the analyst taking care not to overweight any extraordinary earnings on such investments?

There are legitimate situations in which a company's revenues are being collected more slowly (and thus reporting rising days' sales outstanding figures). The company might be shifting from a sales model to a leasing model. The company might be selling more of its products or services to the government, larger companies or to foreign customers, all of whom typically take more time to pay their invoices.

- It is generated by companies that can harness the data related to the purchase to enhance future customer experiences. For instance, every time you make a purchase from Amazon or view a movie via Netflix those companies' intelligent recommendation engines become more accurate. Millions of Amazon and Netflix customers actually welcome recommendations from these companies.

- It comes from a diverse customer base. Companies that rely on one or two customers for an overwhelming portion of their revenues could be devastated by a key customer defection. When the audio company Audience saw its revenues from Apple Computer plunge from 82%

to 1% of its total revenues, its share price plummeted from $22 to less than $6. Thus, analysts should inquire about the percentage of revenue that a company receives from its top—let's say—two customers. However, there are situations where seemingly high levels of customer concentrations are not terribly problematic. If a vendor is selling into several divisions of a large company, each of which has spent a great deal of effort qualifying the vendor and jumping through regulatory hoops, then selling into each division may be more akin to selling to different companies.

- The revenue can be aggressively pursued without damaging the underlying business. Most businesses become healthier as revenues increase. However, banks that too aggressively market loans to consumers run out of qualified borrowers and thus resort to making credit available to customers with high risk profiles.

Demand Generation

Despite how many of the demand drivers that a company or its products meet, no one should be naïve enough to believe that a compelling customer proposition is sufficient to create a thriving business. The company will have to make concerted efforts to generate demand. A good rule of thumb for entrepreneurs is that their investments in product development should be matched by their investments in promoting the new product. Many marketing and advertising textbooks have been written. If the textbook methods for generating demand are working, fine. If they are not working, then more aggressive and less traditional methods of generating demand must be primed. Two of my favorite examples of this include:

- When Steve Jobs demoed the iPhone before the world at San Francisco's Moscone Center in 2007, the iPhone was full of bugs. Among the Apple team's many concerns was that the signal would not reach the phone that Steve Jobs was showcasing. Thus, Apple had AT&T install a portable cellular tower right behind the curtain. There was still concern that the signal might not be at maximum strength. So, Apple engineers coded the demo phone to always display five full bars of signal strength.

- In 1957, Sony introduced its TR-63 "pocket-size" radio, a phenomenal feat in miniaturization at the time. Sony was excited about the marketing leverage that would be gained by putting its radio in a shirt pocket. However, just as the radio was about to hit the market, Sony discovered that its radio was still slightly larger than a businessman's shirt pocket. Akio Morita, Sony's CEO, solved this marketing problem by ordering special shirts for his salesmen that had pockets slightly larger than normal.

It is often a savvy strategy to market your product without it appearing that you are active in marketing your product. Examples of such subtle marketing efforts include when Red Bull places crushed cans of its energy drinks on the floors of restrooms of popular night clubs, when new beers are promoted by "leaners" at bars who ask pub patrons to relay their drink requests through to the bartender, and marketing new cameras by asking wealthy tourists to take pictures of the marketers with such cameras. In its early days, it was alleged that Match.com had several of its attractive female employees feign interest in the men listed on that site when their memberships were about to lapse. Once these men renewed their memberships, they never heard from these attractive ladies again.

The music industry has had many interesting methods for creating demand. One way that record labels ensured that their performers' songs received air time on radio stations was accomplished with the help of independent promotion companies (also known as "indies"). These companies purported to 'promote' radio stations. Their assistance was in the form of helping radio stations maintain maximum listeners by advising it which were the best new records to play. And to persuade the radio stations it was worth paying attention to its advice, the independent promotion companies paid each one a large sum of money. Let's say $100,000 a year. Once an indie had 'claimed' a radio station in this way, the record companies were advised that they would be invoiced (e.g. $1,000) each time that station added a song to its playlist. Thus, if a radio station added four new songs a week for fifty weeks of the year that would be $200,000 worth of invoices to the record companies. The result was that the indie earned $100,000 for each radio station it claimed.

Revenue Traps

Investors and business professionals should be wary of a company's revenue projections especially if they come from a venture funded company or a management team with no experience in preparing financial projections. In determining the feasibility of such revenue projections we should apply the thinking behind the Diffusions of Innovations Theory (see above). We should also take into account Hofstadter's Law which tells us: "It always takes longer than you expect (to generate revenue), even when you take Hofstadter's Law into account." Project managers have used Hofstadter's law to modify their programmers' estimates of delivery times by doubling the number of units at the next higher level. So when a programmer says he can fix a bug in one hour, the project manager will expect the solution in two days. Our lesson from Hofstadter and project managers is to reduce the revenue expectations given to us by inexperienced entrepreneurs by 50% at double the timeline. So, if an entrepreneur says that his company will generate $5 million in revenue in two years, we would expect $2.5 million in revenue in four years.

> **Analytical Consideration** When reviewing a company's financial projections, one of the first things that I ask the management team is how much experience they have in preparing such projections. A follow up question—if the management team answers that they are experienced in this regard—is how accurate their past modeling has been. Another relevant question along these lines is how much input did the modelers receive from the various product managers.

Is the Revenue Real?

It is of crucial importance to make sure we are clear on what the definition of a company's revenue is. As I write these pages, Amazon's annual revenue stands at about $75 billion while Alibaba's revenue is roughly $8 billion. This doesn't sound proportional, does it? The disparity is due to Alibaba not including in its revenue the sales prices of the goods it sells; rather it only reports as revenues the commissions and fees that it receives for facilitating sales through its website. Amazon includes its selling prices in its revenues.

The issue of understanding a company's real revenue is critical when applying the price-to-sales valuation ratio. I have seen situations where investors thought the shares of recruitment firms (or employment agencies) were incredibly inexpensive. However, these companies aggressively recorded the entire compensation of the people they placed as revenues and not the smaller but cleaner commissions that the recruitment firms were entitled to receive. If you were assessing an auction firm, you would want to make sure that the revenues reported represented the auctioneer's commissions, not the selling prices of antiques that it sold. If you were analyzing an advertising agency that maintains custody of its clients' entire budget for television advertising, you would want to focus on the fees generated from creating and placing the commercials rather than the total budget since a large portion would go to television stations airing such advertising. If you were reviewing a cigarette kiosks' or a liquor stores' revenues, you would want to remove any excise taxes collected from those retailers' reported revenues.

Is the Revenue Worth It?

Even when revenue is appropriately reported, it is important to review how expensive it is for a company to collect that revenue. Start-up companies often pay their salespeople extremely high commission rates because of the risk that they are taking by joining a pioneering company. Thus, even when sales are made, a large portion of the revenue is not retained by the company. A similar phenomenon is at work in the Asian gambling industry. Junket operators that recruit high-rollers to gamble in Macau typically receive 1.25% of the gambler's rolling chip turnover, or the aggregate of bets made. This equals 44% of gross revenue from high rollers and 29% of the casinos' total revenue. On the other hand, business that is generated too inexpensively can portend problems down the road: The Lending Club has achieved low underwriting costs by economizing on the verification of the information its prospective borrowers provide.

In some cases the collection of revenue forebodes decreasing prospects for a company. If the sales process is overly aggressive—as is often the case when electronics store salesmen push warranties onto customers—the likelihood of customer defections increases. Also, if customers deem particular service charges so annoying—as was the case with Blockbuster's late fees—customer resentment may motivate their exodus.

The receipt of some revenue carries corresponding liabilities. Auto makers, for instance, are on the hook to pay for recalls should their vehicles need to be repaired due to manufacturing defects. Aircraft manufacturers offer resale guarantees which means that if their planes' resale prices fall below certain thresholds, the manufacturer may need to make up the difference. Thus, the more new aircraft sold, the more risk the manufacturer has in terms of inadvertently suppressing the prices of older aircraft and triggering resale guarantees.

We should be careful that we do not allow press releases to attribute more revenue potential to a company than it deserves. Suppose that you own shares of a defense contractor and Wall Street expects that the company will generate $10 billion in revenue in the current year. You are being a prudent investor by monitoring the press releases that this company issues. It seems to you that every few weeks the defense contractor is announcing contract wins for tens, or even hundreds, of millions of dollars. You might start to get swept up in all these promising announcements. You might be ready to buy more shares in light of all of the positive news coming out of the company. Let this paragraph be a reminder to you that the company must report such wins if it is to reach its projected $10 billion in annual revenue.

Does the Revenue Portend Problems Ahead?

Companies can boost revenues at the price of profit erosion. Retail chains can report rising company-wide revenues by opening more stores. This, of course, could cannibalize the results from individual stores and thus weaken the entire chain. A corollary to this issue can be found among homebuilders that post higher sales contracts because they are opening new residential communities, rather than selling more of their inventory in existing developments.

Analytical Considerations Not all revenue carries precedential value. For instance, it is common for companies to sell their initial products to their employees at discounted prices. Cable companies that launch new services have done this as did Better Place when it made its battery operated cars available in Israel. These employees-customers are reticent to voice any dissatisfaction they have with such services or products and future sales will be adopted less readily by the broader target markets.

Also, companies that generate their revenue through enabling their clients to test new technologies are in positions of vulnerability. For instance, Hortonworks's revenue comes mainly from providing tech support to companies experimenting with Hadoop, an open-source framework for distributed storage and processing of massive amounts of data. According to a 2014 Gartner Inc. report, "Through 2017, 60% of big-data projects will fail to go beyond piloting and experimentation and will be abandoned."

A surge in revenues can indicate that the long-term prospects for a business are bleak. When there was concern about restrictions on purchasing guns in the aftermath of the Obama re-election and school shootings, sporting goods retailers that carried guns, such as Cabela's, experienced a rush of gun sales. When new restrictions on members of the US Army having tattoos (below the elbow) were announced, there was a spike in business at tattoo parlors. However, this spike should not have been extrapolated into the future since the rush to get tattoos was a function of the reduced demand that would soon come about. On the other hand, a literal catastrophe can be an elixir for higher property and casualty insurance premiums. For example, in the aftermath of the Little Tujunga fire in California, the state insurance commissioner approved what amounted to $115 million in increases in premiums for State Farm, Farmers and Allstate.

The acceleration of revenue recognition enables companies to report higher revenue levels in the current quarter even though the reality is that customers have stopped using the product or service. For instance, when people use mobile games for shorter periods of time (maybe because they are bored of the game) and buy less virtual durable goods such as superhero characters, game makers reduce the average period in which the item will be used. Thus, the accounting of the revenue collected from the customer is compressed into few quarters.

Appropriability Analysis

Appropriability is the extent to which a celebrity or innovator has the ability to capture profits generated by their fame. Licensing is a common method for ratcheting up appropriability. A sports team or celebrity can quickly license their names to an almost limitless variety of products. (Of all the things we worship about our favorite celebrities—beauty, charm, wit, talent—by far the easiest and most affordable thing to emulate is their clothing. Thus, many celebrities wisely try to appropriate their fame by introducing lines of clothing and fragrances.) Similarly, Disney's characters are highly appropriable because Disney derives revenues from their appearances in movies, Broadway plays, books, and theme parks as well as through licensing their likenesses.

On the other hand, it does not do much good if there is a great deal of talk about famous people or innovative products if the celebrities or creators cannot profit from such discussions. Chatter is not equivalent to revenue. More people are talking about Twitter than using Twitter and far more people are talking about Thomas Piketty's book "Capital in the Twenty-First Century" than reading it. Further, creators often do not benefit from downstream commerce. For instance, when popular games produced by Electronic Arts are sold on the secondary market as used titles, Electronic Arts receives no revenue.

It seems that GoPro is struggling with appropriability. GoPro users must have filmed at least tens of thousands of hours of their activities that GoPro would like to turn into programming. In its Investors' Prospectus, GoPro indicated that that its reach included the following:

- Facebook: over 7.2 million "likes;"
- Instagram: over 2.0 million followers;
- Twitter: over 950,000 followers; and,
- YouTube: over 450 million video views and over 1.8 million subscribers.

As of December 31, 2013, GoPro had not derived revenue from the distribution of, or social engagement with, such content on its GoPro Network. It is not clear to me how GoPro can profit from its customers' use of their cameras. Genuine demand would have to exist to view so much content and rights would have to be secured from customers to use their content. GoPro will have to split any revenue that it generates with its social media partners, such as the 45% share that YouTube charges its partners. If GoPro were to go it alone, it would incur significant launch costs and would have to spend huge amounts of money hosting millions of videos.

Substitutes Impact Revenue Projections

When projecting the intermediate-term or long-term revenue of a company you should always consider the risk of a substitute product or service displacing the subject product or service. Fracking is a substitute for solar powered panels. Grocery stores are substitutes for restaurants while pharmaceuticals are often substitutes for medical devices. Trucking is a substitute for moving containers by rail while the streaming of movies is a substitute for patronizing movie theaters.

Other examples of products and services that are threatened with substitutes include:

- Dish Network, the satellite operator, could compete with wireless telecom operators since it has billions of dollars of wireless licenses.

- Prescription glasses are losing revenues to Lasik surgery.

- Generations of people grew up with disposable toys and consumer electronics which were powered with disposable batteries. Now the disposable battery business is in permanent decline as consumers shift to smart phones and tablets that have built-in rechargeable batteries.

- Nickel cadmium batteries were replaced by nickel metal hydride batteries which were replaced by lithium ion batteries.

- Now that millions of people are getting their weather information on weather.com or on weather-related apps, they need not watch the Weather Channel. Thus, it should not come as a surprise that DirecTV demanded a reduction in the fees it pays to carry the Weather Channel.

- Apps such as MyFitnessPal, Lose It!, and SparkPeople.com that track caloric intake as well as the number of calories burned during physical activity threaten to snatch business away from the likes of diet management companies such as Weight Watchers and Jenny Craig.

- Adhesives such as glue are replacing welds, rivets, screws and bolts in many manufactured products, ranging from airplanes to smartphones.

- Discount air carriers are a substitute for buses.

- Under some scenarios, recycling cell phones and other electronic gadgets could be a cheaper means of obtaining gold than mining it from the ground. This is because each ton of phones contains ten ounces of gold, a much higher gold yield than you will find in a ton of even high-grade ore.

Derivative Impact of Industry Developments

When assessing the future potential of a company, efforts must be made to determine how the subject industry will be affected by the fortunes of similar or adjacent industries. For instance, if home sales are soaring, it is likely that home improvement retailers such as Lowe's and Home Depot will prosper as home owners will tidy up their homes so as to realize higher selling prices. At the same time, new home buyers often want to renovate their new house so that it reflects their personas. Other examples of the fortunes of one industry being impacted by developments occurring in adjacent industries include:

- If home prices deteriorate and the velocity of home sales decelerates, assisted living facilities operators such as Capital Senior Living could disappoint their investors. This is because a large number of seniors that would like to move into an assisted living facility may not be able to afford to do so if they cannot sell their houses or if they only realize depressed prices.

- When students are burdened with repaying ever-growing student loans, it will take longer for them to afford a down payment or qualify for a mortgage. Instead of buying houses, they will continue to live with their parents or roommates. Thus, the higher student loan debt rises, the more pressured home building companies such as Lennar and Toll Brothers will become.

- If sales of new vehicles plunge, it is likely that auto finance companies will be pinched. However, after-market auto retailers such as AutoZone may benefit as people retain their cars for longer periods of time.

- Regulation can spark a derivative impact. For instance, the government is putting pressure on banks to make sure there is no discrimination in lending. In turn, the banks are putting pressure on car dealers to make sure that they do not exercise discrimination in making loans available to car buyers. This is a serious issue as about 20% of the gross profit generated by dealerships' new and used car sales comes from income earned on finance and insurance services, according to the National Auto Dealers Association.

- If steel prices rise, auto manufacturers' profitability could be adversely impacted.

- If drought causes the price of grain to rise, Outback Steakhouse could suffer in the near-term because the price of steaks will rise as it becomes more expensive to feed cattle. Grain prices could also rise if there were a lack of rail cars—perhaps due to crowding out by shale oil and gas operators—used to deliver grain from the Midwest to cattle ranchers.

  On the other hand—if you were trying to gauge the direction of beef prices, because you are considering investing in Texas Roadhouse or Darden Restaurants (in order to play LongHorn Steakhouse)—you would probably come to the conclusion that beef prices are headed lower (which is accretive to the profitability of such companies) if feed costs were declining. One indicia of some persistence of feed costs declining is if ranchers are retaining more young female cattle (heifers) to produce new animals. Another signal that feed costs are likely to remain lower for some time is if the percent of US cattle that are located in areas currently facing drought is declining.

- Proposed Food and Drug Administration regulation regarding the beer industry's disposal of spent grains could trigger rising prices for cattle feed. This would result in higher costs for beef which could pinch the profit margins of steakhouses such as Ruth's Hospitality Group and Morton's The Steakhouse. The dynamic at play here is that beer brewers have long made good money selling spent grains (which are left over after barley, wheat and other grains are steeped in hot water) as animal feed instead of throwing them away. However, a proposed FDA rule change would impose new sanitary handling procedures, record keeping and other food safety processes on brewers. For the brewers, the impact of the regulatory change would not only deprive them of revenues but would force them to bear the expense of disposing spent grains at landfills.

- The armored transportation and vending machine industries as well as banks that use high-speed coin counting machines could experience disruption if the price of zinc continues to rise. The composition of pennies is 97.5% zinc and the price of zinc has been rising significantly, sparking discussion about finding substitutes for the metal. If a zinc substitute is used in the composition of pennies, industries that value coins by weight and size or by their electromagnetic signature could be confronted with malfunctioning machines and logistical challenges.

- When Google's Gmail service decided to directly route promotional emails to a dedicated promotions folder, this must have hurt companies such as Groupon and the Gilt Groupe which depend on pushing emails to customers. (I do not think Groupon's strategy—announced subsequent to Gmail's shift in managing promotional emails—of enticing people to go to its site instead of responding to emails will be successful.)

- As home entertainment systems continue to improve, movie ticket sales are likely to continue to decline. Indeed, the number of tickets sold fell nearly 11% between 2004 and 2013. One concomitant lesson here is that an increasingly out-of-favor industry can partially disguise its plight by increasing prices even when volumes are deteriorating. Thus, it is important to review trends in unit sales and average selling prices as well as trends in company and industry revenue.

- Self-destructive messaging platforms such as WhatsApp, Secret, Snapchat and Cyber Dust threaten the traditional $120 billion annual global SMS text-messaging system used by telecom companies.

- The ever increasing accuracy and speed of Internet search engines could mute the success that should belong to domain name registration companies due to the proliferation of domain suffixes. One would think that companies such as Web.com Group and Register.com would stand to profit from the growing number of domain extensions, especially since the annual fees for maintaining such extensions are expected to be as much as three times the cost of domains that have common suffixes such as .com or .net. Anyone wishing to locate a business can simply type in the name of a business and the engine will almost invariably find the site regardless of the extension. Incidentally, another factor that could thwart the success of domain name registration companies is that they are losing prominence as more Internet traffic funnels through mobile apps and social networks.

- The ubiquity of high-quality latex condoms, which reduce the risk of (usually lethal) breakage when digested by drug couriers, may lead to heightened demand for technologies designed to detect traces of drugs.

- Companies that manufacture the components that are inserted into highly popular devices—such as iPhone and Xboxes—often benefit from the success of the end product. However, many manufacturers of these hot-selling products forbid their suppliers from disclosing the fact that their components are incorporated into such end products. To determine whose components are included in top selling end products, you have to wait until tear-downs (that is, the disassembling of products to identify their components) are released.

- The proliferation of smart phones is accretive to dating sites. Even when singles attend singles events, they can't stop gazing at their screens. Their inapproachability ratchets up the utility of dating sites.

Pickaxe Companies

It has been said that fortunes were made selling pickaxes during California's Gold Rush that began in the late 1840s. Levi Strauss certainly sewed up a fortune supplying miners with pants initially cut from tent cloth.

Thus, when you spot a trend, you can play it derivatively by investing in companies that enable or supply those trends. If you have determined that server farms will continue to proliferate, you can review the prospects for real estate firms, such as Digital Realty Trust, that house data centers. If your research indicates that exploration for natural resources is poised to soar, you can take a look at logistics companies—such as Civeo, Fleetwood and Horizon North Logistics—that build lodgings for the affected workers. When hearing that fracking activity is surging you will discover that it can take four million pounds of sand to frack a single well. Thus, you can review the prospects for sand miners such U.S. Silica Holdings, Emerge Energy Services, Fairmount Minerals or Hi-Crush Partners. If you believe that the installation of solar panels will soar, you might want to consider investing in silver commodities or silver mining companies as silver is a major factor in catching the sun's rays and transforming them into energy. In addition to generating demand for silver, solar panels reduce the supply of silver since that metal degrades when used in photovoltaic cells.

Analytical Consideration When reviewing real estate companies that house server farms and data centers, you should inquire as to the concentration of their customers utilizing computing power for purposes of mining bitcoins. As the complexity of mining bitcoins increases, the costs of electricity and hardware surge, which could cause bitcoin miners to retreat or fold.

Sometimes pickaxe plays lie at the convergence of two industry trends. For instance, there is a proliferation of micro-brewers and the movement to sell beer through cans instead of bottles. (As mentioned earlier, cans provide better seals than bottles and prevent light from striking the beer, which can make the beer taste bad. Also, since a case of cans weighs about a third less than a case of bottles, money can be saved on shipping.) Anyway, one opportunity that lies at the cross-section of these two industry developments is mobile canners such as Mobile Canning Systems which haul their equipment to breweries, spend a few hours filling cans, and then move onto the next customer.

Selected Accounting Issues

This book is not meant to be a primer on accounting issues. Nevertheless, there are a few accounting issues related to assessing business models that I think are important to consider and I will address them here.

Earnings Normalization There should be some attempt to normalize earnings. At a minimum, do not invest in a cyclical business based on its peak earnings. Rather, take an average of such company's earnings over several years.

Also, suppose you are considering acquiring a privately-held business. You may not run that business in the same manner that the current owners run the business. Maybe the current owners are paying themselves salaries far below what the market suggests they deserve (perhaps to make earnings appear more robust), skirted some regulatory licensing issues (perhaps a bar has not yet renewed its liquor license), and carries excessive insurance (because the owners are not as savvy insurance buyers as you are). To get a cleaner picture of how profitable such business would be in your hands, you should add back executive compensation and regulatory compliance costs to bring those figures to market levels and reduce your projected outlays for insurance premiums.

Cost Management It is extremely dangerous for one company to allow other companies to manage its costs. Grain companies which buy from farmers contract for most shipping, even though farmers bear the cost of shipping their wheat to market. Another example of this phenomenon relates to university textbooks. Professors that receive lecture notes and quizzes from publishers often require their students to purchase the corresponding textbooks for hundreds of dollars each.

Inventory Management You should avoid companies that have very high costs of inventory and only a small window to sell such inventory. For instance, Chegg has been very active in selling used textbooks. The problem is that used textbooks are not that much cheaper than new textbooks. Since textbooks are updated very frequently—it is not uncommon to see twentieth editions—there is little time to sell used textbooks and a large risk of getting stuck with expensive inventory.

However, some companies have a knack for making a virtue of their aging or available inventory. When restaurants offer customers their "specials," they are often trying to dispose of aging food. One of the factors that Netflix used to recommend DVDs to its customers was the availability of such movies.

Margin Analysis Analysts should consider not where a company's profit margins are today, but where they are likely headed in the years ahead. At the time of this writing, Mobileye derives most of its revenues from selling advanced driver assisted systems to the large original equipment auto manufacturers. Mobileye is sporting profit margins of 50%. Substantially no companies outside of the software industry maintain 50% profit margins for any length of time. I cannot imagine that the auto makers would allow any of their suppliers to earn such lucrative margins into the distant future. Thus, it appears to me that Mobileye's profit margins are at risk of being significantly compressed. Similarly, server manufacturers' margins are at risk of being squeezed as cloud storage is resulting in the mix of their buyers shifting from individual companies (which have little negotiating power) to server farms (which have massive negotiating power).

In the mid-1990s, I could not understand why the leveraged-buyout firm Kohlberg Kravis & Roberts was investing so heavily in supermarket chains. (KKR acquired, or was a major investor in, Safeway, Bruno's, Stop & Shop and other stores.) Grocery stores—which traditionally only generated one percent net profit margins—were expected to generate net profit margins of two percent in the near-term. Why was such a successful investment firm interested in an industry that was delivering anorexic net profits margins of two percent? It took me some time to realize that the grocers were expected to deliver a profit margin expansion of 100%.

Leverage of Creditors There is a prescient expression, "If you want it bad, you get it bad." This means that if a company is in dire financial straits but finds an equity investor or creditor, the terms of the financing will be oner-ous. The company's initial owners might suffer draconian dilution, have to comply with covenants that severely restrict its operations, and may be subject to steep interest rates. The takeaway here is that if the company is in financial difficulty, you must perform more analysis of its balance sheet, financial structure and financing terms than if it was financially strong.

Abnormally Large Severance Payments When a company pays abnor-mally large severance payments to its departing employees, the motiva-tion could be to conceal misdeeds. Sure enough, not long after American Apparel paid out large severance packages, its CEO was accused of having sexually harassed some of that company's employees. It would be extremely troubling to see a controller or treasurer leaving a company with an unex-plainably generous severance package.

Conflicts of Interest Warren Buffett said, "Never ask a barber if you need a haircut." It is risky to have the same company that provides inspections also provide repair work. One of Caterpillar's subsidiaries, Progress Rail Services, inspects railcars. It has been alleged that workers at that company charged with inspecting the railcars feel pressure to produce billable work. When the railcars are not in disrepair, it has been said that some of these inspectors have resorted to smashing brake parts with hammers, gouging wheels with chisels or using chains to yank handles loose.

A similar conflict of interest risk exists with surgeons who are also inventors of medical devices or have a financial interest in promoting such devices. For instance, in 2014 the U.S Justice Department sued a neuro-surgeon for allegedly performing unnecessary spinal operations which benefited an implant distributorship that he owned.

Payback Period The faster a company can earn back its customer ac-quisition costs or invested capital, the less money a company will need to raise. Thus, more rapid payback periods reduce the dilution of current shareholders.

Selected Risk Issues

Below are a few of the issues related to risk that business development professionals and investors should consider:

The Strategy Paradox

The Strategy Paradox is a super hyped-up version of the Pareto Principle (discussed a little further ahead) and holds that the more focused a company is in seizing its most promising opportunity, the greater risk there is that the company will implode. Let's say we are managing a pharmaceutical company that has a lot of legacy drugs that will soon lose their patent protection. Our firm is also conducting some research into stem cells. If our research bears fruit and the market for stem cells ripens, our firm could make a fortune. Further, our investment banker tells us that if we were to divest our company of everything except for stem cell research, the stock market would reward our shares with a 3x multiple expansion. Let's say we follow our investment banker's advice. If the stars align, the managers will be heroes. However, if any of the stars fail to fall into place, the company could plunge into insolvency.

Mismatch of Commitments

Companies place themselves in vulnerable positions when their commitments to suppliers exceed the commitments obtained from their customers. This can happen when companies accept cancellation penalties from their suppliers but allow their customers to make refundable deposits. For instance, Better Place collected $5,000 deposits from each of its customers but such reservations were not binding. At the same time, Better Place allowed many of its suppliers to insert high minimum orders and cancellation penalties into their contracts. This created more than $100 million of off-the-record liabilities and contributed to Better Place's collapse.

Questionable Rights

There is an adage which holds that you should never put your money where you can't get it out. Well, if you buy a piece of property with no title or with questionable title, you are taking a major risk. Surprisingly, such risks could manifest themselves when buying a co-op in the toniest buildings in Manhattan because many co-ops in New York City do not own the land beneath their buildings. Eventually, these land leases approach the end of their terms or reach resets (legal triggers that cause lease payments to rise). These events cause apartment values to plunge as the co-ops' shareholders are required pay skyrocketing assessments to cover the purchase of the land.

If investments are made in land with dubious title in developing countries, liquidity risks are compounded with repatriation risks. Many sovereign wealth funds have been acquiring rights to huge swaths of land in the developing world in order to secure food supplies for their populations. For instance, China has leased 6.9 million acres in the Democratic Republic of Congo for the world's largest oil palm plantation. Saudi Arabia has leases on over one million acres in each of Indonesia, Tanzania and Ethiopia. The United Arab Emirates leased 800,000 acres in Pakistan and as many as 250,000 acres in the Ukraine, and a million acres in Sudan. Hedge funds such as Jarch Capital have also been acquiring rights to farmland in emerging countries while KKR, the leverage buyout specialist, invested in Afriflora which is an Ethiopian grower of flowers.

These transactions seem very risky to me as the optics look very bad. Programs that divert food from countries which have huge populations of starving citizens to much wealthier countries would be easy targets for exporting governments to oppose as well as politically difficult for supranational organizations to enforce. Hedge funds making investments in farmlands of developing countries would receive even less sympathy. These concerns are in addition to nonexistent or extremely weak property rights and judiciaries in developing countries. However, if you were to look for a case study in how professional investors can force countries to honor their obligations, you can research how Elliot Management, NML Capital, and Aurelius Capital Management are forcing Argentina to make good on its obligations to holders of its government-issued debt.

Analytical Consideration The business models of some smart-phone app providers are predicated on monetizing rights that do not belong to them. For instance, purveyors of parking apps make markets in public parking spaces that fall under the authority of local governments.

Distribution of Disappointment

Let's say that you are considering investing in a retailer with 100 stores. The company has been losing money for the past several years. In its most recent year the company lost $30 million. One important question to ask is, "How is the pain distributed?" In other words, "Is the chain losing $30 million because all of the stores are losing a little bit of money or because some stores are making money while other stores are losing considerable amounts of money?" I would prefer the answer to be the latter. This is because the retailer could close the underperforming stores and then the entire chain should be able to achieve strong profitability. On the other hand, if all of the stores were losing money, the concept is not successful anywhere and the chain would be doomed.

However, if I were reviewing a bank that was heavily exposed to originating and serving residential mortgages, my answer would be different. If such a bank told me that its average loan-to-value ratio was 75 percent, I would ask, "Are you averaging 75 because the loan-to-value of most loans in your book is between 70 and 80? Or are you averaging 75 because you have a concentration of 50s and 60s along with a concentration of 95s and 100s?" Mortgages with down payments of 5 percent (a 95-percent loan-to-value ratio) would be like time bombs as they would be vulnerable to any downturn in housing prices.

Compounded Risks

There are self-contained risks and then there are compounded risks. You would rather your companies be exposed to self-contained risks than compounded risks.

Self-contained risks mean that a misfortune of one industry player will have a neutral or positive impact on other industry players. For example, if one airline experiences the tragedy of a fatal crash, other airline operators will learn from that mistake and become safer. They will also stand to gain customers due to defections from the befallen carrier. If the retail chain that I alluded to above closed some of its stores, its surviving stores would stand to benefit from receiving the shuttered stores' customers.

Compounded risks mean that the failure of one industry player renders it more likely that other industry players will fail. If our bank discussed above experiences a rise in mortgage defaults, it can expect to experience even more mortgage defaults. This is because when one of your neighbors sells his house at a fire sale price, he is basically repricing every house in the neighborhood at a lower level since new buyers will use home sales data from websites such as The Zillow Group in their negotiations. Successive home sales by mortgage holders may be below their mortgage pay-off values, thereby triggering losses at the bank. Further, since banks often hold interbank loans, the failure of one bank can start a chain reaction. The risk of defaulting debt cascading throughout the economy is more pronounced in China where there is a high incidence of company-to-company debt.

Delivery companies such as UPS and FedEx are exposed to compounded risks during times of inclement weather. Not only does cold weather make on-time deliveries harder but more people accelerate their Internet ordering because they are confined indoors.

Overrating Black Sheep Discounts

It is important that business strategists and investors understand that eliminating one poorly-performing line of business will not always be as accretive to the company as one might think. The removal of one division will have ramifications for the remaining divisions. For instance, when IBM sold its Personal Computing Division to Lenovo Group, IBM's remaining businesses could have been adversely affected: IBM's server business could have faced higher prices for circuits and processors since IBM had less buying power when it no longer needed to procure components for its personal computers. Similarly, when General Electric sold its appliance business to Electrolux, GE's finance unit should have expected to realize reduced profits since there will be less demand for the financing of GE's products.

Mandatory Retirement

Professional services firms that adopt mandatory retirement by a stipulated age put themselves at risk. Let's say your firm adopted mandatory retirement at 62-years of age as did Arthur Anderson. Let's say that the senior engagement partners, most of whom are in their mid-fifties, are heavily incentivized to bring in as much new business as possible. The risk is that these partners may not be so sensitive to risk because it might take three or four years for liability resulting from sketchy clients to surface and then another five to eight years to reach a settlement. By that time, the culpable engagement partner will be enjoying his retirement.

Business
Model
Analysis

Supply Chain Analysis

Generating demand is a crucial factor in developing a successful business. But once demand exists, companies must have the ability to produce the goods that customers crave. While a fragmented supplier base enables the subject industry to negotiate favorable procurement of supplies, the supplier base must be consolidated enough to efficiently produce the materials required by the subject industry. Thus, the importance of supply chain analysis, a few points of which are touched on here.

Let's say that your company wants to tap into the demand that exists for hamburgers and chicken in the developing world. What kinds of supply chain obstacles could your company face?

Well, if you wanted to bring hamburgers to Africa you would find that there is a shortage of refrigerated trucks and warehouses to keep the patties fresh. Solving this immediate supply chain issue would land you right in the middle of the Icarus Paradox. Chains such as Johnny Rockets Group, Burger King and CKE Restaurants (the parent company of Carl's Jr. and Hardee's) have found that demand for beef in Africa is growing faster than cows can be raised. And the cattle that are raised are too scrawny to yield much saleable meat. Looking further upstream you would find that it is hard to grow grass for grazing in drought-stricken areas. Related endemic water shortages may pressure your company to build water treatment plants.

Or maybe you want to sell chicken in China. First, your company will likely be required to purchase expensive land on which to build chicken farms. Your selection of land will be limited to plots adjacent to other poultry producers so as to mitigate the spread of disease to humans. (But wouldn't this heighten the risk that your chickens would catch diseases from neighboring chicken farms?) Obtaining the necessary government approvals can take years and your firm might be required to build roads and bridges and install electrical lines.

Analytical Consideration There are redeeming features associated with supply bottlenecks. A lack of supply can at least partially mute the ferocity of the entrance of a potentially dominant competitor into an industry. For instance, Wal-Mart is making an effort to become a significant player in the retailing of organic foods. However, at the time of this writing, suppliers are not at sufficient scale to handle the volume that Wal-Mart demands. For instance, organic milk suppliers are rationing supplies and customers for organic beans are being rejected.

Some supply chains benefit from deadheading which is what happens when a transporter returns from a delivery with an empty load. For instance, companies that ship their merchandise to China can often obtain very inexpensive shipping rates because, come hell or high water, boats are going back to China and they need ballast to balance in the water. Interestingly, in the early 1900s, United Fruit solved its deadheading problem by converting its cargo ships, used to import bananas into the United States from the tropics, into luxury liners. These luxury liners offered cruises to Americans when the boats were dispatched to retrieve new bunches of bananas.

Risks of Outsourcing

Let's see if you can detect the following sleight of hand: The costs to an American company for having its products manufactured in China are much lower than in the United States because the average factory worker earns $0.63 per hour in China while the average employee in the United States earns $21.11 per hour. Do you see the sleight of hand? It does not matter what the average Chinese worker earns because an American company will usually not directly contract with Chinese workers, but rather with Chinese manufacturers, and those Chinese manufacturers will retain a good bit of the wage differential as their own profits. It does not matter if a Chinese worker earns $0.63 per hour if your company has to pay the manufacturing company significantly more per hour.

There are significant challenges to contracting with outsourcing manufacturers. These problems can begin when the prospective client inspects the quality of the outsourcing companies' work. In some cases, the outsourcing company purchases finished products from other companies and showcases them as their own. While the initial prices that outsourcers charge may be quite attractive, those prices are likely to rise consistently. Also, the quality of the outsourcers' production deteriorates as those manufacturers skimp on the quality of the materials that they use. It is very difficult for the client to disengage from its relationship with its outsourcing contractor because that contractor likely has significant knowledge about the production of the goods and can therefore make a credible threat to compete against its client.

Also, the client (let's say a paint brush company) likely has demands placed on it for rapid delivery from its clients (let's say chains of home improvement stores). This means that if the paint brush company terminates its relationship with its manufacturer, it has very little time to recruit, retain and train another outsourcing manufacturer. Any hiccups in a smooth transition could mean the termination of the paint brush company's relationship with its home improvement customers. And who is to say that another outsourcing company would be any better? The initial outsourcing manufacturer is aware of the predicament that its clients find themselves in and sees no urgency to accommodate its clients.

> **Unique Business Model** Brew Hub has a very interesting business model that skirts many of the problems that arise when working with outsourced manufacturers. That company leases temporary space at its big brewery to craft brewers and allows its lessees to brew their beers under the supervision of their own brewmasters. Thus, specialty brewers can ensure that their beers are produced to their own specifications while avoiding the costs associated with building new breweries.

Supply of Labor Labor is a necessary element in producing products and services. For a business to retain earnings, it must have some leverage over its employees. Otherwise, all of its revenues—maybe more—will be paid out to employees. This concern is pronounced in the investment banking and filmed entertainment industries. In any case, the analyst and business development professional should assess the leverage businesses have over their employees.

In highly competitive industries, employees are often in the driver's seat. For instance, alternative taxi operator, Lyft, allowed its drivers to retain all of the revenues collected from its "prime time" pricing. One sign that the demand for labor is overheating is when companies offer their employees bounties for recruiting additional employees. However, in some cases, when the price of labor is unreasonable, businesses try to circumvent employees. For example, television and movie studios have eliminated a lot of demand for actors by relying more heavily on reality programs that feature regular people as well as more tightly embracing animation. Several cement companies are aggressively researching self-pouring and self-applying cement for similar reasons.

In some industries, employees have no leverage. Let's consider the shipping industry. Imagine you are a cargo handler and have a dispute with your supervisor while on a cargo ship. Since there are no phone lines, cellular service or Internet access, you will have to resolve the issues on the ship. You will have to represent yourself without the benefit of union representatives, a police force or any semblance of a governmental agency or judiciary system. Even if you had access to such dispute resolution authorities and processes, who would you complain to, when you are employed by a Manila manning agency on a ship owned by an American, flagged by Panama, managed by a Cypriot, in international waters?

Separately, companies are at risk of scandals erupting over the terms that the workers who produce their goods have with the intermediary outsource contractors. Because of the demands that the client companies place on outsource contractors, the contractors drive their employees as hard as they can. So hard, that Foxconn had to place nets around its workers' dormitories, to catch those employees who attempted to commit suicide by jumping off of the roof.

Scrutiny of Supply Chains The situs of finished products and raw materials should be assessed. Most industries try to minimize their inventory levels and accelerate their sales cycles because the value of inventory in many industries falls over time. However, the wine industry takes great efforts to retain its inventory of wines for prolonged periods of time since wine increases in value as it ages. Thus, the location of wineries is an important issue. Wineries in Napa Valley, California are at much greater risk of suffering from earthquake damage than their brethren in France.

Under regulations spawned by the 2010 Dodd-Frank legislation, companies whose financial reports fall under the purview of the Securities and Exchange Commission must describe their efforts to determine if tantalum, tin, tungsten or gold used in their products have ties with armed groups in the Democratic Republic of Congo. This scrutiny could impact the semiconductor, mobile phone and the electronics industries. There are similar regulations in place that require the monitoring of companies' use of North Korean gold in their supply chains.

Distribution Channel Analysis

Even when end consumers crave a product, revenues will not be generated unless that product is delivered to the marketplace. In some situations the path to the market will become smoother, such as when the Panama Canal widens and as the polar ice caps melt. Remember, however, that we, as business professionals and investors, must remain relentless in looking for hindrances to conducting business. Thus, it is crucial to determine which obstacles might obstruct distribution channels.

In many developing parts of the world, distribution is rife with challenges. Infrastructure can be inefficient at best and at worst treacherous. Literal highway robbery (or at least highway bribery) is not uncommon in many parts of the world. Even something as seemingly innocuous as multiple levels of required resellers (meant to boost employment) can eviscerate profits when selling perishables.

> **Analytical Consideration** While distribution channel analysis is important, the end customer should remain paramount. When Google acquired Motorola Mobility in 2012, it learned that when Motorola referred to customers it was not alluding to its end users, but rather to its carrier partners.

Other obstacles to distributing a product to the marketplace can take a variety of forms including:

Geography American ethanol producers desire to export ethanol. However, shipping costs are prohibitive because the ethanol companies are located in corn-producing areas which are not in the vicinity of ports. Russia and the Ukraine have problems shipping wheat to Europe because some Black Sea ports freeze up during the winter. Separately, selling into archipelagic nations such as Indonesia presents an obvious set of logistical challenges. As in the case of Indonesia, these challenges are compounded by dozens of dialects used.

Permits to Access Roads Since beer—and the containers in which it is delivered—is heavy, beer delivery trucks are sometimes restricted in some of China's cities. In some cases, equipment (such as that used in mining) is so long that precise calculations must be performed to ensure that the railroad tracks on which the equipment will travel does not curve more than a proscribed number of degrees. General Electric has an evaporator machine that extracts crude oil from the depths of the Canadian oil sands. But the only way to move this 322-ton machine is to use a road that a federal judge says is off limits for such a haul. Similarly, companies that planned to move crude from the oil fields of North Dakota to the West Coast by rail are encountering obstacles in terms of receiving permits to build rail yards and tank farms in California and Washington.

Regulation Let's take a look at the rising challenges to distributing beer in Russia. While there used to be very little regulation regarding beer sales in Russia, there is now quite a bit of regulation: new laws require licenses to sell beer while late-night beer sales have been prohibited. Also, bans on advertising were introduced and there has been a steady rise in excise duties.

Government Favoritism In the Chinese computer industry, the Chinese government's procurement rules favor domestic players such as Lenovo. Also, there is tremendous demand for foreign movies in China and almost 14 new screens a day are being built in that country. However, China only allows those screens to show 34 foreign films a year.

Economic Inhibitors In some cases, there is no economic way to market a product to a customer base. This marketing dead zone can occur when the number of potential customers is large, the price points are low, the product is sophisticated, the product is infrequently used and the buyer of the product could lose their job if they authorize the purchase of it. Let's say you developed a software product that helps lawyers track their annual training in terms of meeting their continuing legal education requirements. The addressable market is large but very fragmented. You could advertise in legal magazines, but the software is probably too tricky to learn quickly and independently. The episodic use of it further retards the learning curve. The software is not expensive enough to justify hiring a salesforce. Even if you decided to limit your marketing efforts to the largest law firms that have staffers dedicated to administering their lawyers' CLE credits, you would be marketing a product that could make their positions obsolete.

Regionalism Even the big Chinese retail and restaurant chains often focus on only dedicated regions of China rather than blanketing every Chinese city with outlets. For instance, Peacebird, a Chinese apparel chain derives roughly half of its revenue from three Chinese provinces while Little Sheep, a hotpot chain, has situated nearly half of its outlets in just five of China's 23 provinces. (Due to Chinese cuisine requiring more ingredients and more complicated preparation regimens than western food, Chinese food is simply more expensive to prepare and thus less scalable than American fast food concepts.) Thus, the question to western companies that think they can penetrate the entire Chinese market is, "If Chinese companies can't penetrate all of the Chinese provinces, what makes you think your company can?"

Due to concerns associated with triggering ethnic strife in developing countries, market segmentation along religious or ethnic lines is not always feasible. While India's Muslim community is estimated at 170 million citizens, Indian companies do not advertise their products as suitable for Muslims because they are concerned about alienating the majority of their potential Hindu customers. Similar concerns likely exist in China.

Incumbents' Control of Distribution Channels Often, the incumbent players enjoy control of the distribution channels which presents a barrier for new entrants. For instance, as part of the terms of its deal with Keurig Green Mountain, Dr. Pepper agreed to refrain from sharing its carbonated drink brands with other countertop drink machine makers such as SodaStream.

Franchise Laws In the United States, state franchise laws give car dealers exclusive rights to sell most new cars. Georgia law caps sales of electric vehicles sold direct by a manufacturer to 150 per year while Pennsylvania and New York cap the number of locations from which Tesla Motors is allowed to sell its vehicles, limiting Tesla's ability to penetrate those markets.

Instability One problem with laying pipelines to tap gas reserves in Nigeria is that saboteurs throw grenades under what few gas pipelines exist in an attempt to extort protection money from Nigeria's government.

Access to Technology Large chains of pizza shops can afford to develop apps that facilitate placing orders with smart phones. Small, independent pizzerias cannot afford to make such investments. The result is that the large chains of pizza shops that take orders by apps are taking market share away from smaller shops that are not accepting orders via apps. Incidentally but importantly, one reason that many customers prefer ordering online versus over the phone is that doing so gives them more time to decide how to customize their meals.

Technological Complementarity The technical facets of the product being distributed should complement the technical dimensions of the distribution channels. For instance, jazz music diffused much faster and more widely than classical music in the early days of broadcast radio. While jazz punched through the compressed, tinny sound of early AM radio speakers, the expansive dynamic ranges of symphonies failed to penetrate radio static and ambient noise. The blast of Louis Armstrong's trumpet sounded better on radio than the subtleties of Bach.

Analytical Consideration Going to market through Original Equipment Manufacturers is often cast as an elixir to market penetration. Yes, there are few potential OEM customers to address which means that the OEMs can be solicited with a small marketing budget and a lean salesforce.

Nevertheless, there are significant drawbacks associated with trying to reach the market through OEMs. Small suppliers are at the mercy of OEMs. Your parts might be difficult to integrate into the large product being produced. You might be required to participate in—and contribute to the funding of—testing conducted by the OEM. If other parts of the OEM's products are not functioning properly, you might feel compelled to offer free consulting just to get the project back on track. Under the best case scenario, you should not expect to receive revenue for a long time because most OEMs have very long product cycles and are slow payors.

Stakeholder Alignment Analysis

There are always problems with aligning the interests of all of a company's stakeholders. Reducing prices may be great for customers but problematic for shareholders. The wholesale termination of employees could be accretive to shareholders, at least in the short-term, but terrible for the affected employees.

In addition to determining how closely aligned the primary stakeholders are, you should consider the impact that other interested parties—such as unions, first responders, animal rights activists, environmentalists and the government—might have on the business model under review. If your idea threatens the livelihood of a constituency or the tax receipts of a government, there is a pretty good chance that they will oppose your plan. Uber is opposed by taxi drivers and Airbnb is facing opposition from the hotel industry. Both business models face scrutiny from local officials. After you identify who might pose a challenge to your business model, you need to strategize as to how you will avoid the issues, work with the opposition or overpower the opposition.

Shareholder Alignment

Shareholders should be largely aligned with management. It is important that the vast majority of shareholders have the same timelines and embrace the same management styles. An example of misaligned timelines between investors and managers would be for a venture capital firm that focuses on smart phone applications (which may have a three month timeline to market) to invest in a biotech or graphene company (as these companies may need as much as ten years to begin selling products). Another example of misalignment of interests due to differing timelines can occur when some shareholders pressure a company to reduce its research efforts in order to make the next few quarters appear more profitable. The concern of companies subject to such pressure is that they would risk losing their star researchers and would be hampered in bringing innovative products to the marketplace.

> **Analytical Consideration** Alignment—between a franchisor and its franchisees, for example—should not be too tight. Franchisors that put too much effort into ensuring the success of their franchisees often find that such efforts backfire. One of the reasons that Boston Market went bankrupt is that it obtained loans on behalf of its franchisees. This overburdened Boston Market's balance sheet and resulted in more complacent franchisees. Franchisees must be exposed to commercial risks and work hard to make their businesses, and their relationships with their franchisors, successful.

Many private equity firms require their portfolio companies to prepare detailed financial reports on a very frequent basis. Sometimes, they expect to receive these reports every week or even every day. In cases where the portfolio businesses are analytically driven and have the resources and temperament to comply with such close supervision, the private equity firm's micromanagement may not be a problem. However, in view of such issues, some companies are not well-suited to become private equity funded. For instance, ship owners tend to be free-spirited entrepreneurs who often rely more on their instincts about market timing, rather than on financial analysis, when it comes to making crucial business decisions.

Financing and Shareholder Alignment

The instruments used to fund start-up companies can introduce fissures between management and investors. Consider convertible debt. Management teams of emerging companies typically want the initial rounds of venture capital funding to occur at high valuations. However, convertible noteholders often demand valuation caps on the initial rounds of financing so that they will not be overly diluted when their status changes from note-holders to equity-holders. To illustrate, suppose an angel investor subscribes to a $100,000 convertible note. A year later, if the company's initial round of venture capital funding yields a post-money valuation of $1 million, the investor will own 10% of the company when he exercises his conversion rights. However, if the first capital raise places a $10 million value on the company, the investor will only own 1% of the company.

Private equity firms' interests are not always in line with those of their portfolio companies. It can be argued that monitoring fees are redundant given that private equity partners receive compensation for acting as directors and usually have coveted that their guidance would be granted gratis. Similarly, transactions fees—imposed by some private equity firms on their portfolio companies when they have liquidity events—seem more like a tax than consideration for value added services. Dividend recapitalizations—which consist of private equity firms forcing portfolio companies to take on substantial debt and then pay private equity investors large cash dividends—seem to be a blatant example of a misalignment of interests.

Analytical Considerations It is difficult to manage—and risky to invest in—publicly-traded private equity firms because they are accountable to two masters: their limited partners and the holders of publicly-traded shares. Both of these constituent groups have different agreements with, and stakes in, publicly-traded private equity funds. Here I will provide just two examples of the disparity between the two constituent groups. First, holders of the publicly-traded shares have instantaneous liquidity whereas the limited partners are greatly restricted in pre-maturely liquidating their investments in private equity firms. Second, the former investors readily pursue shareholder litigation if they believe that malfeasance has occurred while the latter group of investors is reticent to litigate for fear of being blacklisted from other private equity funds if they develop a reputation for litigiousness. The challenge of straddling the fiduciary duties owed to these two groups of stakeholders is akin to navigating around Scylla and Charybdis.

Also, a potential conflict between a company and its shareholders can arise in the Real Estate Investment Trust sector. Externally managed REITs—such as American Realty Capital Healthcare and Senior Housing Property Trust—are akin to external managers that run mutual funds; they do not own the assets entrusted to them. The concern is that since the external managers generally make more money as their assets under management grows, the managers may be more incentivized to grow the asset portfolios than profits.

It is common for private equity firms to collect commissions from channeling their portfolio companies into group-purchasing programs.

These programs, ostensibly designed for the benefit of the portfolio companies, utilize the combined purchasing power of private equity firms' portfolio companies to arrange discounts on many goods (e.g. computers) and services (e.g. health insurance) such companies need. While these programs can be a win for all, there is a risk that a private equity firm could have negotiated an arrangement with a vendor that delivers a more attractive commission for the private equity firm than value for the portfolio company.

Some transactions are designed to cause friction between existing shareholders and new shareholders. For instance, some hedge funds intentionally craft "loan-to-own" lending agreements so that the borrower will inevitably violate at least one of the covenants, triggering a default and thus an entry point for the fund to acquire shares on the cheap. Also, some companies that are in dire of need of capital are doing "Happy Meal" raises with hedge funds. Happy Meals consist of raising capital from hedge funds by issuing convertible debt. Another condition of Happy Meal raises is that the company must pledge a large percent of its shares to the hedge fund which wants these shares to sell short. Thus, the provider of capital may actually make more money if the company fails. This seems like a glaring misalignment of interests to me.

Partner Alignment

Partnerships are very difficult to manage. Egos clash. Missions are muddled. Divisions of responsibility are not clearly delineated. In many cases, B-level or below executives are assigned to represent their companies in the partnership. And when one partner wishes to remove itself from the partnership, it often finds no bidders other than its legacy partner, which results in a suppressed valuation. Interestingly, joint ownership of patents can be downright scary as either co-owner can assign or license the patent to any willing party without the consent of the other co-owner.

A few years ago, I did some work for a company that promotes utilities' services to new homeowners. When a new homeowner moves in, this company presents a range of services—such as electric, cable, telephone, burglar alarm systems and the like—to the new occupant. The occupant places an order for the services he wishes to receive and this company earns a commission when routing the order to the service providers.

Not a bad business model, right? Well, one problem reoccurred with some regularity. The ultimate service provider often upsold the customer that my client delivered. For instance, my client could have told the cable company that the Jones family at 100 Main Street would like to order basic cable service for two television sets. By the time installation was complete the customer could have been sold lots of premium channels for four television sets as well as high-speed Internet service. The service provider's position was that no commissions need be paid to the originator for the extra services because such sales were not reported by the originator. In some cases, the end service provider could claim that the entire sale was non-commissionable because it was modified to be outside of the agreement between the originator and service provider. The originator, of course, believes that it is entitled to commissions on the entire order because the service provider may not have been able to secure that account without the originator's efforts. The lesson of this story is that when your partner is also the arbiter of discrepancies, the ties go to the partner.

Finally, it is very dangerous when companies receive loans from customers. Case in point: Apple lent GT Advanced Technologies a total of $578 million to help get a large sapphire factory in Arizona up and running. As part of the conditions for the loan, Apple restricted the extent to which GT could sell sapphire to other companies while Apple was under no obligation to buy a set amount of product from GT. When GT's cash fell below $125 million, Apple was allowed to demand repayment of about $440 million in loans it had advanced. At the time of this writing, the Apple-GT relationship has unraveled and GT has filed for bankruptcy protection.

Talent Alignment

While there are many benefits to be had from retaining consultants—their expertise, fresh perspective, and the pay-as-you-go cash outlays, for example—a company that relies on freelancers and consultants will suffer from a major misalignment with its talent. Part-time or adjunct consultants are just not as dedicated as full-time employees since freelancers must often juggle several gigs simultaneously while searching for their next assignments. The freelancer is inclined to present work product that justifies his fee but not much more than that. It is a misalignment of accountability when developers of products will not be around when their products are evaluated or when their products need to be maintained. If you can't recruit the right full-time talent, then that is a reflection on the quality of your current vision, team or market opportunity.

Analytical Consideration Companies often try to foster alignment with their employees by grating them stock. When a company distributes its shares to its employees, those employees own a given percentage of that company. At any point in time, this percentage does not change if the company splits the stock or effects a reverse stock split; nor does its value. If at 9 a.m. you own 10,000 of your company's shares and each share is worth $12, you have a $120,000 stake in your company. If at 10 a.m., the stock splits two-for-one (causing you to now have 20,000 shares, each worth $6) or reverse splits on a one-for-two basis (causing you to have 5,000 shares, each worth $24), you still have a $120,000 position in your company's shares. Under any of these scenarios, you would still own the same percentage of your company.

Companies are sometimes compelled to effectuate reverse stock splits. Resulting higher share prices may be necessary to attract early-stage investors or to meet stock exchange listing requirements. However, in many cases, share-endowed employees at start-up companies do not view reverse stock splits logically. Rather, they value their shares based on the best case scenario unfolding. In our example, if you owned 10,000 shares at 9 a.m., you might value the shares based on them reaching $50 apiece, or $500,000 collectively, in the near-term. Thus, in the minds of many emerging company employees, a one-for-two reverse stock split slashes the value of their portfolios by 50%.

Let's consider a company that needs to develop software. Since new technological ground is constantly being broken, consistency among the programmers is crucial because various generations of code need to be made to operate seamlessly. Companies that retain for-hire programmers are at their mercy. Outside programmers implicitly lack high motivation to solve key challenges because any one of their customers only represents a small portion of their overall revenue. Other problems associated with reliance on freelance programmers include their high day-rates and the fact that managers often do not know enough about programming to give the adjunct programmers direction.

Even when third-party developers are extremely capable and dedicated, they cannot be easily controlled. While the project manager for Google Glass insisted that that product only have limited email functionality, the outside developers delivered full functionality.

Opposition from First Responders

One overlooked area of potential challenge to business models is the stance that first responders—such as the police and firefighters—might take against a product or service.

Police forces may oppose legalized marijuana dispensaries. This is because a lot of police forces rely on asset seizures from marijuana purveyors for some of their force's funding. The growth of marijuana dispensaries results in less raids, fewer seizures of the culprit's assets, less fire-sales of such assets and less money flowing into the police departments' coffers. In short, the legalization of marijuana means more funding problems for police forces.

Police department policies are reducing the appeal of burglar alarms. Due to stratospheric levels of false alarm rates—an average of 97% in Colorado Springs in recent years, for example—police departments are requiring that homeowners register their burglar alarms, imposing fines for repeat false alarms and opting out of responding to excessive false alarms connected to given addresses.

Some firefighters oppose the placement of solar panels on rooftops. This is because solar panels can create the risks of roofs collapsing due to their weight, an inability to gain footing (they introduce slipping and tripping hazards) and even potential electric shock. In a conventional building, firefighters typically cut off the electricity leading into the house before entering. However, as long as sunlight hits solar panels, voltage continues to be sent down from the roof throughout the building even after power is shut down. Another danger associated with solar panels is that they obstruct rooftop ventilation.

Analytical Consideration   At my twins' (Zachary and Zoe) four-year birthday party, I got to talking to one of the other fathers. This gentleman was an engineer with an expertise in installing solar panels on buildings. I asked him about the risk of firemen getting hurt by the flow of electricity throughout a building during a firefight. He told me that this was not a problem because there are ways to shut off the flow of electricity in solar-powered buildings. Then, about six months later, I was with my oldest son when the local fire department came to Daniel's school. The firemen did a fine job of educating the children about fires and the like. I asked the firemen the same question about the risks of fighting fires in solar-powered buildings. They said that such buildings are of great concern to them. So whose opinion matters more? The engineer's or the firemen's? The firemen's perspective on solar panels matters much more since it is they that have to navigate the solar panels when extinguishing fires. So what is the lesson of this story? When expert opinion and tactical practicality are in conflict, the practitioners' opinions will have more influence on the business model.

Fire departments and other first responders are concerned that they are not prepared to respond to accidents that result from trains carrying crude oil. These concerns could limit the ability to move crude to its intended markets.

Opposition from Animal Rights Activists

Some business models find themselves in the crosshairs of animal rights activists. For instance, the film Blackfish's unfair depiction of SeaWorld Entertainment's treatment of its animals, damaged attendance at that company's theme parks. Perhaps, the two industries most at risk of receiving the ire of animal rights activists are the apparel and pharmaceutical industries. Animal rights activists have long deplored the use of animal furs in coats as well as (alligator) skin placed on belts and shoes.

Pressure from animal rights activists has put large pharmaceutical and personal hygiene companies such as Merck & Co., Glaxo-SmithKline PLC and Colgate Palmolive in a Catch-22 situation. These companies ended testing in chimpanzees because of the opprobrium they received. The problem is that the FDA generally requires animal testing for proposed new drugs to measure markers such as how much of a drug is absorbed into blood, and chimps have long been desired for such purposes, due to their close genetic connection to humans.

Interestingly, solar farms are at risk of attracting the attention of animal rights activists. This is because solar farms can be spread over several square miles, maintain towers as tall as 40-story buildings and can have hundreds of thousands of garage-door sized mirrors. To the angst of animal rights activists, these solar farms sometimes scorch birds that fly through the one-thousand-degree heat surrounding the towers.

Opposition from Environmentalists

Some thought should be put into the potential for environmentalists to oppose a business initiative. As a case in point, a consortium of some of the most successful private equity funds, together with Warren Buffett, completed the world's largest leveraged buyout when they acquired TXU Electric Utility for $45 billion in 2007. TXU, the largest regulated utility in Texas, had growth plans that revolved around building coal-fired electricity generating plants. However, TXU, later renamed Energy Future Holdings Corporation, faced opposition from environmentalists and its coal-fired expansion strategy was stymied. Even in a state not known for acute environmental sensitivity, environmental opposition played a role in Energy Future Holdings Corporation declaring bankruptcy in 2014.

Opposition from Unions

Business development professionals should consider the risks of union opposition impeding their business models. Union opposition can precede a business venture or can strike an existing business. For instance, the American Postal Workers Union opposes the partnership between Staples and the U.S. Postal Service whereby Staples would provide postal services. Elsewhere, the Air Line Pilots Association has called for the U.S. Department of Transportation to reject Norwegian Air International's application for a foreign-carrier license. Norwegian Air strives to keep its costs low by using crews and planes from low-cost countries. This seems like a logical business model to me but has been characterized by the ALPA as illegal and promoting a "race to the bottom" on labor and working conditions.

Analytical Considerations Analysts should consider the extent to which innovation will be blunted because unions are adverse to the utilization of it. For instance, in the shipping industry, there are more efficient roll-on/roll-off containers and new loading and unloading tools. However, if the unions refuse to use them, there won't be much demand for such tools and the shipping companies will not be able to enhance the efficiency of their operations.

The following are among the trends you can track to determine whether union influence is rising or waning at a particular company or factory:

- The number of unions represented at a plant;
- The number of job classifications at a plant;
- The number of pages in governing labor contracts.

If all of the three metrics above are declining, then labor relations are likely improving.

Opposition from Government

Government policies can have consequences—ranging from unwelcome to catastrophic—for the affected businesses. Makers of snack foods are disadvantaged when taxes—such as the Mexico's 8% tax on high-calorie foods like potato chips—are levied. In other cases, governments thwart transactions, as happened when the Canadian government blocked Manitoba Telecom Services' sale of its Allstream unit to Egyptian investors.

Industries that are targeted for extinction by governments have no chance of survival. For instance, student loan origination and servicing companies were legislated out of business by a bill that was paired with the Affordable Care Act. Both Sturm Ruger and Smith & Wessen ceased selling their handguns in California. That state's microstamping law (which requires that each bullet be stamped when fired so that the bullets can be traced back to the owner of the handgun) triggered the exodus of those companies. Those firearm manufacturers believe that the intent of the law was to remove handguns from the market by requiring gun makers to incorporate a technology that cannot possibly work. Similarly, although not completely eradicated, finders (individuals who helped companies raise money in return for finder's fees) essentially no longer exist in the United States because the registration process is so onerous.

Industries that operate with tenuous government approval are at risk of being purged from the playing field. These industries include publicly-traded master-limited partnerships, real estate investment trusts, litigation lending, and secondary exchanges on which shares of privately-held companies are traded. The fact that it is taking so long to promulgate governing regulations for crowdfunding is a source of concern for the future of such platforms.

On the other hand, regulation can be an elixir to a company's growth. Cases in point include:

- Fire codes that require buildings to have phone lines installed ensure some base level of demand for the traditional phone companies. Sergey Brin and Larry Page considered not having phone lines installed in Google's new office complex but were informed that failing to do so would be a violation of the local fire code.

- Emerson Electric's InSinkErator garbage disposal business benefits from local building codes that give preference to that product. (These favorable building codes are especially important for selling the InSinkErator since it is expensive—often $400 to $800—to retrofit disposals into old homes.)

- H&R Block and Liberty Tax could benefit from the Affordable Care Act because enforcement of that Act is tied into the tax code.

- As of the time of this writing, the Obama administration committed to spend at least $75 million on body cameras and data storage equipment for police agencies. This government action should be a boon for companies such as Digital Ally that makes cameras specifically designed for police forces as well as Ambarella which makes the chips that power cameras produced by companies such as GoPro.

Thoughts on Customer Service

Sometimes customers expect exceptional customer service in terms of the rapidity with which they are served or to the degree of pampering they receive. Even though MasterCard's average transaction speed is a lightning 130 milliseconds, it and rival major credit card companies continually try to become faster by testing a variety of contactless payment instruments. FedEx's sorting process—which includes capturing a package's physical dimensions, weight, destination zip code, and where it is in the process at any given moment—is completely automated and measured in milliseconds. The burrito chain Chipotle has implemented several policies—such as making sure that no trainees are scheduled to work during peak times—to improve the number of transactions it processes per hour at peak times. Amazon expended great treasure patenting and protecting its one-click check-out application.

Lessons from India's eStamp Initiative

Seemingly small delays in processing was one reason that India's eStamp initiative failed. India believed that enabling thousands of vendors throughout India to print stamps electronically would reduce forgeries and alleviate the inconvenience of traveling to post offices. However, each stamp took roughly five minutes to process and print. Other contributors to India's eStamp failure include:

- Since vendors could not make a profit on small commissions—given the personnel, Internet and electricity costs—they charged premiums to the face prices.

- Paper was not a cost reimbursed by the Indian government. Similarly, vendors resented the fact that there was no reimbursement for data entry or printing mistakes.

Virtues of Seemingly Shoddy Customer Service

On the other hand, it makes sense to provide more dilatory customer service when trying to impress upon customers that great efforts are being made to achieve high levels of excellence. There is a custom bike manufacturer that could fill orders for custom bikes in a few days but purposely waits two weeks before shipping in order to reinforce in the minds of its customers that it is expending extra care in custom building each bike. In other cases, slow customer service is viewed as commitment that a gift giver demonstrates to the giftee. One of the popular souvenirs at Tokyo Disneyland has been a leather bracelet, on which couples have their names painted or embossed. The long lines contribute to the bracelet's allure as the couples equate the long wait times with the strength of their commitment to their romantic partners.

Incidentally, I think that patience, or lack thereof, is one of the reasons that Build-a-Bear has a much larger retail network than Ridemakerz. Based on my observations, little girls have more patience to build things than do little boys. Also, both mothers and fathers seem to have sufficient patience to help their daughters create stuffed animals but only fathers have patience to help their sons build model cars.

Art galleries are notorious for their intentionally terrible customer service. It has been said that a customer can self-immolate at an art gallery and he still wouldn't be offered a glass of water. (Art dealers view themselves as cultured art advisors to their high-net-worth clientele, rather than uncouth painting peddlers in need of stooping to the indignities of educating and haggling with people of unknown means and lineage.) In the early days of what became Warner Brothers, after showing a silent movie, the brothers would start singing. They knew their singing sounded horrible. But there was a reason for ending the show with an auditory assault on their patrons. The Warner brothers needed their patrons to file out of the theater quickly so that they could run the film again for the next audience.

Finally, there are situations in which faster processing speeds is a liability. For instance, press-release publisher Business Wire was reprimanded for granting brokers direct access to press releases related to corporate earnings reports while everyone else only was granted delayed access.

Internal Consistency

Most of the discussion revolving around business model validation throughout this book has focused on assessing how external factors will impact a company. We should not forget to consider how internal dynamics will impact a business model. Customer consistency, values, inertia, culture and internal cooperation and competition are important factors in the business models that firms adopt.

Customer Consistency   It must be determined if a firm's product offerings and sales efforts are consistent with its target customers. For instance, it appears that the message at the Noodles restaurant chain is muddled: with the presentation of its wines and wine glasses, the ambiance strives to be classy but its staff often sports the grunge look. Also, the merger of insurers Unum Group and The Provident Companies got off to a rocky start. Unum was a group disability insurer that sold its coverage to groups of employees based on statistics and actuarial tables. These sales were typically made to human resources managers. On the other hand, Provident's policies required much greater knowledge about its individual customers who operated businesses in a wide variety of industries and who made their own insurance buying decisions.

Name Consistency and Relevance

"What's in a name? That which we call a rose by any other name would smell as sweet."

William Shakespeare in Romeo and Juliet

When it comes to naming emerging companies and new products, I disagree with Shakespeare: names matter.

Names of emerging companies should be easy to pronounce, related to the business at hand (after all, names are a marketing tool), and suited to the community that the business is designed to serve. Names can be cute if the business is directed to children, cool if directed to teenagers, but must carry some degree of gravitas if directed to professionals.

Upon their introduction in the late 1940s, potential customers' receptiveness to photocopying machines was hampered by the use of the term "copy." The Oxford English Dictionary makes it clear that during earlier centuries there was an aura of deceit associated with the word; indeed, "copy" and "counterfeit" were nearly synonymous. In the more recent past, I have used SurveyMonkey to conduct surveys. However, I stopped using SurveyMonkey because the name of that company is very unprofessional and ill-suited for the people that I wish to recruit to participate in surveys. My sending requests for participation in SurveyMonkey surveys would reflect poorly on me and my business. This is a shame as SurveyMonkey is a very good tool.

It is best if a name of a company translates worldwide. For instance, Kodak is pronounceable in just about every language. On the other hand, it was a mistake to call an automobile "Nova," which means "doesn't go" in Spanish.

It is an advantage to use names that begin with the letters at the beginning of the alphabet because such names will be listed at the top of directories and trade show listings. Trademark issues notwithstanding, names—such as Google or Venmo—that could morph into verbs, help diffuse brands.

Since domains will invariably be acquired to support the brands, it is important to consider a few issues that could result in discounts being applied to domain name valuations. With these issues in mind, the names should not be difficult to spell, should not be hyphenated, not be too lengthy and should not use symbols (for instance, "accelerate" is preferred to "acceler8").

Values A business's revenue growth will be impeded to the extent that selling products is incongruous with its values. For instance, healthy food or natural food stores do not want to sell cigarettes or beer in view of the obvious contradiction in values. Recently, CVS/pharmacy decided not to sell cigarettes because that drug store chain is becoming more active in providing medical services such as flu shots. McDonald's restaurants decided not to allow Redbox to install its movie dispensing kiosks at its stores because the "R" rated movies in Redbox kiosks were inconsistent with the fast-food chain's children-friendly mandate. Cracker Barrel Old Country Store tried to repel investor Sardar Biglari's efforts to obtain a board seat, in part, because Mr. Biglari's acquisition of the racy men's magazine Maxim was inconsistent with that restaurant's family-friendly image. Finally, humanitarian organizations are more likely to purchase drones that were produced by stand-alone drone manufacturers, rather than defense contractors, because of the inherent mismatch in organizational missions.

Inertia   Most managers dedicate themselves to achieving the goals set out for them by their firm's senior executives. Thus, it is difficult for businesses to pivot every time it is confronted with an opportunity. Virgin Hotels miscalculated banks' willingness to diverge from their business models when executives of that hotel chain thought it would be able to scoop up real estate held by delinquent borrowers at fire sale prices. This plan did not materialize as most banks opted to roll over debt as opposed to foreclosing and then selling real estate on the cheap.

Culture   The rate of decision making at a firm is not likely to change greatly in the short-term. In industries governed by voluminous regulations or shaped by prevailing cultural proclivities to hierarchy, a pensive decision-making process should be expected. On the other hand, decision-making should be much more rapid in industries (such as mobile advertising) that are unregulated, populated with young people and fueled with venture capital investment. Separately, there is a risk that companies driven by the founder's or CEO's ego may not be well-managed since these self-absorbed leaders sometimes tend to recruit less talented managers.

Internal Cooperation and Competition   Another issue along the lines of assessing a firm's internal dynamics is the extent to which employees compete against one another. Restaurants have generally done a better job of managing this issue than automobile dealerships.

Many casual dining and upscale restaurants have adopted a policy of having each store's wait staff pool and equally distribute the tips they collect at the end of each shift. I believe that this policy leads to a better dining experience for the patrons as well as a pruning of less competent servers. If a customer needs another napkin or fork and their server is not in sight, the closest server will be motivated to look after the customer. And the servers will detect which of their colleagues are contributing the least to the tip pool and will likely apply subtle (but effective) pressure on those lower performers to improve or resign.

In other contexts, having largely independent professionals compete against each other is an effective strategy. I have no problem with investment banks or real estate brokerage firms having their bankers and real estate agents compete against one another in closing deals. In these situations, one's success does not necessarily hurt their colleagues in the way that is common in businesses—such as automobile dealerships—that have interlocking dependencies.

Auto dealerships are built to foment internecine rivalry. Every department in an auto dealership is a business unto itself with a budget and income expectations. For instance, at most small and medium-size dealerships, the pre-owned department is the service department's largest customer. The pre-owned department pays nearly the same labor rates as the average customer who has their vehicle serviced at the dealership. This causes constant in-fighting over costs of repairs, turnaround times, requested repairs not performed, and unnecessary repairs.

Another source of inter-departmental friction at auto dealers occurs when the new car salesmen put higher-than-called-for-numbers of used cars into trade-ins so that they can reach the new car sales benchmarks set by the manufacturers. While the new car salesmen are collecting back end money from manufacturers, pre-owned managers must often sell the excess inventory at a loss or eventually take it to auction (and sell at a loss there).

Perspectives on Competition

Usually, the less competition a company faces, the better. Direct rivals siphon off customers, spark price wars, poach talent, compete for raw materials and force companies to market more aggressively. However, it is rare for a company to avoid competition for a long period of time. Either another entrant will break into the market or a substitute for the product will arise.

One way to discern that an industry is experiencing excessive competition is if aggregators arise. The existence of Yipit—a daily deal site that aggregates deals from more than 800 different services including Groupon, Living Social, Tippr and Yelp—indicates that the local deal and referral spaces are completely saturated.[10]

Many of the factors that determine the level of competition that exists in an industry—such as barriers to entry, switching costs, and data exhaust—are discussed elsewhere in this book. However, one determinant of the extent of competition that I will discuss here is the issue of excess capacity. Excess capacity in an industry increases the degree of competition. For example, since professional sports teams cannot operate without opponents, professional sports leagues have excess capacity. All teams in a league invariably survive because many of their local fans remain loyal to them no matter how frequently, or by what margin, they lose. In any other business, if not all eighty or one hundred teams were doing well, there would be pressure to shut some of them down. The result is that the more successful teams attract fewer fans and generate less revenue than they would if excess capacity were to be squeezed out of the leagues.

An analog of excess capacity is excess cash flowing into an industry.

---

[10] Somewhat related to this concern is that startups such as Tapad, Drawbridge and BlueCava allow advertisers to target specific people by selling tracking services and software that links smartphones, tablets, and PCs to a distinct though anonymous person. These services enable advertisers to spend less money since once it is determined which devices a person is using, a coordinated campaign can be implemented.

Many hundreds of millions of venture capitalists' dollars have been flowing into alternative taxi companies such as Hailo, Uber, and Lyft. Much of this money is being used to slash fares as well as to compete for, and compensate, taxi drivers. In many cases, the incremental margins associated with fares are negative. And then these alternative taxi companies have substantial fixed costs. It seems that the funders of these companies might just as well distribute their money to passengers and drivers without first routing it through the alternative taxi intermediaries.

Some readers might point out that since I mentioned that pizza chains are gaining advantage by developing apps so too should alternative taxi companies. However, the analogy falters in that the alternative taxi companies will be subject to regulations (crafted to ensure that the public has access to taxi services), whereas the pizza chains will not be subject to any regulations of the sort. Also, the alternative taxi companies are dependent on independent contractors (their drivers), many of whom relish their independence and are skilled in carving prime clientele away from their paymasters. (For instance, livery drivers often try to cut side deals when they offer to take their out-of-town passengers to the airport.) In contrast, the pizza chains' business models do not orbit around disloyal intermediaries.

On the other hand, if one company so completely dominates an industry, none of the other companies will inspire any confidence. Going back many years, when Microsoft was the undisputed goliath in the software space, every other company was considered to being reduced to conducting research for Microsoft. As was said at the time, if another software company shows promise it will either be acquired by Microsoft or crushed by Microsoft. Another consequence of Microsoft's dominance was that whenever another software company told investors about a new software product it was going to launch, the response was, "That's interesting. But how are you going to compete against Microsoft when it enters the space?" (Another manifestation of Microsoft's erstwhile competitive streak occurred when that company talked up its vaporware; software that Microsoft indicated would soon launch but in reality would be delayed for a long time, if not indefinitely. Such vaporware was extremely damaging to competitors as customers delayed purchases of existing software in anticipation of the eventual release of Microsoft's competing product.)

Benefits of Competition

Sometimes competition is good. At the outset of my career, I researched a coffee company called Chock Full o'Nuts. At that time, Chock Full o'Nuts was just about to launch a line of iced coffee. When I met with management, they were very excited to see their iced coffee hit retail shelves. I asked them if they were concerned that the large beverage players such as Coca-Cola, Pepsi and Nestle would be a competitive threat as they were also preparing to launch iced coffee. The response was that they welcomed the competition since the large players would give the category credibility. With the big players purveying iced coffee, the supermarkets would allocate more shelf space, dedicate marketing resources and prominently display signage.

Proprietors of pornographic websites benefit from competition. Online porn promoters collaborate with one another in that when visitors enter one site, ads for other sites pop open. The idea behind constant website redirections—known as circle-jerks in the vernacular of the porn industry—is to wear out the viewer so that he will capitulate and subscribe to one of the sites.

Online retailers such as Amazon might be better off with competitors such as Barnes & Noble and Best Buy remaining on the retail landscape. To some extent, bricks-and-mortar-based retailers serve as showrooms where consumers can review products and then order them online at reduced prices.

While it might sound counterintuitive, a company can experience severe disadvantage when its competitors declare bankruptcy. These financially weakened competitors stand to benefit from being able to favorably renegotiate labor contracts, vendor agreements, and pension obligations in the context of bankruptcy proceedings. These renegotiations result in lower costs structures for the bankrupt companies which enables them—to the detriment of the stronger companies—to reduce their prices. (In some cases, a financially challenged company's fate is sealed in advance of its filing for bankruptcy protection. For instance, Corinthian Colleges could not file for Chapter 11 bankruptcy protection because doing so would likely have disqualified the company's schools from receiving federal funding.)

The Delusion of Relative Performance

The delusion of relative performance holds that a company's positive performance can be inconsequential, even lethally misleading, if another company in the same, or adjacent space, is threatening to upend the subject company's performance. For instance, there must have been periods of time during the early 2000s that Circuit City was performing very well. During some quarters, that electronics retailer must have delivered impressive revenue gains or wider profit margins. Similarly, a few years later, Borders (a once thriving chain of book stores) must have demonstrated reasons for optimism. Many of its stores must have reported impressive year-over-year same-store sales growth during the 2008–2010 timeframe. However, none of these ephemeral operational improvements mattered in view of Amazon completely upending the retail sector. The same dynamic was in effect when Skype trounced Vonage despite the latter posting a variety of improving financial metrics.

Barriers to Entry

Most executives would prefer to operate a business that faces limited competition. Thus, investors and business leaders often seek businesses that are protected by moats. Barriers to entry, one form of moats, protect business from the vagaries of competition. For instance, electric utilities such as Consolidated Edison benefit from a multitude of barriers which include capital intensity, regulatory requirements and high switching costs for customers. It would seem that the pharmaceutical industry would enjoy the same barriers to entry. However, there is at least one noteworthy difference. That is, there is a great deal of switching in the dispensing of medicine. In many cases, a pharmacy might fill a prescription for a branded drug with a generic unless the prescription specifically states "DNS" which is an abbreviation for "Do Not Substitute".

The following are among the forms that barriers to entry can take:

- **Capital Intensity.** It takes an inordinate amount of capital to form a competing aircraft manufacturing company or a nuclear power plant.

- **Possessing a Regulatory License.** If you don't have approval from the Food and Drug Administration, you cannot sell pharmaceuticals. Without the appropriate approvals a telecom operator cannot lay fiber optic cables. State licensure of physicians may inhibit the emergence of telemedicine. Without a liquor license a restaurant cannot sell liquor. The existing outdoor billboard operators are permitted to maintain their leases on the land underneath their billboards. However, to a large extent, the Highway Beautification Act restricts the placement of new structures along America's highways. This provides a significant benefit to legacy outdoor billboard operators such as Lamar Advertising and CBS Outdoor Americas.

The barriers to entry rise in lockstep with the difficulty of obtaining regulatory approvals. For instance, if approvals are required by authorities at the local, state and federal levels and multiple agencies must sign off on permits to operate, then there will be far fewer competitors than if only one agency's approval is required. With this concern in mind, Facebook requested European Union antitrust regulators examine its $19 billion acquisition of WhatsApp so as to avoid antitrust reviews by multiple EU countries where there would likely be sympathy towards local telecom companies. Since China would have to amend its constitution to authorize casinos outside of Macau, the chances that casinos will be permitted on the Chinese mainland are remote.

The precision with which a product is defined for regulatory purposes can pose barriers to entry. At the urging of Brown-Forman, the maker of Jack Daniel's whiskey, Tennessee passed legislation in 2013 requiring anything labeled "Tennessee Whiskey" not just to be made in that state, but also to be made from at least 51% corn, filtered through maple charcoal and aged in new, charred oak barrels. Similarly, the British government is creating a public register of firms authorized to produce Scotch. The French government polices Champagne and Roquefort cheese in much the same way. These registers give listed companies much more legitimacy than imitators excluded from this list.

Interestingly, not all companies seek regulatory approval to put a product on the market. Companies such as Uber, Lyft and Airnbnb, enter a variety of markets and strive to make such an influence in the local communities that regulators will be left with no choice other than to accommodate the new entrants. In hiring David Plouffe, one of the Obama campaign's most high-profile operatives, Uber seems to be trying to accelerate this process.

- **Possessing Patents.** The essence of patents is to exclude others from practicing the inventions covered by a patent. It is my understanding that the overwhelming impetus that Amazon had for acquiring Kiva Systems is that Kiva had so many patents covering automation technology for distribution centers that Amazon would inevitably infringe Kiva's patents and could consequently be subject to an injunction that would shut down Amazon's fulfillment centers. Separately, in the world of 3-D printing,

3D Systems asserted some of its patents against Formlabs. Before this dispute was resolved, it caused tremendous consternation for Formlabs as customers distanced themselves from this dispute and as investors became wobbly.

- **Enormous Brand Loyalty.** Securities traders are so attached to their Bloomberg terminals that they would rather take a pay cut than lose access to their Bloomberg machines. Harley Davidson enthusiasts are so dedicated to that brand that they emblazon it on their bodies in the form of tattoos. When a flood destroyed one of its Texas stores on Memorial Day 1981, loyal friends and customers of Whole Foods pitched in to clean it up, enabling the store to reopen just a month later.

Owing one's life to a service provider has a tendency to instill loyalty, or at least to avoid applying tremendous scrutiny to such companies. Blackwater USA (now Academi) was one of the largest US-based military contractors. During its heyday, in the aftermath of the second Gulf War, Blackwater was charged with protecting American officials in Iraq such as Paul Bremer and visiting Congressional delegations. While Blackwater had a perfect record of ensuring the lives of its protectees, its employees were accused of using excessive force in carrying out their missions and specifically of wantonly killing 17 innocent Iraqis in Baghdad's Nisour Square in 2007. There was a Congressional investigation into the matter but it was difficult for Congress to investigate Blackwater when that company protected many of its members during their visits to Iraq.

- **Extent of the Competition.** An excessive number of new companies approaching the same pain point and the same customers can inhibit the success of the entire sector. A few years ago there was an explosion of companies determined to compete with the traditional credit card providers. Many of them had very intriguing ideas about offering customers rewards, helping merchants better predict demand and manage their inventories, and tie-ins with local charities. But look at the situation from the perspective of a local merchant who is overwhelmed by all of the solicitations he is receiving from payment providers. Each offer is confusing (as dozens of kinds of fees are charged), the longevity of these new players is far from assured, and it is not known to what extent patrons or other merchants will settle on one or two new payment facilitators as the standard setter. It is easier for the merchant to stick with the legacy credit card providers.

- **Ferocity of the Competition.** The taxi app companies are engaged in an extremely brutal rivalry. In mid-2014, Uber was offering $250 for referring a new driver to its service, $500 for referring a Lyft driver, and $1,000 for signing up a Lyft "mentor," which is an experienced Lyft contractor who helps train new drivers. It has been alleged that, at least one of these companies jam their competitors' capacities by having their employees order rides from rival taxi app companies and then cancel their orders or terminate the rides within a few blocks. (Interestingly, one reason for such intense rivalry is that these two companies' headquarters are located within just a few blocks from each other.) On the other hand, it does not appear that there is a great deal of rivalry among the manufacturers of electric vehicles. Yes, most car makers sell an electric vehicle, but most of these efforts appear to be symbolic offerings to meet California's air-quality regulations.

> **Analytical Consideration** Henry Kissinger once said, "The reason knives are so sharp is because the pie is so small." What this means is that executives compete ferociously when their industry produces scant profits. On the other hand, executives behave in a more genteel manner when their companies and industries are producing greater levels of profits. Those readers who have not worked with hedge fund managers would be surprised at how extraordinarily polite and gracious they are. In my experience of interviewing hundreds of management teams, I have found a correlation between the demeanor of the interviewees and the success of the company. I believe most readers would acknowledge that they are in better moods when their businesses make more money than when their profits are pinched.

- **Expected Retaliation.** The International Cotton Association (ICA) keeps a list of firms that renege on contracts. The ICA also keeps a list of companies that do business with companies that have reneged on their contracts. ICA members are prohibited from trading with second generation reneging firms, risking expulsion from the ICA if they do.

Any book publisher that dares defy Amazon's demands does so at the risk of having its books excluded from Amazon's personalized recommendation push email campaigns, having their books shipped later than necessary and suffering erosion in the discounts that their customers expect.

A particularly ferocious embodiment of retaliation occurs when serving a prison sentence becomes a real possibility. Legal services companies—such as those that sell legal forms and assist their customers with relatively minor procedures such as name changes and incorporating businesses—have been attacked by local bar associations all over the United States for allegedly practicing law without licensure. In some states, the thresholds for practicing law are vague while the penalties for unauthorized practice are severe. In Florida, practicing law without a license is a felony punishable by up to five years in jail.

- **Bottlenecks.** Controlling supply chain bottlenecks presents a significant barrier to entry. John D. Rockefeller seized on this strategic advantage by gaining control of all of the metal belts that sealed oil barrels. Without these belts, other oil producers were constructively barred from selling oil.

  Apple Computer provides more recent case studies of bottlenecks—or chokehold strategies—in action.

  o **Example One:** Apple commits many billions of dollars in terms of pre-payments to parts and equipment making companies, essentially financing the building of factories in exchange for exclusive access. (These deals are essentially "quasi-acquisitions".) This means that if a rival produces a competing tablet or smart phone that customers are clamoring for, the rival would have difficulty producing it in mass since many of the contract outsourcing manufacturers are excluded from accepting such business.

- o **Example Two:** To ensure that its translucent blue iMacs would be widely available at Christmas several years ago, Apple paid $50 million to buy up all the available holiday air freight space. The move handicapped rivals such as Compaq that later wanted to book air transport.

- o **Example Three:** Several years ago, Apple design guru Jony Ive decided he wanted a new feature for the next MacBook: a small dot of green light above the screen, shining through the computer's aluminum casing to indicate when its camera was on. The problem was that it was believed to be physically impossible to shine light through metal. However, the Apple team learned that a customized laser could be used to poke holes in the aluminum small enough to be nearly invisible to the human eye but big enough to let light through.

A large number of these lasers were needed to match the scale of Apple's computer production. Apple's supply chain team found a U.S. company that made laser equipment for microchip manufacturing which, after some tweaking, could do the job. Apple convinced the seller to sign an exclusivity agreement and has since bought hundreds of such lasers to make holes for the green lights that now shine on Apple's MacBook Airs, Trackpads, and wireless keyboards.

- **Data Exhaust.** Having tremendous information regarding customers' buying habits, preferences and wish lists is an enormous asset and extremely difficult to compete against. If you could raise $50 billion to compete against Amazon or Netflix, you very likely could acquire lots of inventory and build state-of-the-art fulfillment centers. However, it would still take you many years of effort to develop the rich data sets that these companies use to predict which products its millions of customers would like to buy. Similarly, Mobileye feeds torrents of data—collected from millions of drivers all over the world and in every conceivable driving condition—into its ever improving algorithms which control its advanced driver assisted systems.

- **Switching Costs.** Switching costs are the costs that a customer experiences when switching from one vendor to another vendor. The costs involved can be monetary or in the form of inconvenience. The higher either of these costs are, the more locked-in customers are to their current vendors. For example, there are significant switching costs associated with changing set-top cable box providers. In addition to the customer having to uninstall the set-top box, he may have to personally deliver it to the cable company. Then, the second cable company will have to install the new set-top box which will require the scheduling of a home visit and possibly the tearing up of your carpet and walls during that installation.

The following are some of the common denominators associated with switching costs:

o   Switchers lose something. For instance, Apple iOS users who purchase movies, TV shows, and applications from the iTunes store are unable to transmit these media to Android or other portable devices (while music is transferrable). iCloud adds another layer of switching costs by synchronizing media, photos, notes, and other items across all Apple devices. Thus, an owner of an iPad is less likely to switch from an iPhone to an Android phone if it means that the individual will be unable to sync or access a portion of his content.

o   Sunk investment—which can be in the form of having scaled a steep learning curve—precludes switching. Software programs and medical devices that take years to learn to master meet this condition. Also, it is much harder to switch bank accounts from one bank to another now than a decade or two ago. This is partly due to the spread of electronic bill-paying services which require defecting consumers to update their banking information with every firm that they pay electronically.

o   Switchers are inconvenienced while benefits are unclear. The perceived benefits of switching from one money manager such as Fidelity Investments, to another, such as Vanguard, are uncertain. (Remember, past performance is no guarantee of future results.) But since the hassle factor is high, many investors take the path of least resistance and remain with their current money manager. A similar phenomena occurs when electric utilities try to convince their customers to sign up for dynamic pricing (i.e. paying more for electricity during peak times and paying less during off-peak hours). The process of reading, understanding and enrolling in such programs has proven to be a barrier. Also, most customers find committing to 12 months of uncertain electricity costs unsettling.

o   High risks associated with switching vendors. Let's say that you run a hospital or a textile mill. You are approached by a start-up electricity provider who is offering you significant savings if you sign up with that company. Despite the compelling costs savings potential, the risks of even a one-second interruption in electricity supply would be catastrophic and thus would probably dissuade you from switching electricity suppliers.

- **Backward Integration Risk.** Another source of competition can come from other companies backward integrating into your market. For instance, if your company produces entertainment for television, your firm could be adversely affected by Netflix backward integrating by creating programming including "House of Cards" and "Orange is the New Black." Similarly, if your company sells servers, you could see your server sales falter as companies such as Google and Facebook now make their own machines.

- **Forward Integration Risk.** As contract manufacturers learn more about the products they produce, they can become a threat by forward integrating. After having produced so many millions of Apple's products, Foxconn is making efforts to produce its own electronics, especially flat-screen televisions. Also, GoPro (in which Foxconn has taken a nearly 9% equity stake) is attempting to forward integrate by producing its own drones.

- **Economies of Scale.** In some industries, companies cannot enter or compete unless they possess enormous economies of scale. Take the packaging business, for instance. Since the margins for producing packaging for things such as water bottles or cereal boxes are so small on a per unit basis, the only way to compete is to possess massive production capacity.

- **Difficulty of Replication.** Products that have steep learning curves—such as nuclear medicine and sushi preparation (people cannot prepare it at home)—block potential copycats.

- **Long Production Periods.** Some agricultural products take many years to mature. For instance, planting cocoa trees will not result in the quick production of cocoa as cocoa trees take about 10 years to reach their peak.

- **High Search Costs.** Existing companies benefit when customers wishing to retain such services encounter high search costs. For example, if I was searching for an expert tax advisor in connection with a matter related to shipping through the Panama Canal, I would place much higher value on a referral from a respected figure in the shipping industry than I would from an Internet search. The problem is that it would take me quite a bit of effort to locate someone qualified to give me such a referral. Once I received the referral and contacted the tax expert, I would be more inclined to pay his fee without negotiating for a concession because the search costs (in terms of time and energy) are so high. When the search costs are low, such as searching for a restaurant, it becomes difficult for the service provider to charge excessive rates. It was transparency and the ease of booking travel arrangements that killed the retail travel services industry.

Despite the importance of moats protecting a business, it is important that we do not overemphasize the issue. The more an executive focuses on competition, the less he focuses on his customers. If executives are not careful, they could erect barriers to a business that is bereft of customers. In a similar vein, some buy-and-hold value investors proclaim that they search for companies that will enjoy moats for the next 20 years. I do not believe this is realistic. There is simply too much competition and convergence of industries. There is no way around it: value investors will just have to come to work a little more frequently. Further, as an investor, it is not a good use of my time to philosophize about unknowable events so far into the future. To be blunt, I do not really care if my portfolio companies have sustainable advantages for 20 years. I just want them to produce high returns over the next several years. I too must be a little more attentive to my portfolio.

Barriers to Exit

Unlike barriers to entry that render it difficult for new companies to enter a particular industry, barriers to exit render it difficult for companies to sever their relationships with customers, close their businesses and exit an industry. Barriers to exit can be damaging to an industry because they often result in excess capacity, causing prices to fall and the earnings of all industry participants to be adversely affected.

So what are some of the forces behind barriers to exit that result in excess capacity? A few are discussed below:

Government Policy. State insurance commissioners do not want property and casualty insurance companies to collect premiums from the state's residents for many years and then to terminate their policies a few days before their meteorologists forecast the arrival of an impending hurricane.

Obligations to Workers. If a company is required to maintain stipulated levels of unionized workers for several years or governments render it very difficult to terminate workers, many business will continue production so as to cover such obligations. Under a law passed in France in May 2013, companies that want to fire workers have to negotiate with them, with any agreement needing the backing of authorities. With this backdrop, French Prime Minister Jean-Marc Ayrault warned Alcatel-Lucent that authorities would not approve the company's planned layoffs of 900 staff in the country unless it negotiated a good a deal with unions, and saved as many jobs and sites as possible.

Sunk Costs. If tremendously large amounts of capital have been invested in a business, that firm may feel compelled to run the business so as to recover such sunk costs.

Barriers to Exit – Barring Customer Defections

Another permutation of barriers to exit is the difficulty that customers face when they attempt to sever their relationships with companies. These barriers to exit are akin to switching costs on steroids. Companies that achieve customer lock-in benefit from long-term revenue streams while reduced customer churn makes it unnecessary to spend heavily on recruiting new customers. However, boa constricting customer lock-in runs the risk of legal retribution and reputational degradation.

The following are examples of how companies erect barriers to customer defections:

- Hedge funds require that their investors lock up money with the fund for a defined period of time. Longer lock-up periods help hedge funds take advantage of less liquid investment opportunities and relieve hedge funds of the pressure associated with frequent redemption requests.

- There have been quite a few consumer complaints regarding the risks of leaving a company that can tarnish their reputations or credit scores. Some customers have said it is very dangerous to cancel Dun & Bradstreet's Credibility service (which provides frequent updates to its customers' credit histories) because they worry about their credit rating becoming the victim of retaliation.

- Partners who leave a flailing law firm before it dissolves have a duty to return any profits from client work sourced from the flailing law firm that they perform at their next law firm. While this issue is usually not sufficient to discourage partners from abandoning a sinking ship, it is a potential barrier to exit that partners in such a situation might wish to entertain.

- Companies that lease their equipment are often successful in ensnaring their lessees for longer than the lessee wishes to lease the equipment. Equipment leases often require lessees that do not wish to renew their leases to notify the lessor within a designated window of time that elapses several months before the lease terminates. For example, if you take a three-year lease on a copying machine on July 1, 2015, the lease may automatically renew on July 1, 2018, unless you notify the lessor sometime between November 1, 2017 and February 1, 2018. These termination windows are designed for lessees to overlook.

- It can be very difficult to cancel service with Customer Relationship Management software providers. Similar to the situation with equipment leases, to cancel these automatically renewing agreements, customers must notify their CRM provider at a certain point before the annual contract is scheduled to renew. But this is one arduous and enervating process. Emails are not returned and it is not possible to navigate the phone number given for cancelling subscriptions (even if you can find the phone number which requires quite a bit of persistence). If you run out of stamina to cancel, your subscription rolls over for another year. Also, it could be very difficult for CRM or cloud storage services customers to leave their vendors because doing so results in the abandonment of their customer data and files.

Despite the near-term advantages companies enjoy when they lock in paying customers through click-through agreements (a.k.a. evergreen contracts, which are the one-sided agreements that you accept when you install software or purchase a subscription via a website), there is a risk that the party could come to an end. There is a strong argument that these contracts of adhesion are completely unfair. Contracts are supposed to involve consent by each party to give up something of his own to obtain something he values more. However, in many click-through agreements, there is a lack of the basics of what contracts are supposed to involve. For beginners, there is no negotiation, massive information asymmetry, and an obvious and concerted effort to make the agreements highly complicated so as to discourage the other side from reading them.

Should these click-through agreements suffer judiciary defeat or challenge from the likes of the Department of Justice, companies such as Salesforce.com that rely on customer retentive contracts would suffer a tremendous blow.

- Interestingly, there is a cogent argument for eliminating contractual barriers to customer defections. Preferred Freezer, which offers temperature controlled cold storage warehouses, does not even use contracts with its customers. Since Preferred Freezer's employees would know that their employer has long-term contracts in place with customers, they would not be terribly motivated to provide stellar customer service. Second, if there were long-term contracts in place, such contracts would provide the competition with a roadmap to presenting competing offers to Preferred Freezer's customers. Competitors would approach Preferred Freezer's customers about six months before the agreements were to expire. Managers of the client companies would also have a defined point in time to assess its vendor relations and would be receptive to reviewing proposals from competing companies. The combination of suboptimal customer service and a defined entry point for competitors could prove lethal.

This notion of eliminating barriers to customer exit is not applicable to all situations. Preferred Freezer has an unfair advantage in that it can perfect senior liens on its customers' inventories of perishable foods.

Leverage in Business Models

Companies that can produce massive volumes of the same product enjoy leverage in that the fixed costs associated with a production run are almost zero. For instance, 60 million LEGO pieces may be produced from a mold that costs no more than $80,000. In most businesses, as a company's demand for supplies rises, that company gains leverage as it can receive concessions from its vendors. On the contrary, the music streaming business is not leverageable because musicians and their recording labels are not willing to grant volume discounts on the royalties they are owed. (Further, music streaming customers demand lower subscription rates while wanting to listen to more songs per month.)

Business models that have a great deal of leverage typically have high fixed costs and deliver earnings gains (and losses) that are disproportionately large compared to their revenue improvements (deterioration). Amazon's business model appears to have a lot of leverage. Based on my very cursory review of books that I purchase from Amazon, Amazon seems to sell its products at a 40% discount to list prices. Barnes & Noble gives its members a 10% discount on their purchases. Thus, Amazon could raise its prices by 10 percentage points and still offer its merchandise at a compelling 20% to 30% discount to competing retailers. With its volume, such price increases could be tremendously profitable for Amazon.

Google is likely to have benefitted from leverage in its business model when it changed its keyword advertising policy so that its advertisers can no longer bid on keywords for separate devices. This change meant that advertising keywords on tablet computers now cost the same as advertising keywords on desktops. This decision should boost revenues at Google as keyword bids for tablets were 20% to 40% lower than for desktop clicks.

Hotels are highly leveraged. When occupancy rates rise, hotels have very little additional costs as they only need to provide the guest with clean linens, together with furnishing a little bit of electricity and water. Thus, most incremental revenues from higher occupancies flow to the bottom line. When room rates rise, all of the excess revenue flows to the bottom line.

Gold miners with high fixed costs are also highly leveraged. When gold prices are too low to justify extracting gold, the miner still has expended enormous resources on, among other things, the geological surveys, permitting, environmental studies, and positioning earth moving equipment at the site. However, when gold prices rebound, it does not cost the mine operators very much to hire the miners to extract the gold. Thus, the value of gold mines can rise from zero to something significant very quickly.

Real estate brokerage firms such as Coldwell Banker, Long & Foster and Keller Williams are highly leveraged. Typically when a house is sold, the commission is split four ways with the buyer's real estate broker, buyer's brokerage firm, seller's real estate broker, and seller's brokerage firm, each receiving roughly 25% of the commission. However, the best real estate agents do not split their commissions evenly with their real estate firms, rather they receive larger commissions than their firms. Instead of a 50% split with their firms, their commissions can be 70% or 80%. These top-performing real estate agents are most likely to sell during periods of sluggish home sales. However, when the real estate market recovers, brokerage firms have tremendous leverage. Not only are more agents selling more homes and buildings at higher prices, but as the second and third tier of real estate agents are now making sales, they are receiving smaller portions of commissions than the top producers, which means that the brokerage firm retains much higher commission levels.

From the point of view of investing in residential real estate, some neighborhoods have more leverage than other neighborhoods. Which ones? Of the many factors that should be considered, three are discussed here. First, the greater the disparity of median home prices in one neighborhood to those in an adjacent and more desirable neighborhood, the better. Let's say that you want to buy an apartment near Midtown Manhattan, where the median price of suitable apartments is $1.3 million. So, you begin to search the Kip's Bay and Murray Hill neighborhoods, both of which you believe are increasingly popular enclaves that abut Midtown. If the median price of suitable apartments in Kip's Bay is $1.1 million and $700,000 in Murray Hill, Murray Hill would offer more leverage. The older the housing stock, the better, because neighborhood renovation would likely occur earlier. Further, the lower the rate of homeownership among the people that live in the neighborhood, the better, because the absentee landlords would be much more receptive to selling to developers than those who have made their homes in the neighborhood.

Airline operators have more leverage in their business models than express delivery companies such as FedEx and United Parcel Service. When the price of fuel rises, the airlines must absorb all of the price increase while the express delivery companies are usually contractually permitted to pass on the higher costs to their customers. (Although, in some cases, vendors decide not to pass all of their higher costs on to their customers for a variety of reasons including the desire to maintain goodwill among their clients.) When the price of fuel falls, the airlines retain all of the cost savings while the express delivery companies are usually required to pass along most of the fuel savings to their customers.

Analytical Consideration The more active a company is in hedging, the less leveraged it becomes. For example, U.S. airline operators typically hedge less of their fuel requirements than European airline operators. If the price of jet-fuel surges, U.S. airline operators will suffer more than European airline operators. However, if the price of jet-fuel plummets, U.S. airline operators will benefit much more than their European counterparts.

Collection companies that purchase aged accounts receivables from banks have leverage in those negotiations. This is because 180 days after a debtor stops paying his credit-card bill, the banks can no longer classify such accounts as assets, because the money might not be collected. Banks then "charge off" the accounts, taking a loss. Collection agencies, in effect, offer banks cash for problematic debts that would otherwise be counted as losses.

The notion of leverage can also apply to the ability to build out a business. Consider the early days of online dating sites. It probably seemed to many that enormous capital, marketing and luck would be required to become the leader in such a network effect, winner-take-all situation. However, Match.com founder Gary Kremen realized that there could be much more leverage in building out his dating site for singles. His idea was that one well-connected woman could get 50 other women—who could get 5,000 men to join the site. Thus, Match.com began to target the small proportion of women who were already online by advertising on female-focused chat sites such as Compuserve's Women's Wire.

Leverage Through Offloading Infrastructure

Another permutation of leverage arises when a company avoids investing in infrastructure. For instance, when several of the on-demand taxi services started up, they were able to leverage off of the smart phone handsets and service contracts that taxi drivers already had in place, enabling these emerging companies to avoid such expenses and to preserve scarce capital.

A new generation of grocery fulfillment businesses (e.g. Instacart) have a better chance of success than their forbearers (e.g. Webvan) due to the former companies' reduced commitment to infrastructure. During its short existence before declaring bankruptcy, Webvan stocked its own warehouses with food, furnished its own delivery trucks and maintained a massive payroll. The newer grocery fulfillment business model is much sleeker: Instacart maintains no real estate, no inventory of food, no fleet of delivery vehicles, and minimal headcount. How so? Instacart relies on independent contractors stationed at its partner grocery stores to perform the roles of shoppers and couriers (who own their own cars) to fulfill and deliver its customers' orders. Further, Instacart's market entry is much more propitious than was Webvan's in the late 1990s. Today, Internet connectivity (a crucial factor in placing orders for many items) is much more robust, GPS navigation is dramatically more precise and backend supply chain management software drives much greater efficiency at participating grocers.

Value of Endorsements

Many companies point to endorsements when attempting to validate their business models or prospects for their products' success. While having testimonials are better than not having any testimonials, some should be weighted more heavily than others. For instance, I do not weight endorsements that come from Chambers of Commerce very highly because Chambers of Commerce want every business in their city to succeed and are therefore promiscuous in granting testimonials. I am more impressed with a glowing article about a start-up company's technology or business model that comes from the trade press than a local newspaper. Trade magazines are more likely to have conducted a comparative analysis of similar products throughout the country (or world) or at least have reporters that are more familiar with a given beat than a hometown paper. I recommend being cautious about endorsements that come from peers at the same accelerators and incubators because the rendering of such endorsements could have been a function of pressure placed on the endorser by the operator of the accelerator or incubator.

Finally, testimonials are more meaningful when they come from people who know something about the product or service they are endorsing. This sounds obvious but many people have a tendency to overrate testimonials coming from superstars. For instance, both Bill Clinton and Shimon Peres—neither of whom knew anything about cars—profusely praised Better Place, which failed miserably.

The Network Effect

Does your business benefit from network effects?

Network effects hold that a product becomes more valuable as more people use it. The first fax machine wasn't worth anything because you couldn't send or receive any faxes. However, as more people purchased fax machines, the utility of fax machines rose geometrically. The same phenomenon occurs with social media sites. LinkedIn, Facebook or Twitter would not be worth joining if only a few others were already members.

Similarly, vehicle-to-vehicle communications systems—which include sensors that inform one car of an approaching car—would not be worth installing on your car if no one else does so. Waze (acquired by Google in 2013) provides another example of the network effect. Waze is the world's largest community-based traffic and navigation app. Waze uploads and synthesizes user input on changing road conditions as evidenced by the speed, location and routes of its users. Users are also rewarded for making accurate reports. If only a small number of users were to use the Waze app, it would not be able to provide useful information.

Typically, network effects are "winner take all" propositions. That means that since network effects require the participation of large numbers of users, there are not enough subscribers to give critical mass to many (or any) competing platform providers. In other words, there is no reason to have a variety of professional networking sites (akin to LinkedIn). People do not want to be bothered engaging in multiple media platforms, especially when they are providing the site's content which entails considerable user effort.

Further, some network platforms are becoming so dominant that, in many cases, people are compelled to use them. For instance, if a job candidate or potential business associate were to contact you, you would probably want to check his profile on LinkedIn. If that person did not have a LinkedIn profile, you would probably be reticent about proceeding with the interview or meeting. If you are single and getting ready to go out on a blind date, you would likewise feel more apprehensive about your date if he didn't have a Facebook or LinkedIn profile.

Many restaurateurs dislike OpenTable, which allows patrons to book reservations online. While OpenTable enables restaurants to better manage its reservations, it is very expensive in view of its high per-person booking charges and fees for the use of its computer equipment. OpenTable even charges a per-person fee for guests that book through a restaurant's own website. To top it off, OpenTable emails one restaurant's customers recommendations to other nearby restaurants. Nevertheless, OpenTable has engrained itself in the reservation routines of so many customers that most restaurants have no choice but to accept reservations through OpenTable.

Concerns with Network Effects

A few words of caution with respect to network effects are in order. First, network effects that rely on the replacement of an installed base will diffuse slower, especially if the replacement and product development cycles are long as is the case with automobiles. So, vehicle-to-vehicle communications will take time to become ubiquitous.

Not all technologies that become more valuable in lockstep with growing numbers of users are beneficiaries of the network effect. Messaging systems allow users to form groups of friends, each of which represents a different dimension of their lives. Many teenagers like to message with Kik while WhatsApp is well-suited to messaging with family and friends located throughout the world. Colleagues might feel comfortable using iMessage while Facebook enthusiasts message via Facebook Messenger. Twitter junkies use direct messaging. Reasons for messaging platform agnosticism include:

- The real platform behind messaging apps is the phone's address book. Since all apps can access the phone's address book, it is easy to communicate with friends and colleagues via whatever messaging service they prefer.

- Most messaging apps have a basic texting feature that looks the same regardless of the app.

- The process of entering text, picking a friend, and hitting send is the same in all apps which means that there is no learning time.

- It is easy to respond to a message using the same app that the initiator utilized.

Finally, there is a conflict between network effects and the Pareto Principle (also known as the 80/20 Rule). Let's see how Mark Zuckerberg of Facebook wisely steered clear of the Pareto Principle. In the early days of Facebook, it is easy to see how a management consultant may have advised Mr. Zuckerberg. The management consultant would have probably told Mr. Zuckerberg to focus on the core 20% of his users who, according to the Pareto Principle, accounted for 80% of Facebook's value. Fortunately, Mr. Zuckerberg focused on enticing the casual and infrequent users—but even more importantly, those who were not yet using Facebook—to join that social media platform.

Scalability Analysis

Business owners typically seek scalable businesses. For a business to be scalable it must be able to expand without incurring significant additional fixed costs. An accountant is much less scalable than accounting software provided by Intuit. If tomorrow five hundred customers were to seek to engage the accountant, he would have to turn most of that business away. He simply would not be able to handle the surge in demand for his services. However, Intuit could easily activate five hundred additional customer licenses. Another criterion of scalable businesses is that such businesses must have tremendous opportunities for growth. It does not help a company when it has the capacity to scale but not the demand to warrant such expansion.

Scalable businesses are more typically found in the manufacturing world than in the service sector because machines are easier to manage than people. Also, for standardized goods that are produced in factories, the customers do not care from which factory or in which container the goods originated. However, where the service quotient of a product is high, such as in delivering health care or financial or legal advice, tremendous value is yielded to the client by the professional. Thus, it is much more difficult to ensure that each service provider will deliver the same quality of advice and attention. It is also easier for service professionals to start their own firms than it is for a factory worker to build a rival production facility.

Unlike in the service sector, when a manufacturing company produces tremendous volumes (e.g. of batteries as Tesla is gearing up to do) it can design custom equipment which can much more efficiently process each step. Scale also yields negotiating leverage to reduce the profit margins at suppliers which they often accept in return for large volumes.

Concerns with Scalability

Abraham Lincoln said that logic does not have the consistency of cobbed corn. What does that mean in the context of business model validation? Very simply, companies must have some scale to operate efficiently but the largest companies face diminishing returns from their growth. Just as in the animal world, in the business world there are limitations to the ability to scale a company.[11] The top management of a large and growing corporation becomes progressively more removed from the multiple touch points with customers, suppliers, and partners. (Sometimes, this is literally the case as senior executives are prone to occupy the offices on the top floors of buildings, far from the hustle and bustle taking place in their stores at the street level.) This reduces management effectiveness, eventually causing scale to become a disadvantage and providing competitors with an opportunity to beat the incumbent.

Major companies that currently enjoy large scales of production are threatened by disruptive technologies as well as by universal service requirements. Let's look at how an electric utility operator could be threatened by more people installing solar panels on their homes. Since the solar panel industry receives a variety of governmental subsidies, those companies are becoming more price-competitive with the utilities. While the electric utility loses customers to solar panel operators it is still required to maintain the electric grid. These costs are spread over fewer kilowatt-hours due to customers defecting to solar panel companies. These higher costs are passed on to the remaining electric utility customers, thereby making solar power even more compelling and pushing people to adopt it in a vicious circle. Hawaiian Electric Industries has experienced this cycle of events as 10% of its customers have avoided paying roughly three times the U.S. average for electricity on a kilowatt-hour basis by installing solar systems.

Some business models are just not built to scale. A few examples follow:

- Companies that impose revenue limiting policies on themselves will be hindered in their attempts to scale. Many years ago, then Caterpillar CEO, Donald Fites, said that he did not want to make the investments

---

[11] There have never been mammals much larger than an elephant, perhaps because mammals are warm-blooded and need energy to survive. It gets progressively more difficult for the heart to circulate blood to the extremities as a mammal grows bigger.

necessary to build manufacturing capacity that would be needed to fill orders of his company's earth moving equipment during periods of peak demand. The reason was that Mr. Fites did not want to be saddled with excess capacity and tied-up capital during the non-peak periods. While Square, the payments company, is making valiant efforts to diffuse its technology in order to capture more transactions—it also limits the amount of money per transaction that can be sent through its payments network.

- Companies that have revenue limiting policies imposed on them will be hindered in their attempts to scale. Governments limit defense contractors in terms of to which countries they may sell their weapons systems. When several countries jointly-develop a weapons system, the potential market is further restricted. Take Israel's Iron Dome which was partially funded by the United States. Despite its roughly 90% success rate for intercepting missiles Hamas fired from the Gaza Strip during the summer of 2014, there are not many countries that have both a need for such missile interception technologies and that are acceptable to both the U.S. and Israel.

- Products that are meant to be niche-oriented, exclusive, or counter-culture cannot scale because the wide acceptance of such products would reduce their appeal in the eyes of their most loyal customers. Similarly, it is important to realize that if companies are using a product to emphasize their uniqueness, this is not a signal that the product will become mainstream. For instance, the online dating site OkCupid began accepting payment with Bitcoins. In a related announcement, the site's senior management stated, "We pride ourselves on being the nerdiest online dating site." Thus, if you were trying to gauge the uptake of Bitcoin, adoption by companies such as OkCupid would not be a strong signal of that medium's prospects.

- Companies that are affected by the Law of Large Numbers cannot scale. An example comes from the money management industry. The larger a mutual fund or hedge fund becomes, the more difficult it is to produce strong returns. The combination of a limited number of investment opportunities that will yield the best returns in the realm of the manager's expertise and the fact that those opportunities can only accommodate limited investment means that large portfolios must allocate the majority of their assets to investments that will provide lower returns.

- Companies whose products have outgrown their supporting infrastructures have trouble scaling. For instance, most airports are unwilling to modify gates and widen runways to make room for the 500-plus seat Airbus A380. Similarly, there are few ports capable of accommodating the largest container ships while canals run greater risks of blockage when these enormous vessels pass. (Also, the larger container ships become, the more difficult it is to find capable crew and the more devastating accidents become. Moreover, the largest ships experience more metal fatigue due to phenomena such as "springing" which occurs when waves cause disproportionate vibration on the hauls.)

- Multiple layers of regulatory authorities in the value chain impede scalability. For instance, financial services apps scale and diffuse much slower than game apps because the former are regulated differently in every country while the latter face very light regulation throughout the world. Businesses that are subject to regulations on a national level usually find it easier to grow and leverage their costs than businesses that are regulated at the state level. Litigation finance companies and property and casualty insurers are some businesses that are burdened with having to comply with a quilt of 50 regulatory mandates just in the United States, whereas pharmaceutical companies only have to meet the regulatory approval of the Food and Drug Administration. Conventionally grown crops can scale better than genetically-modified produce. While conventionally grown crops undergo no government testing in the United States, genetically-modified seeds must be reviewed by the Department of Agriculture, which is followed by a voluntary check from the Food and Drug Administration, which (if the GM seed includes insecticides or pesticides, as most do) is followed by a review from the Environmental Protection Agency. The disparity between drones and sharing companies is even more dramatic. Drones are regulated at the federal level and will therefore have more scalability than sharing companies such as Airbnb and Uber, which must appease city—which are even more Balkanized than state—authorities.

- A strong balance sheet and a large centralized organization are not helpful in the fracking industry. Onshore wells are a fraction of the cost of drilling offshore. Shale development requires intensive drilling of many wells rather than the handful common to a conventional project. Since drilling wells faster, experimenting with the number of fractures per well and other operational tweaks are tried at the field level, there are no efficiencies with executing such a micro approach in large, centralized organizations.

- Too much selection can backfire. This is certainly the case for retailers selling men's apparel. Most men will become bewildered and annoyed with too much selection. As they do not want to shop for clothes, they would rather retreat from the store than wade through excessive selection. In another realm of retailing, Wal-Mart is trying to compete against GameStop by allowing customers that trade in used video games to spend related trade-in proceeds on anything in the Wal-Mart stores or on its website. However, Wal-Mart's expansive selection is probably not of interest to young, mostly male, gamers.

- Localized businesses have difficulty scaling. Software typically scales less robustly than computer hardware because software must be accompanied by manuals written in a multitude of languages. Not so for hardware manufacturers. Because the cement business is so localized—due to its very low value-to-shipping costs—there is little ability to achieve scalability in this industry. It is only economic to transport cement a few hundred miles (at the most) from a kiln. Thus, if Lafarge from France acquires a cement producer in South Korea, Lafarge will not likely be able to achieve significant economies of scale by ramping up its production in France and exporting to South Korea. Even if Lafarge were to operate its newly acquired business in South Korea, its negotiating power in Europe would not translate very well to South Korea. Lafarge would have to pay local limestone and coal suppliers as well as purchase electricity and hire locally. (However, Lafarge would be able to transfer its know-how relative to more efficient production processes to South Korea. Also, there is some opportunity for cement companies to reduce interest costs through acquisitions, as Cemex (from Mexico) did when it became eligible to raise capital in the United States when it acquired several American cement companies.)

- Businesses that are consultant-heavy or allow their employees to work offsite. Aside from it being difficult to determine exactly how much work remote employees are actually performing, disparate workforces are hard to scale. I just can't see myself having the patience to train someone remotely and offsite workforces make learning by osmosis impossible.

Market Spoilage

Market spoilage occurs when a negative experience or bad press causes potential customers to avoid using a product. Many years ago, I bought a sophisticated coffee maker. Maybe I didn't use it properly, but after a few uses it stopped working. I repeated the process of buying and trying coffeemakers a few more times, but had no luck with any of them. I am not willing to try the Keurig coffeemaker even though its technology and reliability may very well be much improved from the coffeemakers that I tried to use some 15 years ago.

Thomas Alva Edison, the inventor of direct current electricity, tried to spoil the market for the rival alternating current electricity which was invented by George Westinghouse. Edison lobbied for New York State to adopt alternating current electricity as its official form of execution by electrocution. The horrific electrocutions that ensued scandalized alternating current electricity with respect to a variety of end uses. Separately, maybe the lingering images of the Hindenburg disaster will spook auto buyers away from hydrogen-based cars.

The most vivid example that I can think of regarding market spoilage in recent times comes from BATS Global Markets, which is one of the largest platforms for high-frequency computer-driven trading. BATS intended to offer 6.3 million shares at $16 apiece during its initial public offering. The stock debuted on BATS's own exchange, but was halted several hours after it began trading due to a technical snafu of its own making. When its share price plunged to 4 cents, BATS Global Markets withdrew its initial public offering.

Another instance of market spoilage relates to the financial sector. Fund of funds managers receive performance and management fees from institutional investors in return for performing due diligence on, and selecting, suitable hedge funds and private equity funds. When some of the most prominent fund of funds managers, such as Fairfield Greenwich and

Tremont Group Holdings, funneled enormous sums of money into the Bernard Madoff Ponzi scheme, the merits of retaining any fund of funds managers were brought into question.

Disappointing performance by one industry player can damage the appeal of other companies in the sector. Many years ago, there was a proliferation of dental and orthodontic related companies going public. The fortunes of the dominant dental company—which was called Orthodontic Centers of America—impacted the perceptions of every publicly-traded company in the space. When OCA reported positive results, the entire peer group got a boost. When OCA disappointed, all of the dental stocks took a beating. In one presentation at a conference that I organized at the New York Society of Security Analysts, an executive of Orthodontic Centers of America joked that it would be in the industry's interests if all of the publicly-traded dental companies donated 10% of their profits to OCA.

The perception of entire countries can be stained by recent conflicts. For instance, Israel, Rwanda and Columbia are much safer than the general public might think. These countries are also welcoming to businesses and have strong entrepreneurial communities.

Optionality Implicit in Business Models

There is option value in being able to delay investment decisions, quickly pivot from one business initiative to another, and to remove one's self from a cratering business. While a discussion on options analysis is more suitable for another time and place, we can readily see that some businesses have more option value than others. For instance, there seems to be more optionality in farming (where farmers can plant different crops with relative ease) than in the medical device industry (where changing the mechanics of a device or its intended use requires painstaking regulatory review).

Some restaurants offer their customers more optionality than other restaurants. Sandwich shops like Subway allow their customers to not only create their own sandwiches but to also determine how many calories they will ingest. On the other end of the spectrum would be the restaurants in Japan where the chef decides what the customers eat.

Manufacturing operations can be designed to enhance optionality. A company that makes both nipples for baby bottles and condoms is much less sensitive to changes in the birth rate than a company that makes either one of them alone. There are quite a few similarities in pet-food and chocolate factories. Both manufacturing processes use similar equipment and require very high hygienic standards. Also, it is important that the end products will have the right density and look. Thus, it is not surprising that Mars, Incorporated enjoys the flexibility associated with producing both pet-food and confectionary products.

Building owners' optionality is impacted by the tenants they currently have. Usually the second tenant of an auto dealer will be another auto dealer because most other prospective tenants will be averse to establishing their businesses where there may be exposure to spent solvents, used oil, gasoline, and other pollutants and contaminants left behind by the first auto dealer. Landlords that lose a restaurant as a tenant are largely resigned to securing another restaurant operator because the costs of removing the kitchen equipment are prohibitive. Finally, once doctors' offices begin to fill vacancies, other doctors may have to be enticed to take adjacent space. This is because other businesses such as restaurant operators are concerned that the perception of their patrons will be that the patients visiting the doctors may have contagious diseases and that the disposal of needles and bandages presents health risks.

Similarly, tenants' optionality is affected by their landlords. For instance, shopping mall-based businesses have less optionality than strip-mall and stand-alone stores. Stores sited in shopping malls must keep their doors open during the hours that the mall operator sets. If the store thinks it could generate more profit by remaining open two hours later on Saturday evenings and opening one hour later on Sunday mornings, the store is out of luck. If a yogurt shop wants to drum up more business by giving out free samples, it is much more restricted from doing so if it is located in a shopping mall than it would be if it were in a strip mall or located on a street downtown.

The structure of a company is partially determinative of its optionality. Privately-held companies have more optionality than do publicly-traded companies because they have fewer constituents—such as securities regulators and research analysts—to answer to. A publicly-traded company may be reticent to pivot its business because doing so would cause it to lose coverage from its research analysts. Companies financed with equity have more optionality than companies financed with debt. Banking covenants are rigid and not in-tune with enabling companies to act opportunistically whereas equity investors are often accepting of their portfolios losing money while they are growing their businesses. Companies with smaller numbers of investors and directors have more optionality than do companies with larger numbers of investors and directors because changes in the strategic direction of a company require less consent.

Optionality and Start-Up Companies

Start-up companies are often designed with optionality in mind. Emerging companies that pioneer new industries and realize that they may have to pivot might be better off hiring younger, more malleable employees as opposed to older employees with high degrees of skills in specific disciplines.

It is true that businesses should have the ability to adapt to changing circumstances and to seize new opportunities. One or two pivots in a business model are acceptable. However, too many pivots indicate that management failed to put thought into its planning while excessive pivoting confuses investors, employees and customers. Companies that pivot too frequently end up with employees that are not suited to help the company reach its new goals. No investor wants to invest his money in a company and not have any idea as to the general direction the company is going.

Investors in start-up companies often view such investments as options. These (largely) sophisticated investors realize that their entire investments could become worthless. Thus, it may be rational for CEOs of such companies to behave irrationally, albeit not recklessly. If their aggressive gambits work, all stakeholders will be happy. If their gambits fail by a wide margin, their shareholders should not be shocked. Narrowly failing to miss milestones might be the worst situation for leaders of cutting-edge companies as they will receive neither adulation nor will their failed efforts be readily dismissed. Instead, they will be perceived as deficient managers. Thus, Steve Jobs might have been acting rationally irrational when he timed the initial public offering of Pixar to occur during the same week that the film *Toy Story* was released. The movie's box office success contributed to Pixar raising $140 million which was the largest IPO in 1995. If *Toy Story* had flopped, it would have been difficult to raise money anyway.

Optionality in Research Funding

The way in which a company manages its research initiatives will impact the degree of optionality inherent in that company. First, there is more real options value if the method for funding research projects more closely resembles that of the Howard Hughes Medical Institute (HHMI) than the National Institutes of Health (NIH). The HHMI method is to fund the researcher while the NIH method is to fund the research project. Since researchers funded by HHMI are freer to explore where there is potential, while NIH researchers are required to seek approval for deviating from the approved research path, the HHMI researchers are more likely to discover breakthroughs.

Second, companies with long procurement cycles for acquiring research equipment and supplies will have a lower propensity to discover breakthroughs than companies that expedite the acquisition of such equipment and supplies. An ossified procurement process inhibits experimentation in the short-term and demotivates researchers in the intermediate term.

Options Are Only Options

It is a common mistake for investors to overweight the importance of a large company taking an equity stake in a start-up company. Too often, investors jump to the conclusion that the large company's investment validates the smaller company's technology, business model or market position. However, we should remind ourselves that these investments often represent very small commitments, or options, on the part of the large company. A more diligent analyst would try to determine how many similar options the large company has taken in the given industry. For instance, Visa owned a 5.5% stake in Monitise and accounted for as much as 15% of Monitise's revenues while Visa Europe owned 6% of the stock and accounted for about 15% of Monitise's sales. Did these equity stakes and transactions levels prove Visa's commitment to Monetise? No. Visa said it will invest more in its own mobile-banking initiatives.

Similarly, being a legacy supplier or owning stakes in client companies does not guarantee business. For instance, an Intel chip will replace a processor from Texas Instruments that was included in the first version of Google Glass. As this book goes to press, Foxconn has not won any manufacturing contracts from GoPro despite owning nearly 9% of that company.

Icarus Paradox

In Greek mythology, Icarus (a flying Pegasus) burned its wings when it flew too close to the sun. The lesson is that excelling to extremely high levels can have unwanted consequences. For instance, companies that grow at exponential rates often find it difficult to terminate employees that under-perform. They need all hands on deck to pursue their ambitious portfolio of initiatives. The problem is that poor performers linger at the company, dragging down productivity and morale while bloating payroll costs.

The Icarus Paradox could singe the wings of Kickstarter, one of the most successful crowdfunding sites. Kickstarter allows companies, artists and hobbyists to raise capital for their projects. In return for paying an amount of money set by the creators listing on Kickstarter, supporters are entitled to receive a demo product. One company that listed on Kickstarter was called Oculus. Oculus raised $2.4 million to develop its Rift virtual reality headset. After development, Oculus shipped its Kickstarter sup-porters the virtual reality headset. The demand for the headsets generated through Kickstarter was a proof of concept exercise that enabled Oculus to raise venture capital.

So far, so good.

Approximately 18 months later, Oculus was acquired by Facebook for $2 billion or 833 times the $2.4 million its supporters contributed to Oculus via Kickstarter. The Oculus story seems to be a success for everyone. Oculus funded its project and successfully developed its headsets. Oculus's sup-porters helped fund something they believed in and received a product that didn't exist before they supported it. The founders and investors of Oculus made a fortune when that company was acquired. In Oculus, Kickstarter has a great story to tell about the power of its platform in connecting in-ventors with potential customers.

However, Oculus's success has caused ill-will towards Kickstarter be-cause many early supporters believe that they should share in Oculus's bountiful exit despite this notion being clearly absent in Kickstarter's Terms of Service Agreement. Although neither Oculus nor Kickstarter have any legal or moral obligation to enrich their early supporters, missing out on such profitable windfalls could reduce the appeal of crowdfunding sites such as Kickstarter.

Another example of the Icarus Paradox at play on Kickstarter comes from Radiate Athletics. Radiate produces workout shirts which feature thermochromatic technology so that the fabric changes color during exercise. These colors highlight the muscles that are getting the most intense workout. Radiate's Kickstarter campaign to raise $30,000 yielded nearly $600,000 within one month. While this validated customer demand for its shirts, it also overwhelmed Radiate, which could not orchestrate the timely production and shipping of 30,000 shirts. Obviously, the delay disappointed Radiate's supporters.

Other examples of the Icarus Paradox include:

Successful Brands. As a rule of thumb, the more successful a brand, the more stridently it will be counterfeited. However, the pain associated with a creator's product being counterfeited is not evenly distributed. When a Gucci handbag is counterfeited there is some possibility that the lady that carries the counterfeit bag aspires to own the original. Maybe one day she will. However, since this dynamic is absent when a movie or book is pirated, there is no potential upside for movie producers or authors.

> **Analytical Consideration** Chinese eCommerce companies such as JD.com, which focus on direct sales to customers, are better positioned to police counterfeit goods than companies such as Alibaba which act as intermediaries by routing customer orders to their networks of merchants.

Cray Supercomputers. Seymour Cray has been called "the father of supercomputing" and his computers ran the fastest in the world for decades. However, Cray had a very difficult time selling his over-engineered supercomputers and at least one of his ventures—Cray Computer Corporation—filed for bankruptcy protection.

Personalized Medicine. The closer a company comes to personalizing medicine based on patients' varying genetic makeups, the more likely it is that their patent applications will be rejected or, if granted, will be invalidated. In the wake of the Association for Molecular Pathology v. Myriad Genetics case, the Supreme Court ruled that the laws of nature and natural phenomenon are not proper subjects of patent protection.

Pain relief medicine that eradicates pain. When a medicine eliminates pain, people may stop taking their medicine as prescribed. Thus, a pharmaceutical company that develops a highly efficacious drug is effectively penalized in terms of receiving reduced revenues.

Predictive Software. Companies that herald the use of predictive software in better managing their businesses expose themselves to shareholder lawsuits when the future unfolds differently than expected. There have been situations in which shareholders are baffled as to why financial results were different than management guidance when the same management team boasted of the power of its predictive intelligence.

Dating and Freelance Sites. Lots of single people purchase memberships to dating sites such as Match.com and eHarmony. However, when they find a spouse, they terminate their memberships. I would imagine the same situation occurs with freelance sites. Once a service provider and client meet, they can take their relationship offline and therefore deprive the freelance site of future commissions and fees.

Document Management and Storage Sites. The more successful companies such as Box and DropBox become in facilitating the sharing of files, the higher the risk of misappropriated proprietary information rises.

Extravagant Service Providers. Some extravagant hotels (such as Four Seasons) and upscale retailers (such as Nordstrom's) pamper their guests to an illogical extent. Sure, they deliver phenomenal customer service but they lose money doing so. These hotels and retailers should moderate their doting customer attentiveness with the notion of earning a return on customer service or return on customer satisfaction.

Backfiring Pricing Strategies. Companies at the opposite end of the luxury spectrum can make the mistake of forsaking revenue while enhancing the customer experience. Economy carrier Southwest Airlines has made a splash in terms of refraining from charging its passengers baggage fees. While customers must appreciate not having to pay to send their luggage they do not truly appreciate the savings because most customers price compare base airfares, those prices exclusive of such add-on fees. Thus, Southwest may be getting the worst of both worlds: lower load factors (percentage of seats occupied with paying customers) because of its more expensive listed base prices and no baggage fees (which totaled $3.4 billion for U.S. carriers in 2013) which other airlines use to cover baggage handling costs, extra fuel, and occasional claims for lost suitcases.

StubHub, an online marketplace operator for buying and selling sporting and performance entertainment tickets, is another company whose pricing strategy has backfired. StubHub introduced "all-in" pricing in which the entire ticket prices are posted upfront, eliminating the need to tack on service fees at the end of the transaction. The problem is that competitors who feature lower base prices (sans service fees) show up favorably when searches are conducted. No matter what StubHub does to impress upon ticket buyers that no other charges will be applied, some people have been conditioned to believe that there is going to be a surprise at checkout.

Defense Contractors. Defense contractors that produce highly lethal technologies may not be able to satisfy the demand that exists for their weapons systems. Their home countries usually have strict controls on such exports and even approved buyers impose restrictions on sales to neighboring or adversarial countries as a condition of sale.

The Babysitter Phenomenon. If you have young children and have finally found a reliable, responsible and available babysitter, you probably don't want to recommend her to your neighbors because she might not be available when you need her. In situations where a highly capable professional service provider—such as an accountant, architect or lawyer—has limited capacity, they might not receive the referrals they deserve.

Other Examples of the Icarus Paradox. One trend in the lawn mower business is to make those machines operate more quietly so as to comply with city ordinances aimed at noise pollution. While leading lawn mower manufacturers such as Briggs and Stratton and The Toro Company are capable of producing low-noise mowers, their overwhelmingly male customers equate the loudness of lawn mowers with the machine's power and are thus less inclined to patronize the manufacturers most successful in reducing the decibel level of their lawn mowers.

Electric vehicle manufacturers designed their cars to run quietly. While this attribute deserves praise for helping reduce noise pollution, it also represents a hazard for pedestrians and the blind. If you can't hear these cars, you are at risk of getting run over. Thus, the National Highway Traffic Safety Administration wrote rules requiring electric vehicles traveling less than 18.6 miles an hour to emit warning signals that can be heard over typical background noise. The NHTSA calculated that these sounds were necessary to save 2,800 pedestrians and cyclists from injuries for every model year of electric and hybrid vehicles.

- One of the problems that confront electric cars is the rapid rate of improvement in the performance (as measured by the ability to hold more energy in less space, temperature robustness, and production costs) of batteries. The more each new generation of electric vehicle batteries improve, the worse the resale proposition of current electric vehicles becomes.

- The initial iPhone's unprecedented and unexpected popularity coincided with AT&T's less than robust cellular infrastructure, especially in view of the surge of video streaming. The result was that a lot of calls were dropped in the early days of the iPhone's release, detracting from the utility of the handsets.

- If HBO is too successful in streaming its programing, it could lose marketing support from DirecTV, an important HBO distributor. For instance, if HBO recruits more than 450,000 streaming subscribers throughout the United States, DirecTV could opt to highlight HBO in its consumer offers for five months per year instead of eleven months per year.

The Las Vegas Conundrum

The Las Vegas Conundrum holds that you do not want to be in a business whereby you produce a product or render a service that your competitors give away for free. For example, you probably would not want to open up a stand-alone restaurant across the street from a Las Vegas casino that gives all of its patrons free—or significantly subsidized—gourmet meals in its restaurants.

I have, unfortunately, had direct experience of being whipsawed by the Las Vegas Conundrum. I had a conference business in partnership with The New York Society of Security Analysts in the 1990s. Together, we developed hundreds of industry conferences in which senior executives of publicly-traded companies delivered roadshow-like presentations to the institutional investors in the audience. This was a great business. I was able to charge the companies thousands of dollars to make 30-minute presentations. The attendees also paid. We had low overhead as NYSSA had its own conference facilities at The World Trade Center. We had a great run but then the investment banks started developing their own investor conferences. Since they developed these conferences for purposes of soliciting investment banking business and to boost trading volumes, they charged neither the companies to present nor their clients to attend. The investment banks could easily afford to run their conferences at the most luxurious hotels and even brought in first-rate entertainment. The encroachment of investment banks on my investment conference business forced me to pivot the direction of that business.

Here are a few other examples of companies that are exposed to the Las Vegas Conundrum:

- In the early days of the iPhone and Android-driven phones, Google's advertising model enabled it to subsidize the proliferation of its Android devices. The more the Android technology diffused, the more searches would be conducted with Google and thus the more revenues would be generated by that company. Apple's profits, on the other hand, were dependent on high-margin device sales.

- Many mergers and acquisitions consultants from the likes of PricewaterhouseCoopers bemoan the fact that investment bankers provide similar consultations to corporate executives free of charge in anticipation of receiving investment banking work.

- Recruiters that specialize in placing professionals with alternative asset managers such as hedge funds face competition from prime brokers that offer their "talent introduction" services gratis.

- Tech companies such as Google (Drive), Apple (iCloud) and Microsoft (SkyDrive) can subsidize their consumer file sharing services with the money that they make from other lines of business in ways that newer and purer play entrants such as Box and DropBox cannot.

- Airline carriers can price the delivery of overnight packages very close to their marginal costs since this business is incidental to their core business. On the other hand, overnight couriers such as Fedex and UPS must charge full freight for such deliveries because such jobs are their core business.

The Tom Sawyer Fence Painting Business Model

In the Adventures of Tom Sawyer, Tom's Aunt Polly punished the boy by making him whitewash her fence. However, Tom inveigled other boys to pay him for the privilege of painting the fence. So too, in business can customers be made to pay a business for the privilege of rendering services to it. For instance, popular programs such as American Idol, X Factor and Britain's Got Talent use their audiences in multiple ways. First, by encouraging the audiences to vote for their favorite contestants, these shows reduce their risks in selecting winners. Voting also indicates the extent to which the artists—that the shows promote after the contests end—have built-in fan bases. Since voters pay to cast their votes when they call in, and since some of that money is collected by the talent shows, the audience is basically paying these shows to vet talent and to plug their favorite contestants.

A similar situation is manifested when you are asked to type in the images you see on a website before your email to a company is sent. These captchas are used to prove that a real person wishes to communicate with a company rather than a bot spamming the company with junk email. However, the other problem that these captcha technologies solve is that the blurry words that you are expected to decipher and enter are actually words and strings of numbers that optical recognition technology cannot decipher. (For instance, Google uses optical recognition technology and captchas when it digitizes books and historical documents.) The captcha tools take the position that if the majority of respondents believe that the indicated word is "skeleton," for example, then that is probably the word that confused the optical recognition technology. So the next time you enter a captcha, you are probably working alongside an optical recognition technology program. While you won't pay to help decipher words, the captcha operator may still make money from the ads placed in front of you, those next to the response box.

While you do not pay companies such as LinkedIn and Facebook when you write posts on their sites, you are still producing needed content to those social media sites free of charge. Companies that sell concentrated detergents and other home cleaning products leverage off of their customers when the buyer is required to add water to use the product. Another example of this dynamic comes from Intrix, a traffic-analysis firm. Intrix offers free smartphone apps which provide traffic information to users and, in return, Intrix receives its users' traffic coordinates. By determining the rate of motion of its users' smartphones, Intrix can determine where there are traffic jams and alert its users accordingly.

Similarly, sometimes businesses consistently receive unintended benefits. For instance, automobile recyclers are paid to scrap cars and they retain the loose change, averaging $1.65, left in junked cars when they are shredded. Since 14 million American cars are scrapped some years, automobile recyclers can inadvertently make more than $20 million per year.

Veto Power

You might think that a company that can attract the vast majority of a customer clique would have a very high probability of achieving commercial success. You would probably be very impressed with companies that win over four out of five potential customers. In many cases, your optimism would be justified. But not when veto power is in effect. Veto power is exercised when the fifth person in our example objects to patronizing a business.

Consider a family deliberating about which restaurant to patronize. As the family is discussing where to dine, any family member (even a six-year old) can prevent the family from going to that restaurant by vetoing the idea. Thus, diners with seemingly endless selections and restaurants like Noodles that serve dozens of variations of noodles are at less risk of veto power than restaurants like Benihana that only serve one type of cuisine. On the other hand, veto power is much less of an issue at auto dealerships as the risk of losing a sale because of a six-year old child's predilections is minimal.

Another example of veto power relates to a software program that is designed to facilitate the rescheduling of meetings. The motivation for developing this software is that once email requests to join a meeting are sent out to several colleagues, at least one of them will seek to reschedule the meeting. The result is that a flurry of emails and electronic invitations must be disseminated to arrive at an agreeable time for holding the rescheduled meeting. The software is supposed to reduce the related administrative burdens by automating the rescheduling. Maybe the software programmers estimated that 95% of the targeted customers use tools such as Outlook or Google for scheduling their meetings. Let's assume that this estimate is correct. The problem is that the one invitee to the meeting that does not use these electronic meeting scheduling tools can render the software ineffective. If one invitee relies on his administrative assistant or maintains his own paper-based calendar, then he will have to be consulted about a convenient rescheduling time via means other than the software. Thus, this individual would effectively have veto power with respect to how meetings are scheduled.

A similar veto issue arose in connection with the staccato release of the movie "The Interview." Sony Pictures Entertainment, the producer of "The Interview," sustained a brutal cyber-attack in which its internal systems were disabled and many documents (relating to employee compensation, for instance) and upcoming films were leaked. This hacking was followed by threats, that if the movie were to be exhibited, acts of terrorism would be perpetrated against participating theaters. One of the issues that movie theater operators had to grapple with in view of such threats was that entire participating theaters could be boycotted due to safety concerns, not just the screens running "The Interview."

Platform Dependence

Buildings require strong foundations to prevent them from sinking under their own weight and to protect them from the outside elements. Similarly, businesses and technologies need stable operational platforms to ensure their agility, resiliency and longevity. Technologies that provide the base for a variety of platforms should demonstrate such characteristics. For instance, programmers are busy harnessing Bitcoin's blockchain technology for end applications as diverse as digital rights management, peer-to-peer property transfers and electronic voting systems. Business models that are platform agnostic are preferred while business models that are reliant on the platforms controlled by other companies are vulnerable.

The more platforms on which a technology or a business operates, the better since that technology or business will serve a larger addressable market and will have more negotiating power vis-à-vis the platform operators. If you are investing in an app, it is better that the app works on both the iOS and Android platforms. Electronic games designed for different platforms, such as the Xbox and PlayStation consoles, are more attractive than electronic games that are captives of only one of these platforms.

Many businesses have been built on the platforms that other companies control. Maybe you know someone whose livelihood is based on their ability to sell products through eBay or Amazon. While these people may be making lots of money today, they would not have any recourse if eBay or Amazon decided to extirpate them from their sites. Should this happen, their entire businesses would crumble at the flick of a switch.

It is not just small time merchants that are dependent on the platforms provided by ecommerce and social media companies. For much of its existence, Zynga was completely beholden to Facebook as its entire business was dangling on a standard click-through license with Facebook. The hit game Candy Crush is highly dependent on Facebook's hospitality as it is largely played on that social media site. Similarly, many of the online micro-lending companies such as Lenddo, Neo Finance, and Affirm use social media to determine to whom loans should be made. Among the issues that go into the algorithms that micro-lenders use are the number of social media followers a loan applicant has, the backgrounds of his contacts, and the repayment history of the borrower's friends. If companies such as LinkedIn and Facebook decide that they do not want data harvested from their sites to be used to make lending decisions, and therefore block algorithms from online micro-lending companies crawling through their sites, the foundations of the micro-lender business model could suffer a serious jolt.

Companies and technologies are also vulnerable to transitioning platforms. For instance, Pandora Media, which traditionally streamed its music to desktop computers, is imperiled by more people listening to music on mobile devices such as smart phones and tablets or through car dashboards. The problem for Pandora is that advertisers are paying less to reach people listening to music through these devices while the artists to whom royalties must be paid when their songs are downloaded are not willing to make concessions to Pandora. Elsewhere, Zynga found it very difficult to transition from displaying its games on large desktop screens to smartphones' smaller screens as the different user experiences required a reworking of the monetization strategy.

Analytical Consideration On a daily basis, companies such as Google, Amazon and Netflix demonstrate how effective algorithms can be. However, developing algorithms based on social media data is fraught with challenges. One concern with building algorithms based on the quality of one's online contacts is that some profiles on social media sites are fictitious: Facebook revealed that seven percent of its overall users, or more than 83 million profiles, are fictitious, duplicative or otherwise fraudulent. Sites such as buy-cheap-likes.com offer 50,000 Facebook Likes for less than $400. Every LinkedIn user must know that endorsements on that site are a joke, as they often come from complete strangers who have no basis to render judgment on someone else's areas of expertise.

Platforms that fuel the fires of competition are often highly profitable. For instance, Google's AdWords auctions off keywords for use in search advertising to the highest bidder. In the traditional advertising model, such as advertising in a magazine, you would not know which company would fill the advertising pages if you elected to forgo your advertising campaign. If your company sold jewelry, the advertiser that takes your abandoned slot could be from the auto, toy, electronics, clothing or any other industry. Thus, you would not feel especially compelled to secure the ad space in the magazine. However, with AdWords-type auctions, you know that the company that wins the bidding for key industry phrases will be a competitor. If you are in the jewelry business and lose the auction for the search term "wedding ring," you can rest assured that you will lose to a competitor. Thus, the stakes in search advertising are heightened.

Alligators

Businesses must remain vigilant so that their products do not turn into prey for alligators. More specifically, you want to make sure that your product is not consumed by another product. This phenomenon has happened to eReaders which were consumed by electronic tablets. This has also been the fate of standalone GPS navigation systems produced by companies such as Garmin and TomTom which have witnessed similar mobile app technologies displace their dedicated GPS hardware. Nextdoor, a website whose raison d'etre is to facilitate neighbor-to-neighbor communications, seems to have surgically placed its business model directly in the crosshairs of several of Facebook's initiatives such as community pages, groups and digital neighborhood maps.

For all of the hype surrounding the future potential of wearable computers, I would ask, "Doesn't just about everyone already have one?" I mean, isn't their mobile phone all the wearable computer most people will need? If you concur, then smart phones have played the part of alligators consuming wearable computers.[12]

> **Analytical Consideration** It is dangerous to offer products that compete with Google since Google's search algorithms are analogous to alligators. Companies that provide services that compete with those offered by Google could have their search results displayed beyond the first page, which are rarely reviewed.

---

[12] There is an argument that smart watches such as Apple Watch save people a relatively great deal of time compared to using smart phones. When you receive an email and only have a smart phone, you have to take the phone out of its case, navigate to the email app, find the right email, open it up, perhaps respond to it and then holster the phone. With smart watches, you just have to raise your arm to see the new message. The seconds that smart watches save wearers could be particularly valuable to stock market investors who have a lot to gain by keeping abreast of breaking news.

Here is an example of how quickly alligators can snap up and spit out promising technologies. In 2007, Pure Digital Technologies made very inexpensive video recorders called Flip Videos. These Flip Video cameras uploaded videos directly by USB drive. At just over $100 a unit, these devices became the top-selling camcorder on Amazon within weeks of their launch. In March 2009, Cisco Systems snapped up Pure Digital Technologies for $590 million. Over the next two years, inexpensive videos became ubiquitous due to video cameras being incorporated into smart phones. Cisco saw the writing on the wall and shut down Flip Video in April 2011 and sold off the remaining inventory at a deep discount.

Business Model Portability

The issue of model portability is similar to that of the Seduction of Extrapolation discussed above. When we see a business attempting to grow geographically or by serving different customer bases, we want to determine how portable the business model is.

Suppose there were two local men's clothing stores that had aspirations of becoming national (or even international) chains. Store A derived more than 90% of its revenues from the young men attending the local university. Store B derived its revenues from a healthy mix of college students, businessmen, men looking for business-casual attire, men in search of formal wear, men from the local military base, retirees, and women seeking gifts for the men in their lives. Which store would be more likely to meet its expansion goals? Of course, Store B.

The following are among the questions that could be posed in trying to determine the likelihood of one store concept successfully competing in other markets:

- How do the demographics—the concentration of various ethnicities and distribution of ages, for instance—compare from the initial market to the successive markets?

- How comparable is the weather from the initial market to the successive markets?

- How do the modes of transportation—walking, public transportation, bicycle riding, cars—compare from the initial market to the successive markets?

- Is the initial store expanding into markets that have large groups of customers that have ordered from the initial store via catalog or Internet?

- How many miles on average do customers travel to the initial store? What is the average number of competing stores that those customers pass on the way to the initial store?

- Is the initial store expanding into migratory markets? Examples of companies following the migratory paths of its customers include a New York-based store expanding into Florida or a California-based store opening up shops in Nevada. Washington D.C. would be a fertile springboard into international markets due to its being a hub of rotating diplomats.

Portability Head Fakes   The early success of a business initiative does not guarantee its portability. Let's say that you were responsible for selecting locations for Starbucks's stores in that chain's early years. Management tasked you with expanding the chain into New York State. There are many sound reasons for opening up the first store right in the middle of Times Square. In addition to its extremely high foot traffic, Times Square attracts a tremendous cross section of people from different cultures as well as socio-economic and psychographic backgrounds. However, the success of that store, in terms of generating traffic, should not be extrapolated throughout the hundreds of other stores slated to open across The Empire State.

Similarly, because of the enormous wealth behind it, the fact that Emirates Airlines is an undeterred purchaser of the $400 million (list price), 500-plus seat Airbus A380 does not mean that other airlines will follow suit. Indeed, as I write these pages, Airbus has found no buyers for its A380 in the United States, South America, India or Africa. Only one Chinese customer has ordered it while the only Japanese customer canceled its order.

The following are a few examples of how impressive data points may not underlie the portability of business models:

- Movies that are more visual oriented fare better than movies that are more dialog driven in international markets. So you would expect that action, disaster and superhero movies would perform better globally than comedies and dramas.

- Strong sales of electric vehicles in Norway do not mean that such strong sales will occur in other parts of the world. Some of the reasons that electric vehicle sales may perform better in Norway than elsewhere include:

  - Policymakers in Norway have exempted electric vehicles from a 25% value-added tax and a registration tax that can reach tens of thousands of dollars a vehicle. Premiums on these levies can be assessed based on the vehicle's weight and emissions characteristics.

  - Electric cars offer great utility in Norway as its fuel prices are among the highest in Europe, with costs of roughly $9.60 per gallon in late 2013.

  - Electric cars also are exempt from tolls, and are granted access to bus lanes on Oslo's highways, thus dodging the congestion that ensnares ordinary drivers during rush hours.

- Garbage collection companies that are successful in San Francisco may not be able to replicate their success in cities such as Houston. This is because the waste haulers benefit from population density in San Francisco (where there are roughly 17,000 inhabitants per square mile) but must travel further distances to collect garbage in Houston (where there are some 3,300 people per square mile).

- Garbage disposals that are sufficiently rugged for western households might prove to be insufficiently rugged for the Chinese market. This is because the Chinese eat less processed foods and have more left-over vegetable peelings, fish bones and other items that need to be ground up.

- The success of scrap yards, tasked with differentiating copper and brass, in Foshan, China should not be projected onto scrap yards in Tianjin, China. Foshan's weather is similar to that of Florida which means that metals can be sorted bare-handed, all year long. However, in Tianjin, where temperatures drop well below zero, the workers must do all of their sorting during the winter months with gloves. Since sorting metals with gloves is less precise, productivity is much higher in Foshan than in Tianjin.

Recursos de Amparo

It is interesting to note that a business mogul's success may not be portable from one country to another. One interesting case in point is Carlos Slim, probably the richest man in Mexico.

Mr. Slim's success in Mexico is, in part, a function of favors bestowed upon him by the Mexican government. For instance, his consortium won an auction to acquire 51% of the voting stock of Telmex, Mexico's telecommunications monopoly even though his bid was not the highest. Instead of paying for the shares right away, Mr. Slim managed to delay payment, using the dividends of Telmex itself to pay for the stock.

When the Mexican Competition Commission declared that Mr. Slim's Telmex was a monopoly, Mr. Slim used what is known as a recurso de amparo, literally an "appeal for protection." An amparo is in effect a petition to argue that a particular law does not apply to you.

Mr. Slim had neither an amparo nor success in his business dealings—his CompUSA acquisition being a case in point—in the United States.

Technology Overfitting

To what extent are you exposed to technology overfitting?

The issue of technology overfitting is a close cousin to the Icarus Paradox. Technology overfitting means that the technological potential of a product exceeds the utility that a user can gain from it. For instance, if an inventor invents a battery for mobile phones that will last more than 100 years, that would be a brilliant invention. It would also be an example of overengineering (or technology overfitting). No handset manufacturer would want it as the handset would be discontinued within a few years of its launch into the market.

One of the selling points of electric vehicles (EV) is that the cost of charging batteries could be less than 20% per mile of the cost of filling a gas-powered automobile. However, to reach the breakeven point associated with purchasing more expensive electric vehicles, an EV driver may have to drive 75,000 miles. The problem is that charging stations are not nearly as ubiquitous as gas stations and the charging regimen is more time-consuming than filling a tank with gas. Thus, drivers of electric vehicles are resigned to driving limited ranges. The convergence of these issues means that cheaper charging is not likely to have positive overall economics for purchasing electric vehicles.

The Hiriko Fold is an electric car from Spain that that can fold from 100 inches in length down to a mere 60 inches which is the width of an ordinary car. The Fold can be parked facing the sidewalk, relieving the driver of the inconvenience of parallel parking. With this parking configuration, three-and-a-half Folds can fit into one parking space. As for the practically of realizing benefit from this last purported advantage, I would ask how likely is it that there will be three Folds in close enough proximity to take advantage of such compactness.

I wrote a Patent Valuation Report on the patents owned by a company that was in the business of shooting electro-magnetic waves through pipelines to determine if there were obstructions, corrosion or holes in the pipe. When I began the research I learned that this company's electro-magnetic waves could produce interpretable data for 250 feet in two directions while a competing technology (guided wave) could produce interpretable data for only some 40 feet in two directions. I was impressed because the greater propulsion of my client's electro-magnetic wave technology meant that it could inspect more than six-times the pipeline than competitors using guided wave technology. However, I later learned that in much of the company's addressable market, there were bends in natural gas pipelines every 30 feet. So the fact that my client's electro-magnetic wave technology could be pushed 250 feet was not accretive to its value proposition.

▋Capacity Head Fakes

Analysts are often impressed with companies that operate at close to full capacity. The thinking is that such high utilization rates are indications of tremendous demand for the companies' products as well as efficient manufacturing operations. However, for every rule there are exceptions. In the airlines industry, operators that achieve 100% load factors (percent of seats occupied with paying customers) might not be maximizing their revenues. Consistently-packed flights could imply that overall ticket prices are too low. Had such operators reserved a few open seats close to departure they might have been able to capture higher-paying, last-minute passengers.

Be careful not to make the mistake of assuming that a company can ramp up its throughput simply by utilizing more of its unused capacity. For instance, as the Internet content delivery network Akamai Technologies operates at only 20% to 30% of its capacity it would seem that that company can accommodate much more traffic without investing in additional infrastructure. This is not true: Akamai operates at low capacity levels so as to ensure it fulfills performance guarantees to customers. A similar dynamic is at work in the media business. If a television station has 100 hours of time dedicated to airing commercials each month, it cannot sell 100 hours of advertising. This is because some of that commercial time must be reserved for make-goods, which are granted to advertisers who received smaller audiences than they were promised.

When a company is consuming high levels of capacity it is reasonable to believe that it will have to invest in expanding its infrastructure. In view of Netflix consuming about one-third of U.S. Internet capacity during peak viewing hours, it seems likely that Netflix will have to expend significant resources on building out its infrastructure or licensing more infrastructure from others.

Africa is said to possess as much as sixty percent of the world's uncultivated arable land. Much has been written about how empty and underworked so much land on the African continent appears to be. However, the seemingly vast unused capacity for farming in Africa could be misleading. These reasons range from traditional farming methods in widespread use across the continent that leave large swaths of land fallow (so as to allow it to recover its fertility) to control of land by local chiefs or kings (who have had a history of keeping land usage under tight rein).

The potential of ethanol presents another example of a capacity head fake. From 2005 to 2014, ethanol production in the U.S. more than tripled. Looking forward, ethanol is slated to account for more than 10% of the U.S. fuel supply. The combination of relatively low penetration and sustained rapid growth seem to indicate that ethanol can capture far more market share.

However, there are structural limitations to this happening. Almost all of the gasoline sold in the U.S. contains 10% ethanol, a blend known as E10. Gasoline marketed as E10 is prohibited from containing more than 10% ethanol. So more gasoline would have to be sold using higher blends such as E15, which contains up to 15% ethanol. This is unlikely to happen because:

- Only about 60 gas stations in the U.S. carry E15 and they had to install new tanks and blending pumps to handle the blend. Some refiners mandate that the only way its gas stations can pump E15 is to install yellow hoses from which E15 must flow. Not many gas stations are expected to wish to incur such costs.

- Autos are not designed to run on gasoline with high levels of ethanol. According to the American Automobile Association, higher blends of ethanol accelerate wear and tear on car engines. Thus, auto manufacturers including BMW, Chrysler, Nissan, Toyota and Volkswagen say their warranties do not cover cars that use E15, while other auto makers such as Ford, Honda, Kia, Mercedes-Benz and Volvo have said E15 use will void warranties.

- Allocating more farmland to corn production for purposes of producing ethanol would lead to higher food prices as corn is a crucial animal-feed product.

Agency Issues

I am concerned about business models that revolve around platforms on which vendors and customers forge relationships with one another. Platform providers whose business models call for earning repeated commissions from the work brokered on their sites could be circumvented. These platforms include introducing babysitters to parents (e.g. Sittercity), housecleaners to homeowners (e.g. Merry Maids), and independent contractors to businesses looking to hire temporary help (e.g. Guru.com). It is rational to expect that these people will find it more economical to take their relationships offline and avoid paying repeated commissions to the platform's hosts.

People are always going to be more loyal to themselves than to their principals. Thus, I do not like business models that have many touch points between employees and customers that are beyond the sight of cameras. For instance, a gardening service like TruGreen could lose money if one of its employees agrees to perform a lawn treatment for a homeowner in return for cash. The homeowner would benefit by paying a lower rate and the employee would make some extra cash. The proprietor of the business, however, would doubly lose out by not only being deprived of revenue but by having its resources (compensation to its employee and materials) expended.

Another example of how agency conflicts could hurt business owners comes from the restaurant industry. Let's say that your waitress is very busy and cannot provide you with great customer service. As a peace offering she tells you that coffee and dessert are "on the house." You are pleased and decide to leave her a generous tip which makes the waitress happy. However, the owner of the restaurant loses out because he is not receiving any revenue for the coffee and dessert and the patron remains seated longer.

In some cases, vendors are more loyal to other industry players than to their clients. Let's say that after thirty years of hard work, a construction crane crashes into a restaurant, thoroughly demolishing it. The restaurant's insurance agent is likely to be less aggressive in collecting on the culprit's insurance policy than the proprietor. The proprietor's life's work was just destroyed whereas, for the insurance adjuster, the restaurant represents just one of the fifty claims that might be assigned to him that month. A similar scenario might enfold with a client caught up in a scandal that seeks the services of a public relations firm. For a variety of reasons, avoiding the media might be in the best interest of the client. Well, the public relations firm already deposited the client's retainer and the client will emerge from the scandal, in one form or another, in a month or so. So, maybe the public relations firm would offer up the client for interviews with media figures with whom the publicist hopes to build a working relationship over the next few decades.

A few years ago, a start-up company called Opez developed a platform that sought to help professionals—such as waiters, bartenders, DJs, models, hairstylists—maintain contact with their clients. Well, the patrons were not always their clients, but rather their employers' clients. While it may not have been the intention of Opez's founders, I believe that this business model abetted the agency issue. For instance, bartenders could boost their followings by giving away free drinks. Among the other problems associated with this now defunct service were:

- Some wait staff were concerned that customer feedback would be relayed to their managers and thus be used as a managerial instrument.

- Opez would pressure managers to determine how to promote the exceptional staffers without antagonizing their less meritorious associates.

- Opez could foment resentment among a stable of waiters or hairstylists if a stream of customers were to enter the store and request to be served by Joe or Jane, causing their colleagues to remain idle.

The Chicken-and-Egg Conundrum

Near-field communications (NFC) illustrates the chicken-and-egg conundrum.[13] Retailers are reluctant to invest billions of dollars on the needed infrastructure (such as payment terminals) unless banks commit to spending billions of dollars needed to issue and market near-field communications technologies.

The following issues are among those that should be considered in trying to determine whether or not NFC will be able to surmount the chicken-and-egg conundrum:

- Is there support among the critical players? For instance, Apple's NFC chip in its iPhone 6 is restricted to Apple Pay. Also, for NFC to work, retailers need to equip their point-of-sale terminals with NFC hardware. However, retailers have resisted making this investment because of the expensive capital outlays as well as because of NFC's limited customer spend per transaction.

- Will stakeholders' interest in rolling out a new technology such as NFC be diluted? Too many players are needed to make NFC work and there is too little for any of them to gain. Yossi Yarkoni, CEO of mobile payment company Digimo, queried: "The question comes down to who owns the customer? Why should Apple or Samsung bother putting NFC in devices if they simply hand over that customer relationship to others?"

---

[13] Near field communications is a set of standards for smartphones and similar devices to establish radio communication with each other by touching them together or bringing them into within a few centimeters proximity. Present and anticipated applications include contactless transactions and data exchange.

Also, Matthew Hudson, head of business development with Transport for London, whose Oyster Card system is one of the most successful NFC systems in the world, rhetorically asked, "With banks, retailers, mobile network operators, device manufacturers and advertisers all fighting for a share of the revenues... How much money is there to make with all these parties trying to get a piece of it?"

- Are there impending collisions with competing technology deployments? Perhaps, the uptake of NFC would be more successful if it did not collide with the rollout of chip-based credit cards.

- Have the operational issues been well thought-out? Security, redundancy and privacy must be thoroughly tested. In terms of facilitating contactless transactions, the technology must work instantaneously. No one wants to spend even 10 seconds re-waving their subway cards during rush hour. If customers are expected to enter personal identification numbers, that would drastically slow down the purchasing process. Also, if the new technology is not sufficiently robust it will less likely be adopted. While a new payment technology may be sufficiently secure and fast, if it does not integrate desired functionality, such as inventory management, it will face adaption hurdles.

- Will retailers or public transportation systems operators have to make all-or-nothing decisions? Will they have to rollout NFC at all of their check-out terminals (or turnstiles) or only some of them? If they make NFC available at some of the terminals (or turnstiles) will customers know which lines to stand in?

- How will NFC impact the merchant fees that credit card companies charge retailers? Will liability for fraudulent transactions be shifted due to adoption of NFC?

Business Model Fragility

It is important to consider the fragility of a company's business model. Analysts and business development executives should try to gauge the degree of risk a business faces if it experiences a mishap. Such mishaps can be operational or reputational.

One example of an operational mishap is losing a key employee. If the solo chef abruptly resigns at a small restaurant, the entire restaurant may have to close until a replacement can be recruited. Another marker of fragility is dependence on licensure. Businesses—such as law firms, accounting firms, bars, restaurants, radio stations, cable operators—are at risk of losing everything if they fail to maintain their licenses. Since operational issues are discussed throughout this book, I will focus the remainder of this section on reputational fragility.

Which Businesses Have the Greatest Reputational Fragility?

Private companies are typically less reputationally fragile than public companies because agitators have fewer allies to help them attack private companies. In other words, more piling on happens at public companies where self-reinforcing pressure from agitators, sympathetic media, activist investors, short sellers, class action shareholder lawsuits and investigations from securities regulators can be brought to bear.

Professional service firms—such as law firms and accounting firms—are particularly fragile. If a lawyer or accountant is accused of doing anything that might even give rise to the appearance of impropriety, his practice could experience a dramatic downturn. However, other successful people benefit from being anti-fragile. That is, they are immune to reputation degradation and might actually benefit from just about anything they do, even behaviors that are inarguably inappropriate. If actors or rock band guitarists are accused of wrecking hotel rooms or are caught possessing illegal drugs, they usually benefit from the related exposure. If an associate at a white shoe law firm was caught revealing a little too much flesh at a Mardi Gras celebration that attorney's career could be doomed. This contrasts to sex tapes igniting the careers of both Paris Hilton and Kim Kardashian.

The more visible a business is, the more fragile it is. It is easier to organize nation-wide demonstrations against a chain of stores such as Best Buy or Starbucks than against Amazon. In the case of the former, demonstrators need only travel a few minutes to find a site to protest but they would have a hard time finding an Amazon fulfillment center. And even when they found a remote fulfillment center, it would be more difficult to attract media attention. Businesses located in regions where there are extreme weather conditions dissuade protesters: The cacophony of the Occupy Wall Street protests diminuendoed in the winter months. Because they are less public and more difficult to identify, contractors and subcontractors are less fragile that contracting companies.

Foreign companies are more fragile than domestic companies because the foreign company can be used as a proxy for venting anger against the unrelated actions of a foreign government. For instance, McDonalds' restaurants located outside of the United States often feel the repercussions of American policy towards their host countries.

Businesses with stringent loan covenants are particularly fragile. It is common for large law firms to have covenants with their banks that, for example, hold that in the event more than two partners leave the firm in one month's time, the law firm's line of credit can be frozen. The inaccessibility to the line of credit often renders it impossible for the firm to meet payroll, causing the law firm to crater shortly thereafter.

Businesses that can shop for certifications and reviewers are less fragile than companies in industries that are only certified or rated by a few authorities. If Michelin and Zagat are the only restaurant rating authorities that matter, then a restaurant has a lot riding on those reviews. On the other hand, there are 81 accredited "certifying agents" that stamp food as organic in the U.S. So if an organic food producer does not win certification from the most prominent certifying agent, it can mitigate the collateral damage by winning certification from another certifying agent.

Fragility Mitigation

How can businesses at least partially inoculate themselves from fragility? One operational defense is to build redundancies (or at least develop optionality) into the business model. In the case of the restaurant at risk for being paralyzed by its solo chef abruptly resigning, the restaurateur can cultivate relations with the local culinary school. The restaurateur might teach a class in restaurant management, so that he will be in close contact with budding chefs that might relish the opportunity to utilize their skills. The same idea is exhibited by professional sports clubs that maintain minor league farm teams.

The more fragile a business model is to reputational shocks, the more important it is for that business to have already retained a public relations firm. When a critical article is published or when a scandal erupts, there will not be enough time to scout, vet, retain and educate a public relations firm. In the aftermath of the bank bailouts, some large American banks adopted a policy of requiring almost every deal to receive a stamp of approval from the public relations department before being allowed to proceed.

The more charitable work a company does on an ongoing basis and the more friends it has in the media, the less likely it becomes that negative press will drastically adversely impact its reputation.[14] (As a side note, charities are fragile in the sense that should they choose to defend themselves, they may be lambasted for expending money on defending the institution and its executives rather than on pursuing the charities' missions.) Of course there are legal precautions to take, such as obtaining indemnifications from suppliers and requiring them to carry indemnity insurance.

Sometimes it is appropriate to suppress negative comments about your company or its products. At a minimum, this can be done by refraining from publishing damaging commentary on your company's website, blogs, and Facebook pages. The letter that I wrote to the management of Crumbs, the cupcake chain, explains my thinking in this regard. Companies such as Reputation.com and Reputation X have tools for suppressing defamatory results when Internet searches are conducted. These tools are needed because many social media sites allow the anonymous posting of defamatory

---

[14] However, the more charities a business supports, the more targets agitators have. For instance, Starbucks' stores in Vancouver, British Columbia were spray-painted and vandalized because Starbucks supported the Vancouver Aquarium, which keeps whales in captivity.

statements without the poster having to prove, in any way, the veracity of such statements. Some business models are simply designed to monetize humiliation. For instance, Mugshots.com offers a service to remove notices of arrests for prices starting at $399.

Finally, because of their emotional attachment to their companies and products, founders and members of family businesses are more likely to retaliate against those attacking their businesses than are hired, professional management teams who assess the merits of combatting defamers through a detached lens. For instance, when he believed that the patents covering the iPhone were being infringed, the late Steve Jobs of Apple Computer said, "I am going to destroy Android...I'm willing to wage thermonuclear warfare. I will spend my last dying breath if I need to, and I will spend every penny of Apple's $40 billion in the bank, to right this wrong." Another example of turning the tables on agitators occurred when several animal rights groups falsely accused the Ringling Bros. and Barnum & Bailey Circus of animal abuse. Kenneth Feld, CEO of Feld Entertainment and son of its founder, which owns Ringling Bros., sued the animal rights groups for racketeering, conspiracy, and lawsuit abuse-related counts. In January of 2013, the American Society for the Prevention of Cruelty to Animals agreed to pay Feld Entertainment $9.3 million.

Nevertheless, an interesting case study of a large company returning reputational fire to its smaller competitor comes from AB-InBev, the large beer producer. Despite its success over many years, Boston Beer Company cast itself as a scrappy start-up battling industry behemoths. Boston Beer's CEO, Jim Koch, often stated that the big brewers spill more beer than Boston Beer produces. Shots fired.

AB-InBev launched a brutal public relations campaign against Boston Beer. The global brewer attacked the microbrewer for the inconsistency in its labeling and contract manufacturing. To wit, AB-InBev pointed out that Boston Beer was, by far, the largest American microbrewer and that it labeled its beers as being microbrewed in New England while the reality was that Boston Beer was produced at larger breweries, often outside of New England. Shots returned.

**Email That I Sent to the Management of
Crumbs Bake Shop on January 6, 2014**

Gentlemen,

Almost every day, customers are posting extremely acerbic critiques about their experiences with Crumbs on the Crumbs' Facebook page.

These postings are very detrimental to Crumbs' brand equity.

As mentioned before, I am asking that someone at Crumbs police this and suppress a good bit of the scathing reviews.

There is a time and place for everything. Customer feedback is important. But, there is no reason why Crumbs needs to expend its resources facilitating damaging commentary on the world's largest social network. Maybe a customer feedback hotline or an electronic suggestion box would be better. Maybe a message on the Crumbs' Facebook page saying "Help Us Improve" and then dealing with complaints off-line and privately would be better. Of course, resolving the underlying issues is critical.

It wasn't that many months ago that Crumbs was talking about licensing / franchising its name. There is no reason why some resources should be dedicated to these ends while other resources are dedicated to facilitating activities that will obviate any licensing / franchising efforts.

Let us not be taken in with the naïve gibberish espoused by social media hucksters about there being any value in voyeuristic self-flagellation. (Let us not be the first company to be accused of facilitating hate speech against itself.) Before social media, no company would compile its most critical comments and then spend resources having them advertised through The New York Times. A little more attention to Crumb's brand on its own Facebook page would go a long way.

Thank you for allowing me to share my thoughts.

David Wanetick
Managing Director
IncreMental Advantage

The Transparency Conundrum

A business model's transparency can be a double-edged sword. It is important that companies' business models be transparent so that investors, customers, vendors and employees will believe the company's business model is sound, offers the prospect of durability, and is at least not obviously engaging in illegitimate activities. If a business model is opaque or illogical, customers, vendors, employees and investors will want to disassociate themselves with that business.

Many years ago, I invested in a start-up company called Osmio, a developer of an online expense tracking tool. Osmio enabled employees of professional services firms—such as law firms, accounting firms, architectural firms and the like—to order their meals from local restaurants and have the related expenses invoiced to the appropriate clients.

Osmio was a close comparable to what is now SeamlessWeb/Grubhub. However, there was one major difference in the business models of those two companies. Osmio charged its clients neither a surcharge on the meals they ordered nor a monthly fee while SeamlessWeb added a surcharge to the meals its clients ordered through their system. Osmio's management thought that it could gain traction quickly as the professional service firms it prospected would rapidly embrace the cost-free proposition.

Unfortunately, this thinking backfired. Since it was unclear to potential customers how Osmio could make money—its only source of revenue was deriving a commission from the restaurants—they were reluctant to sign up as customers. They actually felt more comfortable paying fees to SeamlessWeb because doing so gave them peace of mind that SeamlessWeb would have staying power.

Separately, transparency, in the form of customer reviews on sites such as Yelp, has boosted the revenues of independent restaurants. Much of these incremental revenues have come at the expense of chain restaurant operators. The menus, themes and decors of chains have long been widely known. Not so for independent restaurants. Thus, the transparency provided by restaurant reviews has been a cost-free vehicle for customers to discover independent eateries.

The Degree and Changes in Transparency

Changes in a company's level of transparency can be revealing. For instance, if a company unexplainably cancels a conference call or stops reporting on a particular line of business, that could portend problems ahead. It was not reassuring when Finnish pulp and paper company Stora Enso switched reporting segments twice in less than two years, thereby reducing the transparency of business units that accounted for at least 40% of its sales.

However, as there is nothing to stop customers from reading their suppliers' investor reports, less investor transparency can help a company maintain its pricing and margins. Let me explain. Years ago, I asked the senior executives of what was then Guilford Mills, a publicly-traded textile company, why they did not provide segmentation analysis, which would reveal how much revenues and profits each segment of their business was generating. The reason, I was told, was that this degree of disclosure would cause their customers—namely, the large auto manufacturers—to reduce the prices they pay because they would see that the textile company could afford some profit erosion.

In other instances, reduced transparency can be the harbinger of positive results. A company could be growing its customer base which is usually good. However, some of the new customers could be in the defense industry or have required the company to refrain from revealing their names. Apple is known to forbid its contract outsourcers and suppliers from disclosing that Apple is a client. (Isn't it interesting that Apple is one of the most revered companies as well as one of the most secretive companies?) In isolated cases, there are outright embargoes on disclosing information that would be helpful to investors. When I valued a company that had a patent on incorporating biometrics onto handguns, I learned that the Bureau of Alcohol, Tobacco and Firearms imposed an embargo on the disclosure of the number of guns produced in the United States.

Nevertheless, to the extent a company is seeking to be transparent, such transparency should diffuse throughout the enterprise. Some of the publicly-traded educational institutions provide case studies as to the consequences of failing to do so. As mentioned earlier in this book, there is significant government scrutiny over for-profit education firms that offer student loans.

The government seizes on the inconsistency when these schools inform their investors about very high levels of student default rates but neglect to convey such information to their students. These default rates and related lapses in disclosure are some of the primary reasons behind the demise of Corinthian Colleges and pose a mortal threat to companies such as Career Education, Apollo Education Group and ITT Educational Services.

Analytical Consideration Investors and business professionals should align their money with their knowledge.[15] Today, investors in private companies have a better flow of information about their portfolio companies than do investors in publicly-held companies. Access to executives is guarded and fewer forward looking statements are offered by them. The message that populist, politically calculating and self-avowed Wall Street bashers such as U.S. Attorney in Manhattan Preet Bharara have sent to investors in publicly-held companies is, "You better damn well not invest in any company you know anything about because, if you do, I will indict you for insider trading."[16] Today's conference calls basically consist of the recitation of the numbers that appear on companies' recently-released financial documents. When you strain out all of the filler, investors are left with a meager gruel of insight.

---

[15] I suppose that floor specialists, broker-dealers who are responsible for maintaining orderly markets in the particular stocks with which they are charged, present a bit of irony. In the course of meeting their responsibilities, floor specialists are often required to take risks with their own money against their own better judgment.

[16] In December of 2014, a three-judge panel of the Second U.S. Circuit Court of Appeals said that prosecutors must prove traders knew the person who provided an inside tip gained some sort of tangible reward for doing so. Mr. Bharara's attempts to demonstrate that career advice or friendship constituted such reward was dismissed when the court said that under such logic "practically anything would qualify." These judges characterized Mr. Bharara's cases as being doctrinally novel. I was very pleased to hear Judge Barrington D. Parker say, "Although the government might like the law to be different not every instance of financial unfairness constitutes fraud." (The Wall Street Journal, Christopher M. Matthews, A1, December 11, 2014, Volume CCLXIV No. 138.) While this ruling may have slowed Mr. Bharara's lawfare against investors, by December 19, 2014, he found another man's life to ruin. The U.S. Justice Department and the U.S. Treasury's Financial Enforcement Network (FinCEN) sued Thomas Haider personally, the former Chief Compliance Officer of MoneyGram International. His crime? Failing to stop fraudulent telemarketers from using the money transfer company's service. Thus, Mr. Haider was personally sued for $1 million for suspected malfeasance on the part of other companies when it was the responsibility of the federal agencies that sued him to stop such alleged activities in the first place.

The Dangers of Indiscriminate Transparency

Too often, though, "transparency" is a disingenuous applause line that executives drop in investor presentations in order to evoke a Pavlovian response from ethical jihadists. Trying to run a business in a completely transparent fashion is irresponsible and even deserving of shareholder lawsuits. Disclosing everything means that a company is destroying its own trade secrets as a matter of policy, jeopardizing its patent applications by prematurely marketing related products, broadcasting its intentions to its competitors, and violating confidentiality provisions in its contracts with suppliers and customers. Being too transparent diminishes a company's leverage with its business partners and reduces its customers' search costs.

Those pompous praetorians of political correctness who preach that transparency is the paragon of virtue must never have had to run a business. When a business suffers a setback, and all businesses do, the CEO cannot make his concerns apparent to the workforce because if he does, they will mutiny. Similarly, pre-maturely disclosing succession plans will often result in the defection of highly talented senior executives. One of the advantages of acquiring companies through earn-outs is that earn-outs disguise purchase prices. Thus, earn-outs reduce the risk of serial acquirers trapping themselves into having to pay ever-rising valuations for targeted companies due to the precedents that they themselves set.

Transparency invites myopia. Consider the extreme consumer activism that occurs in professional sports where just about every fan critiques every play of every game. Since everyone second guesses the team coach and demands that any loss result in the immediate reworking of the team's strategy, it becomes very difficult to manage these kinds of businesses for the long-term.

> **Analytical Consideration** Some managers impose myopic behavior throughout their organizations. An example of this perpetual unforced error occurs when publicly-traded companies stream their stock prices all over their offices.

Transparency butchers creative thinking. If there was a video camera in a conference room where a brainstorming session was taking place, the participants would self-censor. Why? Because there are very thin lines between brilliant ideas and idiotic ideas. If one of your ideas later proves to be on the inane side, and a video clip of you articulating it finds its way to YouTube, the remainder of your career could be adversely affected.

Even attempts to instill transparency within a company could easily result in the imprisonment of innocent employees as well as their friends and relatives. If too many people are apprised of their company signing a large contract with a supplier, taking an equity stake in another company, or signing a licensing deal with another industry participant, employees or their relatives who coincidentally bought stock of corresponding companies could be accused of insider trading. Secrecy is designed to reduce the risks of employees and their friends and families becoming ensnared in accusations of insider trading.

Transparency invites mafia-style shakedowns.[17] Consider the transparency associated with crowdfunding. At a minimum, campaigners have perfect transparency as to who on their contacts lists have contributed to their campaigns as well as how much each supporter donated. A holdout co-worker who has not contributed to a campaign when everyone else in the office has could be subjected to ridicule and ostracism. While the public cannot see other contributors' history of supporting listed causes, artists and businesses directly on crowdfunding sites, most crowdfunding consultants advise listers to connect their crowdfunding initiatives with their social media efforts. Thus, without too much effort, one can determine who among his friends, neighbors, relatives and co-workers are contributing to various campaigns. Suppose that ten college students invite an avuncular professor to contribute to each of their campaigns. The professor believes that four of them have promise and makes a $100 contribution to each of them. I would think that such contributions would be a manifestation of the professor's kindness and generosity. However, the six students who did not receive any contributions from the professor could cause quite a ruckus. The professor could be labeled a hater (of whatever ideas the professor elected not to support) or a racist, misogynist, or radical feminist depending upon the genders or selected ethnic characteristics of those who did, and did not, receive contributions from the professor. The professor might relent and shell out another $600 to avoid any controversy. And once

---

[17] Merely suggesting that a company be transparent is a snide request, analogous to a loaded question. It suggests that the company has something to hide. It is the equivalent of asking a husband how long he has been beating his wife.

it's known that the professor is an easy target, what's to stop every other campaigner on campus from shaking contributions out of him?[18]

Nevertheless, there are legitimate reasons for obfuscation. For instance, death care companies and slaughterhouse operators may not want to elaborate on their profitability metrics for fear of being perceived as too crass. When a company is announcing a workforce downsizing it may want to disguise its true earnings results (by accelerating extraordinary charges, for example) in an effort to mute the opprobrium from terminated employees and the media. Shopping malls are intentionally designed to confuse shoppers—notice the sloping floors so that you never know which floor you are on—so that they will spend more time there. Casinos refrain from placing clocks on their premises so as to help gamblers lose track of time. When Starbucks opened its doors in April 1971, the inaugural store was designed to look as though it had been there for decades.

Convoluted Corporate Structures

While excessive transparency brings its own set of problems, so too does an extreme lack of transparency. When investors and business professionals encounter business models that are just not understandable, the evaluation of those companies should come to a halt. Some financing companies' financial statements are simply impenetrable. There are few industries as defiantly opaque as shipping where it is not uncommon to have twelve layers of legal entities between a ship and it beneficial owners. Interestingly, the shipping industry is so noncommittal that it is considered normal

---

[18] Do you think that I am being overly dramatic when I posit that merely refraining from supporting a cause will result in a mafia-like shakedown? Susan G. Komen For The Cure has donated roughly $2 billion to breast cancer research, advocacy, and education since its inception in 1982. Seems to me like a successful organization supporting a wonderful mission. Nevertheless, the Komen charity was pilloried in the media. Why? Because it decided to stop donating money to another organization. In early 2012, the charity decided to stop funding the Planned Parenthood Federation of America's providing of mammograms. (The reason was that Planned Parenthood was under a congressional investigation and the Komen charity had a policy of not funding organizations facing legal or regulatory scrutiny.) No statements were made for or against Planned Parenthood by the Komen charity. Any supporter of Komen that wished to donate money to Planned Parenthood was free to do so. Organizations and individuals should have the right to direct their money, or cease directing their money, to any organization they wish, without being lambasted until they are forced to reverse their decisions, which Komen was pressured to do with regard to funding Planned Parenthood.

that the official Greek ship owners' association refuses to say how many members it has.

There are a variety of penalties for maintaining a convoluted corporate structure. Because it has a unique stock structure which gives its founders enhanced rights on board appointments, it was not possible for Alibaba to list on Hong Kong's stock exchange. Because Alibaba is a Chinese company that is incorporated in the Cayman Islands, it may not be included in some benchmarks such as the S&P 500 index. Exclusion from important indices could act as a major drag on a stock with so much capitalization to support.

> **Algorithm Companies and Transparency** There is a good argument for businesses wanting to shroud their pricing and business models in a bit of mystery. Companies such as online dating services and Klout, whose secret sauce lies in their algorithms are somewhat conflicted. On the one hand these businesses absolutely cannot disclose their trade secreted algorithms. Doing so would enable anyone else so inclined to replicate those trade secrets, causing originators to lose very valuable assets. However, not disclosing at least a few kernels of an algorithm leads to some skepticism about the algorithm; skeptics could say that the algorithm is just a random number generator. Companies, such as Herbalife, that offer nutrition and weight management consumables—for which there are both ardent advocates and fervent detractors—face similar quandaries.

While a convoluted corporate structure may suggest a shady business lying underneath, there are legitimate reasons for such complexity. Sometimes convoluted corporate structures are necessary to navigate labyrinthine tax codes or to reduce the risk of assets being attached during potential litigation. Also, let's take a look at the major movie studios. Despite the major studios having tremendous access to financing, there are two primary reasons why these studios create separate partnerships for each movie they produce. First, these partnerships act as vehicles through which the studios can negotiate attractive deal terms with wealthy investors, who often place a higher value on their brush with fame than the potential for financial returns. Second, so as to reduce the pecuniary expectations of actors and other expensive movie production professionals, the studios position themselves as struggling to raise capital sufficient to fund each partnership.

Transparency and Digital Advertising

There is an old saw in the advertising business that hails from John Wanamaker which is, "Half of all the money I spend on advertising is wasted; the trouble is I don't know which half." The digital advertising industry has trumpeted its ability to help its customers only pay for the advertising that delivers verifiable results. However, the reality is that billions of marketing dollars are being poured down a digital drain.

According to Google, 50% of all online ad spending is wasted. For instance, there were reports that fraudulent websites caused more of the digital ads that Rocket Fuel prepared for Mercedes-Benz to be viewed by computer programs than by live humans.

Many digital ads are not even seen because they are invisible as they are the size of one pixel or they only appear at the bottoms of screens and surfers do not scroll down. In other cases, digital ads are not displayed because they load so slowly that Web surfers migrate off the page before the ad comes up. Some ads are counted when they are cached in browsers even though they may never be displayed on screens.

A significant number of display-ad "impressions" are based on fake traffic as malicious software makes a website think a person is actually on a page and ads are served up to that fake visitor. Also, Twitter's "timeline views" metric counts each time a user refreshes a page on a desktop or mobile device as a proxy for the amount of content consumed.

The better digital advertising companies are developing technologies to combat these problems. For instance, The Mobile Majority has sensors that will prevent an ad from being released, and customers being charged, if it would otherwise appear below the fold or is merely cached in a browser.

Mafia and Corruption

Few books on business development or investing factor in the impact of the mafia or corruption on business or investment decisions. While it may not be a pleasant issue to consider, in some sectors of the economy and in some countries, you will be deceiving yourself if you fail to make allowances for these issues.

How can you detect the presence of the mafia on a business that you are reviewing? Unfortunately, there are no failsafe methods to rely upon. Moreover, legitimate businesses are motivated to downplay their exposure to injustices that they suffer, such as theft and shakedowns, at the hands of the mafia. For instance, a shipping company will not want to admit to its potential customers that it loses some cargo due to corrupt inspections officials, pirates, or thieves. That company may not want to itemize the cash that it reserves for averting such theft to its auditors or shareholders. Nevertheless, here are some signals that the mafia or other corrupt influences might be involved in a business:

- Background checks into the people running the business under review reveal a great deal about their character, criminal record and business associates. You can begin the process by searching the Internet. Reviewing a person's contacts on LinkedIn and friends on Facebook is a useful process. When the stakes are higher, private investigators can be retained. Some industries just attract people with criminal histories, in part, because the owners are former criminals who want to give people with similar backgrounds a chance. For instance, it is not uncommon for former prisoners to work for debt collection agencies one week after their release. Similarly, merchant cash advance lenders that make high-interest rate loans to desperate business borrowers, have a tendency to attract people with criminal backgrounds.

- While learning that a business is run by people with criminal records might deter you from partnering or investing in such a company, if you really want to understand the dynamics that underpin that company's operations, you do not want to talk to sources with impeccable ethics or credentials. Rather, you stand to get a much better understanding as to how that business works by talking to those of its employees that have checkered pasts or more mundane positions within the company. For instance, if you were considering investing in a nightclub, consulting with a professor emeritus who developed a slew of econometric modeling and published numerous articles in esteemed academic journals on the nightclub industry would be worthless. You would glean better insights by talking to the bartender and the bouncer.

- Business transactions that offer extremely large commissions, relative to the value of goods provided, are suspect. They are more suspect when the corresponding agreements are poorly drafted—except for the provision that clearly states there are only miniscule penalties for failure to perform—so as to avoid enforcement.

- Transactions that are encumbered with unnecessary intermediaries, that add no value to the business proposition, could be an indicator of corruption. For instance, western companies that do business with Gazprom, Russia's energy behemoth, have found that the involvement of intermediaries, that provide neither pipelines nor natural gas, are required. The existence of these intermediaries is designed to inflate prices, siphon off profits from legitimate players and enrich oligarchs and government officials.

- Organized crime is more likely to surface where boycott busting and price arbitrage opportunities exist. For instance, back in the days of prohibition (when alcohol was illegal in the United States) the mafia germinated in Chicago which became a natural base for smuggling illicit liquor into the United States due to its proximity to Canada. Today's disparity of excise taxes on cigarettes from one state to another is an arbitrage opportunity that attracts not only the mafia but terrorist groups as well. In other words, organized crime flourishes when it can game jurisdictional triangles. Perhaps, the mafia will take on the task of moving marijuana from the states where it is legal to the states which prohibit marijuana.

I have no knowledge that this is happening. But if it were to be revealed that organized crime figures in countries such as Russia or the Ukraine have developed algorithms to value women based on the responses they receive from their profiles on dating sites or mail-order bride sites and then formulate their asking prices based on such calculations when selling the women into the cross-border sex trade, I would not be surprised.[19] Think about all of the data—number of men introducing themselves, persistency of approaching men, country of origin of the men making approaches, comments and compliments made, number of times profiles viewed, length of comments left for the women, average length of time spent reviewing profiles, number of times pictures clicked, and much more—that could be fed into such algorithms. So too, could data about the women's age, hair color, eye color, complexion, weight, height, and languages spoken. Nefarious traffickers could use their algorithms to de-risk the investments for buyers on the other side of the border as well as to determine which of the women's data sets generate the highest yields when sourcing new recruits.

- Non-native American businesses that are located on Indian reservations, or have partnerships with Indian tribes, may be involved in shady activities. You should ask such a company, "Why, other than the shield of sovereign immunity, did you decide to partner with the Indian tribes?"

- The seedier the neighborhood in which a business operates, and the more successful that business becomes, the more likely it is to be shaken down for protection. Successful bars in Pittsburgh as well as

---

[19] Young women in the former USSR are a fertile source for sex trafficking; they are very attractive and very depressed with their lives in their native countries. Over 50 percent of the models in Paris and Milan are from the former USSR, while six of the seven countries with the highest suicide rates among young females are former Soviet Republics. Further, a massively disproportionate share of online extortion hails from the former Soviet Union. Such shakedown tactics include "ransomware" which occurs when online gangsters impersonate law enforcement authorities (e.g. the FBI) and demand that the victims pay fines to avoid arrest for allegedly downloading pirated content or child pornography.

Buffalo, New York-based collection agencies with lots of expensive cars in the employee parking lots, may not escape the attention of organized crime and drug dealers.

- The mafia is more likely to engage in the theft and resale of products that are physically compact but high in value. These items include semiconductors, diamonds and, as confirmed by my discussions with company executives, Gillette shaving razor blades.

- A business that conducts a large percent of its operations with cash or prepaid cards (when doing so is in contravention of industry norms) should be reviewed with suspicion. Likewise, a business that uses a disproportionately high number of banks and maintains a multitude of bank accounts might be trying to launder money.

- Suspicion should be raised when a company has had its domains suspended numerous times or if it uses hosting firms that have had their accreditation revoked by the Internet Corporation for Assigned Names and Numbers. Similarly, companies that pay excessive website hosting fees to obscure hosting firms are suspect. Doing so could signal that mainstream hosting services do not wish to accommodate such clientele, perhaps because such sites are used for illegitimate activities.

- Caution should be taken when interacting with a company's representatives who each have multiple mobile phone numbers or insist on communicating solely through instant messenger services.

- Another marker of potential corruption is when the period for bidding on contracts is truncated, when few (or no) participants are invited to bid for contracts, or when the contractor has already been chosen and the bidding process is merely a facade.[20]

---

[20] While not connected to accusations of mafia activity, litigation has been brought against eleven private equity funds for their "club deals". These deals consist of various financial players joining together to make bids to acquire companies. The plaintiffs alleged that such joint bidding is a collusive attempt (a form of bid rigging) to reduce asking prices of target companies.

- In most legitimate businesses, the most senior people do not pay an extraordinary amount of attention to their warehouse activity. They delegate such responsibilities to the warehouse manager or vice-president of Supply Chain Management. However, in a corrupt business, the senior-most people might spend a disproportionate amount of effort overseeing warehouse activity because they do not want others to know about sudden surges of stolen inventory being placed in warehouses. Thus, a lack of documentation relative to what goes into warehouses and what comes out of warehouses could signal mafia influence. Without such documentation, a company may be committing "control fraud," which is what the Mafia does when it takes over a business from someone in too deep with loan sharks. The mob orders all the supplies it can to be delivered as quickly as possible, carts them out the back door and then torches the place. The vendors never get paid.

> **Analytical Consideration** While not necessarily related to smoking out the influence of the mafia, a sudden surge in a company's warehousing costs could be a sign of stagnating inventory or channel stuffing.

- When purchasing managers are living beyond their means, there is a good chance that they are supplementing their incomes from vendor kickbacks.

- One red flag concerning internal fraud occurs when employees are unwilling to share duties or who have an unusually close relationship with a customer or vendor. The banking industry requires its employees to take vacations so that if a given employee is committing chicanery, such activities will likely surface during that employee's absence.

- Businesses run by women are less likely to be involved in corrupt activities than businesses run by men.[21] For instance, the countries that rank as least corrupt on the global indices tend to have more women in government. In fact, when Finland ranked as the least-corrupt country

---

[21] According to the work of Professor Donald E. Brown ("Human Universals") as well as the work of Harvard Professor Steven Pinker, it is a universal fact (transcending all cultures and throughout history) that men commit more crime than women.

in the world, its government set the record for having the most women in cabinet-level positions. Interestingly, the accounting scandals at both WorldCom and Enron were disclosed by women.[22] In Mexico City, male traffic officers have been replaced entirely by women on the theory that women are less corruptible. Previously, Mexico City traffic officers were famous for accepting bribes in lieu of issuing tickets. Since the women traffic officers replaced their male counterparts, the number of issued tickets has increased dramatically.

---

[22] Cynthia Cooper, vice president of internal audit at WorldCom, blew the cover on fraud at her company by alerting the board to the executive cover-up of $3.8 billion in losses. Enron Vice President Sherron Watkins warned Chairman Ken Lay about financial wrongdoing and the possibility of a meltdown. Lisa P. McAllister divulged the accounting fraud taking place at American Realty Capital Properties Inc.

Corruption Throughout the World

No matter which countries you are considering transacting business in, there is always the risk of encountering some corruption. So, how can you determine the pervasiveness and depth of corruption that exists in disparate countries? Below are some of the considerations you might want to take into account.

The quickest way to determine the extent of corruption in a particular country is to look up the subject country's corruption ratings as reported by Transparency International. That service reports on a variety of metrics— such as Overall Corruption, Open Budget Index, Judicial Independence, Rule of Law, and Press Freedom—for almost every country in the world.

Corruption is more likely to take place in countries with sclerotic bureaucracies where the only way to get anything done is to grease the palms of officials. According to some studies, half of Indians admit they have bribed a public official, for everything from getting a birth certificate to filing their taxes on time.

> **Analytical Consideration** I find it especially troubling when a country criminalizes the conducting of due diligence. To wit, China sentenced British corporate investigator Peter Humphrey to 30 months in prison and his American wife and business partner Yu Yingzeng to 24 months in prison. If potential investors cannot even assess a country's business landscape or conduct background checks on potential local partners without the fear of arrest, how much confidence can they have committing significant resources to that country?
>
> You should also be aware of efforts business partners might take to discourage you from conducting due diligence. One such gambit was effectively used by Bernard Madoff when he cast himself

as an elite investor whose funds were closed or oversubscribed. If you were given a coveted opportunity to invest in one of Madoff's funds, it would have been perceived as impolite to request to conduct any due diligence.

Corruption and the mafia are more likely to prevail when a nation's wealth is highly extractive. Countries that are natural resource intense inculcate a temperament in their citizens to take rather than to create. We see this phenomenon in effect in countries ranging from Russia to Saudi Arabia as well as to many located in Africa. (However, there is now a good bit of entrepreneurialism in many African countries.) In extractive countries, there becomes a tremendous rush to control and ration scare resources to the highest bidder. Those charged with guardianing their nations' resources are often tempted to cut side deals with customers.

Culture can be a determinant of dishonest business practices. In many parts of Asia, saving face is more important than correcting a business partner's misconceptions, which is unfortunate because it often results in agreements based on misunderstandings. When a culture does not place great value on keeping commitments, there will be more dishonesty. In her outstanding book, *On Saudi Arabia*, Karen Elliot House wrote that Muslims award themselves points when they announce a good intention such as keeping a meeting. So, according to Ms. House's book, Muslims are inclined to make a lot of promises but will not keep all of them. It should give one pause when dealing with Russians, that American metaphors for being sincere and authentic—such as "say what you mean," "going public," and "being straightforward"—do not translate properly into Russian.

Analytical Consideration One method for determining the degree of corruption that exists in a developing country is to review both the number of students that compete for seats, allowing them to study different disciplines at universities, and the starting salaries of graduates with degrees in those disciplines. The way to read the chart below is that there are twice the number of students who would like to become oil industry managers compared to the number of seats available and that profession has a starting salary of $100,000. Each seat to become a civil servant has ten candidates and the starting salary is $20,000. The numbers below are completely random but they illustrate the point.

Candidates per Seat in the Following Disciplines		Starting Salary
Oil Industry Manager	2	$100,000
Airplane Pilot	5	$50,000
Civil Servant	10	$20,000

Do you see how corrupt this country is?

Why would the competition for seats for a degree in civil service be five times as fierce as the competition to become an oil industry manager when the former degree would only yield a salary one-fifth the amount that be could earned by choosing a more lucrative course of study? A disparity of this magnitude likely indicates that young people know that they can earn more than enough money under the table to compensate for their shortfalls in official salaries.

Thus, the greater the percent of the working age population employed by the government, the more likely there is widespread corruption as these government apparatchiks will need to supplement their incomes.

Countries that have high ratios of solitary sports to team sports are more likely to experience widespread corruption than countries with a greater incidence of team sports. Does this sound ridiculous? Well, it is much easier to fix sports competitions such as boxing and sumo wrestling where one athlete battles another athlete on a solo basis than it is to fix games that entail a large number of players such as basketball, football or baseball. Aside from soccer (and cricket in India), where are all of the large team sports in China, Russia, India, Brazil and Nigeria? Isn't ping pong China's national sport while gymnastics, weight lifting, figure skating, and boxing are areas where Russian athletes excel? Keep in mind that it is not just the presence of large teams on the national stage that reflects the degree of corruption but the greater difficulty of fixing team competition—from youth leagues to university leagues, and from community leagues to regional leagues—that render this consideration instructive.

The less fluidity there is among the wealthiest people in a country, the more likely it is that corruption exists. In a dynamic economy, a new cast of entrepreneurs can be expected to displace some of the industry barons of old for the top slots on lists such as the Forbes 500. In corrupt countries, the wealthiest people maintain their ranks at the top of such lists year after year due to their continuing protection from government officials while their enterprising citizens are discouraged from taking the risks associated with championing new ideas, business models and technologies.

Another signal of corruption is when the availability of luxury goods in close proximity to government officialdom is greatly disproportionate to the number of successful civilian professionals. In these situations, luxury items could be used to bribe government officials. China's state media conceded that sales of the country's most famous liquor, Kweichow Moutai, was an index for China's corruption. Indeed, when the Chinese government announced its anti-corruption campaign, the French wine-maker, Remy Cointreau SA, suffered plunging sales. (Interestingly, while China's crackdown on corruption has resulted in diminishing demand for conspicuous luxuries, sales of high-end intimate apparel have skyrocketed.)

Since corruption is very hard to eradicate, one should not be overly optimistic about anti-corruption campaigns. While Chinese Premier, Xi Jinping, has made sweeping arrests of corrupt officials, such movements are probably more reflective of a gambit to enhance his own power than to level the playing field for commercial activity. Culturally, it is difficult to wean recently communist countries off of corruption because under communism, smuggling and bribing were not illegal transactions undertaken by a few hardened criminals, but common survival strategies.

Mafia States

It is dangerous to be right when the government is wrong.

- Voltaire

It is an unfortunate injustice when businesses are subjected to mafia shake-downs as well as suffer from the economic costs of corruption pervading their industry. It is an even greater injustice when it is the government that is perpetrating mafia-like demands on businesses within their jurisdictions because there are few venues in which businesses have any chance of achieving redress against the prevailing authorities.

So, why am I writing about mafia states in a book dedicated to validating business models? Because even companies with the most promising business models have little chance of succeeding if the government becomes determined to bring them to their knees. While one may not win friends by discussing the mafia behavior of governments, it is important for business people and investors to at least have a familiarity of the related risks.

The discussion below indicates some of the mafia actions that three governments—those of China, Russia and the United States—have taken against legitimate businesses.

China The Chinese government seems determined to give domestic companies a competitive advantage by handicapping their western competitors. Within a year or so of this writing, the Chinese government has barraged western businesses with fines. For instance, the Chinese government fined six infant powder companies, including Mead Johnson Nutrition and Abbott Laboratories, $110 million. Contact lens manufacturers, among them Johnson & Johnson and Bausch & Lomb, were fined $3 million while twelve Japanese auto-parts makers were fined $200 million.

GlaxoSmithKline was fined $490 million and Qualcomm is at risk of being fined more than $1 billion.

Companies in China are often forced into confessions of guilt without due process. China's National Development and Reform Commission encourages companies not to bring lawyers to meetings, often does not inform firms what they are being charged with, and tries to force them to sign written confessions. Some Chinese officials even view the request to have a lawyer present as an indication of guilt.[23]

Russia I believe that Russia is truly a mafia state, with billions of dollars being diverted from businesses to the Kremlin each year. Lennart Dahlgren, a former head of Ikea Russia, said that his company had been subjected to years of legal traps that they sought to solve by meeting personally with Prime Minister Vladimir Putin. But a high-ranking official told them that a meeting with Putin would cost $5 million to $10 million. Mr. Dahlgren withdrew his interest in such a meeting. Anyway, the Russian version of the Federal Bureau of Investigations raided an Ikea office in Khimki, Russia in September of 2014, ostensibly due to a land dispute dating back to 2007.

Corruption is extremely prevalent in Russia (from local traffic police to tax collectors to the ministerial level) and businesses (especially western businesses) should not harbor expectations of receiving justice when seeking resolution to disputes.[24] I have heard stories where witnesses for business owners en route to the court house have been detained by traffic police so as to prevent their testimony. Among Russia's business leaders that have been sentenced to prolonged prison terms when their interests conflicted with those of the Kremlin are Mikhail Borisovich Khodorkovsky (formerly, head of Yukos), Vladimir Yevtushenkov (formerly, from Sistema, a Russian holding company with assets ranging from oil to mobile phone operations) and possibly the recently arrested Vladimir Evtushenkov (who has refused to sell his oil company, OAO Bashneft, to state-run OAO Rosneft

---

[23] Scott Cendrowski, "Beijing Pulls Back the Welcome Mat," Fortune, October 27, 2014, pp. 88-92.

[24] Let's take a stab at quantifying the extent of corruption in Russia. The 2014 Winter Olympics in Sochi, Russia cost a reported $50 billion, about three times more expensive than the second most expensive Winter Olympics, those hosted in Nagano, Japan in 1998. Let's say that the quality of the work performed for such investment and the inexpensive labor in Sochi at least compensate for any inflation that occurred between the 1998 games in Nagano and the games in 2014. Using the Sochi Games as a proxy for business in Russia would mean that for every $1 of legitimate investment, $2 is diverted to corrupt channels.

under terms dictated by its chief executive officer, long-time Putin ally Igor Sechin). Even lawyers representing the accused can find themselves rotting away in Russian jails until they die.[25]

"For my friends, anything. For my enemies, the law." This expression has real meaning in Russia. As for its friends, in a meeting with Putin at the Kremlin, the Russian government reallocated half of the stakes that Royal Dutch Shell, Mitsui, and Mitsubishi had in Sakhalin-2 to Gazprom. Russia has used infractions of fire codes to shut down non-governmental organizations and alleged lapses in food standards codes to close McDonald's restaurants.

The United States The overall business climate in the United States is much more antagonistic now than it was even less than ten years ago. Politicians all over the country are competing with each other to require businesses to provide their employees with ever more generous benefits such as paid time off. Labor disputes put before the National Labor Relations Board are overwhelmingly decided in the employees' favor. Businesses are beset with the certainty of higher taxes, higher minimum wages and higher costs of complying with a hail of bewildering government regulations. The flurry of conflicting laws imposed on corporate America are like spring traps set to ensnare legitimate businesses. For example, how are security guard companies or operators of firing ranges supposed to comply with laws forbidding businesses to inquire about candidates' criminal records?

As if the government was not enough of a threat to business owners, the government is actively encouraging employees to act as "whistleblowers." Instead of bringing any perceived infraction to the attention of management, any employee who reports his bosses and employer to a government agency stands to gain generous rewards, with potential book deals and lucrative speaking engagements to follow. And if the allegation is found to have no merit, the employee enjoys immunity while the bosses and company endure great expense defending themselves and suffer from lingering reputational degradation.

Here is just one small example of how ridiculous things have become. I always thought that the notion of internships was a win-win situation. Businesses would receive some free help and young people would receive

---

[25] This was the fate of Sergey Magnitsky who represented William Browder, an American investment banker that helped privatize Russian companies but fell out of the Kremlin's favor.

valuable work experience. There was no coercion on the part of either side. Now, the notion of internships has been recast as exploitive servitude and related litigation waged against grantors of internships is currently a growth driver for the legal profession. (Nevertheless, in another manifestation of contradictory government policy, under the Foreign Corrupt Practices Act, free internships are deemed to be valuable consideration for which favorable dispensation is not to be reciprocated. For instance, giving the child of a Brazilian customs official an internship at your company in return for lower tariffs on your exports to that country would be a violation of the FCPA.)

True. These examples of the piñatatization of businesses throughout the U.S. do not rise to the level of mafia behavior. (But they should not be neglected when assessing or developing business models either.) And in some ways, the mafia behavior propagated by the U.S. government is less repulsive than that committed by the governments of China or Russia. The shakedowns that do occur in the U.S. are much rarer than in countries such as Russia and do not directly enrich prosecuting government officials. (But in many instances, they do support their interests and help advance their careers.[26]) Also, no one involved in a business dispute is murdered, or required to submit to psychiatric treatment (as was the fate of Mikhail Kosenko in Russia and Xu Lindong in China), at the direction of the U.S. government.[27]

---

[26] Unlike in many other countries, U.S. prosecutors are not career civil servants. Since prosecutors in the U.S. are elected or appointed in a partisan fashion, they feel they must rack up winning cases. No matter if it becomes apparent that a defendant is innocent during a trial or tribunal, the prosecutor feels that he must obtain a guilty verdict (despite the travesty to justice) because in the campaign for re-election or higher office, the prosecutor's opponent will make an issue of the cases the prosecutor lost. As Harvard Law School Professor Alan Dershowitz has stated, "That the prosecutor's job is a stepping stone to a higher office is evidenced by the fact that nearly every senator or congressman who ever practiced law once served as a prosecutor."

[27] However, some Americans have committed suicide as a result of overbearing government prosecution. For instance, Dr. Peter Gleason, a Maryland psychiatrist, hanged himself after his assets were seized and his medical license was suspended. More information about this case is available at this link: http://online.wsj.com/news/articles/SB1000142412788732398 1504578174973015235686?mg=reno64-wsj.

Also, at least one of the 85,000 Arthur Anderson employees that lost their jobs when that firm collapsed committed suicide. This was a particularly regrettable tragedy as the government's conviction of Arthur Anderson was unanimously overturned by the Supreme Court in 2005 and the highest court roundly criticized the government's prosecution of that case.

So, why am I drawing attention to the United States' mafia behavior? Because more businesses are getting shaken down by government officials using unjust tactics, and in many cases these shakedowns are retribution for the political persuasion of top executives. A few of the businesses that have been unfairly shaken down are:

- The large American banks have been subjected to over $200 billion in fines. The unrelenting stream of fines assessed on the banks shows no sign of abating as new fines are imposed on the banks on a weekly basis. One has to wonder, have many of the large American banks been nationalized? It seems that targeted banks have been effectively reduced to utilities that are allowed to stay in business just to remit fines to the government.[28]

- Gibson Guitars and Lumber Liquidators were subjected to inter-agency raids—through the Department of Homeland Security, U.S. Fish and Wildlife Service and Department of Justice—on the pretense that these companies allegedly imported lumber from countries such as Russia and India in violation of those countries' laws. These raids occurred despite India or Russia filing complaints against the named companies. Top executives from these companies supported conservative causes. Interestingly, other guitar makers, such as Martin & Co. that used the same imported lumber but whose CEO donated to Democratic politicians, were not raided.[29]

- United Parcel Service agreed to forfeit $40 million to settle a probe into its shipments on behalf of illicit online pharmacies. Similarly, the Justice Department filed charges against FedEx, accusing it of conspiracy to launder money, in connection with its prescription-drug case against the package-delivery company. These companies had no more responsibility to inspect the contents of the packages they delivered

---

[28] Included in these penalties was a $13 billion settlement with JPMorganChase. Note that part of the government's reason for extracting such settlements was a function of the problems that existed at Bear Stearns and Washington Mutual, which JPMorganChase acquired. However, JPMorganChase acquired these companies at the behest of the same government that later sued it for doing so.

[29] This targeting should not come as a surprise in light of the Internal Revenue Service's targeting of conservative groups for aggressive audits.

than the United States Postal Services did. Nevertheless, they had money that the government wanted so an excuse was conjured up to extract it.

Anti-money-laundering laws, which generally require companies to have adequate internal systems for spotting suspicious activity and reporting it to the government, could ensnare operators of armored car services and even companies like Facebook and Amazon that are becoming involved with digital payments. Oh, and guess what? The Las Vegas Sands, run by Sheldon Adelson, one of the largest individual contributors to Republican interests and candidates, reached a $47 million settlement with U.S. prosecutors over a money-laundering investigation.

Kangaroo Court Justice

While one normally associates kangaroo courts with the likes of Russia, China or North Korea, violence is being inflicted upon the notion of justice with greater regularity in the U.S. Dozens of government agencies—ranging from the Securities and Exchange Commission to the Environmental Protection Agency and from state medical boards to the National Oceanic and Atmospheric Administration and from state liquor control boards to the Equal Employment Opportunity Commission—are increasingly bypassing courts altogether and instead are funneling cases into their own administrative proceedings which resemble kangaroo courts.

In such agency proceedings, the government acts as both prosecutor and judge. SEC defendants who cannot afford a lawyer well-versed in securities law have no right to have counsel appointed at government expense as would be the case in a criminal prosecution. For many defendants, the reality is even more Kafkaesque: In Kaley v. U.S., the Supreme Court ruled that it is permissible for the government to seize all of a defendant's assets pre-trial.

The right to remain silent when brought before an administrative proceeding is eviscerated because courts allow the SEC to treat silence as evidence of guilt. The presumption of innocence is largely meaningless as the bar for determining guilt is set at the lowest level of mere "preponderance of the evidence" rather than proof beyond reasonable doubt. In collecting such "evidence," SEC prosecutors are allowed to use hearsay and other unreliable evidence. Unscrupulous prosecutors commonly use inducements such as immunity for defendants' kin, cash stipends and new identities to coerce witnesses to testify against defendants. Defendants are limited as to the kinds of pretrial discovery and defense motions that are routinely allowed in courts. The SEC has even forced some investigative targets to admit wrongdoing if they want to settle and avoid trial, effectively treating agency settlements like criminal guilty pleas. In many administrative cases, the defendants are charged with criminal violations and are threatened with jail.

The behavior of government prosecutors and administrative tribunals has not only debased the notion of justice, but has also redefined "guilt".[30] Guilt, in government cases, can no longer be equated with culpability, but rather with efforts to mitigate the risks of even further governmental retribution.

While SEC prosecutors typically spend years building their cases, the agency's administrative law judges only have a few months after the hearing to evaluate the mountains of evidence presented. These administrative law judges are not life-tenured judicial officers, but rather executive-branch employees who conduct hearings at the direction of agency leaders following procedural rules dictated by the agencies themselves.

Analytical Consideration There is a term in economics called "the repeat player problem." While a process might seem fair to both parties, it will really favor the party that utilizes the process most frequently. If you have a dispute with your stock broker, you may be required to arbitrate. Well, you might go to arbitration once in your life, whereas the stock broker on the other side of the table is a frequent customer. Arbitrators who rule for consumers tend not to get selected for future work. The repeat player problem could occur with home inspectors who depend on referrals from real estate agents. It must certainly occur with administrative law judges employed by government agencies.

When the cases remain within an agency's tribunal, the facts of the

---

[30] The repugnance of some government prosecutors is boundless. As a pastime at the U.S. federal prosecutor's office in the Southern District of New York, staffers would conjure up theories based on obscure crimes to indict celebrities such as Mother Theresa and John Lennon. You can read more here: http://www.slate.com/articles/news_and_politics/jurisprudence/features/2007/american_lawbreaking/introduction.html

case are sealed and precedent is not established. Thus, in the aftermath of such proceedings, it cannot be known what is, and what is not, legal. The lack of precedent together with the avalanche of indeterminable legislation, rules and regulations, leave enforcement of the laws to the discretion of tens of thousands of federal, state and local government employees. Even when an agency such as the SEC loses after a case is brought to trial, double jeopardy does not prevent it from trying to reverse the verdict or force a retrial.

As if agency tribunals were not sufficiently bereft of any notion of fairness or due process in and of themselves, zealous prosecutors often unfairly disparage the defendant before their own kangaroo proceedings commence. For instance, arrests of alleged wrongdoers are arranged with media sympathetic to the prosecutors to ensure that the defendant is maximally humiliated.[31] Prehearing press releases issued by agencies such as the SEC are written by attorneys prosecuting the case and are couched in language that makes it appear as if the defendant were already found to be guilty. And when the agency dismisses or loses a case, it does not always remove its grossly accusatory press releases from its website. Thus, even those who achieve victory in kangaroo regulatory tribunals, such as that of the SEC, continue to have their reputations trashed.

The tendency to shakedown businesses is heightened when the agencies or states are allowed to retain proceeds from settlements and fines. The result is that agencies are crossing jurisdictional lines and tripping over other agencies in their zest to shakedown lucrative targets. For example, somehow the state of Rhode Island wound up with a $500 million payout from Google. Meanwhile, the state of New York has received billions of dollars in settlements from banks because its governor, Andrew Cuomo, threatened to withdraw their licenses to operate on Wall Street. Apparently, these threats resulted from Governor Cuomo being incensed that these banks violated federal law.

---

[31] One of the rare occasions in which overzealous prosecutors refrained from humiliating a defendant by subjecting him to the "perp walk" was in the case of Martha Stewart's arraignment for alleged insider trading. One middle-aged lady manhandled by a phalanx of burly and armed agents ran the risk of evoking sympathy for Ms. Stewart. If government prosecutors are dedicated to seeking justice, why is so much of their energy spent scheming?

What Can You Do?

How can an executive contend with transacting business in a mafia state? While there are neither easy nor failsafe answers to this question, we do address them in my Enhanced Negotiating Strategies course offered by the Institute for Strategic Negotiations. For now, a few quick ideas follow. First, if you know you can't win a fight, the best thing to do is avoid the fight. This means that if you do not have to conduct business in Russia, you may want to avoid entering that market or at least reduce your exposure to that market. Second, if you must operate in a country whose government resorts to mafia tactics, accept the reality. At a minimum, you may have to raise the discount rates in your economic forecasts and reserve funds for mounting a defense in the event that your firm is ensnared in a regulatory trap. Third, hire qualified lawyers at the outset of developing your business and tell them that you expect them to guide your firm around such obstacles. (There are analogs to lawyers acting as Sherpas in Russia and India. In Russia, it is common for companies to have Federal Security Services (the successor to the KGB) officers on staff for the purpose of deflecting shakedowns by other government officials. In India, the corollary is admittedly less reflective of corruption. The retired military officials that are often embedded in Indian start-ups act more like dorm mothers who monitor employee tardiness, petty theft and the padding of expense reports.)

Fourth, you may have to buy protection by supporting the campaigns of, and causes dear to, influential politicians, especially those who chair committees that oversee the agencies that are charged with regulating your business.[32] In a similar vein, Lockheed-Martin subcontracted the production of equipment related to its F-22 Raptor to suppliers in 44 states. The result was that there were 88 senators who had a reason to support funding for the F-22. Finally, partner with the government. For instance, Intuit offers its TurboTax software free to lower-income taxpayers for state-level

---

[32] Here is another contribution that the self-appointed apostles of ethics have bestowed upon us. Because of transparency, one takes a risk in making contributions to the campaign of a challenger to an incumbent. Thanks to transparency, the incumbent office holder will know that you have supported his opponent. When you seek that representative's assistance in getting a locked-on government prosecutor to desist from depriving you of your rights during an administrative tribunal, do you think the incumbent will be more or less likely to accommodate your request for his intervention? Would the response likely be different if instead you sought the representative's help in obtaining life-saving medical treatment?

tax return filing, but only in states that refrain from pre-return filing. (Pre-return filing is when the government sends completed returns to taxpayers who are saved the trouble of preparing their returns if they agree with the government's numbers.)

Analysis of Emerging Business Models

Marijuana Dispensaries

There has been a lot of buzz about the potential for the marijuana industry since at least 2012 when the sale of marijuana for recreational purposes was legalized in Colorado and Washington State. As we go to press, marijuana is legal in some form in 22 states. Demand for marijuana could spike as efforts are underway to turn it into a branded consumer product. For instance, Privateer Holdings is in the process of leveraging the Bob Marley name as it launches lines of Marley Natural heirloom Jamaican cannabis strains, marijuana-infused skin creams and lip balms and accessories such as vaporizers and pipes. In addition to pain relief and recreation, marijuana could penetrate a good bit of the $22 billion market for sleeping pills. However, in addition to opposition from local police forces (discussed above), marijuana growers and dispensaries face numerous challenges ahead.

Government Support for the Marijuana Industry

The marijuana industry is reliant on government support. However, support among politicians for marijuana may wither as it is not clear that marijuana dispensaries will end up producing significant tax revenues for the states that legalize pot smoking. One reason, as contended by lawsuits in Colorado, is that requiring those involved in the legal marijuana industry to pay state taxes would incriminate them at the federal level, where marijuana remains illegal. A second reason that tax receipts might be disappointing is that marijuana dispensaries are exclusively cash businesses—banks and credit card companies want nothing to do with marijuana businesses—where failure to report revenues is relatively easy. The third reason that tax receipts might fall below projections is that, contrary to the notion of legalization driving out illegal marijuana sales, illegal sales of marijuana are likely to rise in lockstep with the legalization of marijuana.

In view of the imposition of sales taxes, marijuana state sales taxes, excise taxes and local taxes imposed on marijuana sales, together with the high operating costs of managing a marijuana dispensary (discussed below), the legalization of marijuana results in higher prices which makes illegal sales more profitable. Since marijuana dealers' criminal histories bar them from working in the legalized marijuana trade, many dealers are likely to remain on the illegal side of the business.

Another concern that politicians might have about further legalization of marijuana is that such actions might lead to the release of hundreds of thousands of prisoners who are serving jail sentences for marijuana possession, use and trafficking. Costs would be saved if these prisoners were to be released. However, it is not clear that politicians want to gamble their careers on low recidivism rates among marijuana smokers and dealers. Moreover, Nebraska and Oklahoma sued Colorado in the U.S. Supreme Court on the grounds that the legalization of marijuana in Colorado has resulted in more interstate drug trafficking. Finally, there is a potential preemption issue at play: when states legalize marijuana they are effectively abrogating international drug interdiction treaties in which the U.S. federal government is a key signatory.

Operational Challenges

Financial institutions are averse to serving marijuana dispensaries despite the U.S. Attorney General assuring banks that they will not run afoul of national banking regulations when providing banking services to marijuana growers and dispensaries. Nevertheless, banks remain reluctant to provide banking services to this industry as they fear being accused of violating laws aimed at preventing money laundering. Also, lenders to the marijuana industry remain on the sidelines as they could be required to make regular reports to the Treasury Department and be responsible for monitoring suspicious activities at marijuana dispensaries.

It is very difficult to operate a business without using banks or having the ability to accept payment by credit card. For one thing, all sales must be consummated in cash. This customer inconvenience and safety risk certainly must inhibit sales. Accepting only cash transactions presents monumental security risks and payment challenges. Brinks will not provide armored transport for the marijuana industry because the drug remains illegal under federal law. Marijuana dispensaries must invest heavily in security in the form of guard dogs, cameras, alarms, safes and armed guards. They often need redundant staff to watch one another handle and account for all of the cash. Payments must be made in person to most service providers such as electric utilities and phone companies as well as to tax authorities. Meticulous records must be maintained, and receipts collected, for all transactions because without such practices there will be no proof of the dispensaries having made payments. Only some vendors will accept cash and when they do, it must be counted and recounted. Other vendors to marijuana dispensaries will only accept payment by money order.

Another issue that the marijuana industry is forced to grapple with is the documentation of marijuana plants, all the way from seed to sale. In the process of being harvested and dried, marijuana plants are often moved around to various rooms–one room for drying, for example, and another for trimming. Growers need to track this process precisely, both to monitor inventory and for compliance reasons. Similarly, when plants die, they too must be accounted for. In Colorado, pot merchants, who must grow most of what they sell, have to put a microchip on each plant so it can be recorded and monitored in Colorado's Marijuana Inventory Tracking Solution.

Under some state laws, such as those of Connecticut, cultivating marijuana for medical use requires meeting standards close to those of pharmaceutical companies. For instance, employees must wear scrubs and a licensed pharmacist must work at every dispensary. There are also requirements to ensure that the marijuana products that have the same names share the active ingredients within ranges as tight as three percent. However, it will be very difficult to ensure such consistency because marijuana is a crop, not a synthetic pharmaceutical.

Since the federal government still classifies marijuana as a Schedule 1 drug, marijuana merchants cannot talk openly about their plants' intended medicinal functions. Neither can marketing materials nor websites discuss the intended functions of marijuana if pot producers want to sell the cannabis in all 50 states or import them into the United States. Marijuana purveyors cannot trademark anything intended for marijuana consumption. (Those entrepreneurs who have created pot-laced drinks and confections—from chocolate to gummy fish to cheesecake—that resemble children's snacks are at great risk of running afoul of labeling and marketing edicts.) Dispensaries cannot advertise their pot with the major search tools as Google, Facebook, and Twitter have banned "marijuana" as an acceptable search term.

Perhaps companies that cater to marijuana growers and dispensaries are safer ways to play marijuana. There are companies such as Agrisoft that develop software for complying with regulations for tracking marijuana from seed to sale as well as for managing the cash payments of the marijuana industry. Advanced Cannabis Solutions leases growing space and related facilities to licensed marijuana operators. Similarly, warehouses are finding more demand as they are being used to grow marijuana. Steep Hill Halent is a quality-control laboratory that tests medical marijuana to determine moisture levels as well as contamination from mold, bacteria or harmful pesticides. GW Pharmaceuticals is developing a portfolio of cannabinoid medicines, including Sativex for the treatment of multiple sclerosis spasticity and cancer pain as well as Epidiolex for the treatment of childhood epilepsy.

Interestingly, there are a few companies that manufacture machines that dispense marijuana. Medbox's machines use biometric identification to document that the user is a registered patient and that the patient has a valid and unexpired authorization from a physician to possess and use the medicine dispensed.

American Green's medical marijuana vending machine uses an advanced ID-scanner to verify age and identity. In addition to these machines adding verification as to whom marijuana is dispensed, they promise to enhance the efficiency of marijuana dispensaries. Some customers are veteran marijuana smokers who know exactly what they want when they walk into the dispensary. Other patrons are new to marijuana. Since they do not know much about the various strains, flavors or other properties of marijuana, they need a lot of time to confer with the staff members. Thus, dispensing machines allow the former customers to quickly buy what they want and then exit the store, leaving more time for staff members to serve the latter group of customers.

Before becoming exposed to marijuana companies, you might want to ventilate issues such as these:

- For how many debilitating medical conditions is medical marijuana approved? What is the incidence of medical marijuana conflicting with other medications such patients are taking? Will insurance companies pay for marijuana directed to medical applications?

- Will marijuana dispensaries face opposition from zoning commissions?

- Do employers in states that have legalized recreational marijuana still have the right to fire employees for using marijuana when they are off the clock?

- Can customers drive away after buying marijuana from a dispensary? Is marijuana required to be kept in sealed bags while in transit or while outside?

- It seems that Uruguayan companies are making money from industrial uses of marijuana including rope, textiles, and paper. To what extent are these end uses feasible ways for marijuana dispensaries to diversify their merchandise?

Electronic Cigarettes

Electronic cigarettes are battery-powered, smoke-free devices that turn nicotine-laced liquid into vapor without most of the carcinogens, such as tar, produced by tobacco combustion. Since e-cigarettes are not combustible, the need for lighters and matches is eliminated and the dangers linked to fire are avoided. Because e-cigarettes emit vapor rather than smoke, e-cigarette users enjoy the fact that their clothes, hair and environment do not absorb smoke. (The odorless nature of electronic cigarettes makes it harder for parents to detect that their children are using e-cigarettes.) E-cigarettes contain no tobacco products and the nicotine is synthetic. E-cigarettes come in many shapes and sizes: many look more or less like long cigarettes, others look like cigars or pipes. Some of the major producers of e-cigarettes are Electronic Cigarettes International Group, Clearette, MarkTen (owned by Altria) and Blu (owned by Imperial Tobacco Group).

The hope for e-cigarettes was that, since they appear to be less damaging to users' health, such alternative cigarettes would face fewer restrictions on marketing and sales as well as lighter regulatory burdens. While it is too early to determine how much success e-cigarettes will ultimately enjoy, the category appears to have lost some of its promise. One reason is that restrictions have been placed on e-cigarettes. My understanding is that electronic cigarettes are banned in countries such as Austria, Brazil and Indonesia. Other countries restrict the marketing and sale of e-cigarettes. One of the many examples of such restrictions is that a French court ruled that tobacconists should have the exclusive right to sell electronic cigarettes. Another reason for the reduced luster associated with e-cigarettes is that they have not delivered enough nicotine to satisfy smokers' cravings. Also, alternative nicotine delivery mechanisms, such as an inhalable nicotine spray, are arriving at the market.

Some of the questions that can be asked in attempting to ascertain the merits of producing, or investing in, e-cigarettes include:

- How easy are e-cigarettes to use? Can anyone inhale e-cigarette vapor on the first puff or is this an acquired effort?

- How much do the devices cost? To what extent are excise taxes imposed? How much of an initial outlay is this compared to buying a pack of regular cigarettes? What percent of traditional smokers can afford this initial purchase? Can electronic cigarettes be sent through domestic mail services? What is the risk of health insurers levying surcharges on e-cigarette users?

- Are the cartridges disposable or reusable? What kinds of excise taxes are imposed? Are nicotine cartridges exempt from tobacco taxes? If they are disposable, where can replacement cartridges be found? Can they be reordered online? Is proof of age required? If they are reusable, how easy or difficult is it to clean them? What is the level of ease or difficulty in replacing them? Are there industry standards surrounding reusable cartridges so that the cartridges are interoperable with the larger device? If the cartridges are reusable, how many times can they be reused before they must be discarded? Are there any protocols regarding the disposal of cartridges that must be adhered to?

- How does the level of nicotine in e-cigarettes users' blood compare to such levels that result from smoking regular cigarettes? What is the ratio of nicotine to liquid content in electronic cigarettes? The higher these ratios are, the more regulatory scrutiny is likely to be visited upon electronic cigarettes. Do electronic cigarettes, in general, result in lower levels of nicotine reaching users' blood than vapor pens? The concern is that vape pens' larger batteries produce more heat, increasing nicotine levels.

- Is Food and Drug Administration approval required to sell e-cigarettes? What are the restrictions on marketing and selling e-cigarettes? What are the restrictions on smoking e-cigarettes? What is the trend in banning the smoking of e-cigarettes in public places? How many countries and states have banned e-cigarettes in the work place? Is secondhand vapor deemed to be pollutant?

- Since e-cigarettes contain no tobacco, are they still subject to U.S. tobacco laws? If not, can e-cigarettes be purchased without proof of age? If so, can they be purchased online? If so, what precautions are e-cigarette companies putting in place to preclude underage people from buying e-cigarettes through the Internet?

- E-cigarettes have won applause for being available in a wide variety of colors and candy flavors. Such flavors include cola, lemonade, peppermint, mint tea, coconut with butterscotch as well as dragon fruit and cream. Is this diverse array of flavors a double-edged sword? What are the risks that this selection could appeal to children and thus spark a public relations or regulatory backlash?

- Are people that experiment with e-cigarettes more or less likely to try traditional cigarettes? If e-cigarettes are deemed to be a gateway for smoking traditional cigarettes, what are the risks of a public relations or regulatory backlash?

- Are smokers using e-cigarettes in place of—or as a supplement to—smoking traditional cigarettes? One way to grapple with this question is to review related marketing messages. If the prevailing marketing campaigns stress the ability to smoke e-cigarettes where traditional cigarettes are banned, that would indicate that e-cigarettes are being marketed as a supplement to traditional cigarettes. In that case, there would be less potential for e-cigarettes than if sales of e-cigarettes were driven by their appeal for replacing regular cigarettes.

- Cartridges are available in varying concentrations of nicotine, including low concentrations and no nicotine at all for smokers trying to quit. If e-cigarettes are directed to weaning smokers away from nicotine, to what extent might they face opposition from pharmaceutical companies? Companies such as GlaxoSmithKline and Pfizer sell nicotine patches and gums that could lose sales to low, or no, nicotine e-cigarettes. Thus, pharmaceutical companies such as these may move to counter competition from electronic cigarettes.

- To what extent do electronic cigarettes compete with other vaporizers? How does the "throat hit" of vaporizers compare to that of e-cigarettes?

What are the risks that vapor bars and vape shops will be reclassified as manufacturers on the theory that these retailers are mixing and bottling liquid nicotine? What would be the consequences of such re-classifications in terms of zoning restrictions and costs of permitting?

Bitcoin

Bitcoins are a peer-to-peer currency whose transactions occur directly among the system's participants. Because there are no intermediaries, such as banks or credit card companies, there are almost no intermediary costs such as currency conversion charges or merchant charges. Rather than issuing tangible bills and coins, bitcoins are based on digital tokens with no intrinsic value and backed by no central bank. New Bitcoins are issued when miners solve increasingly complicated mathematical quandaries. Bitcoins are designed to retain value and, unlike government notes, this currency cannot be promiscuously printed. There is an upper limit of twenty-one million new coins built into the governing software, with the last Bitcoin projected to be mined in 2140.

The process of initiating transactions with Bitcoins requires stamina. On the websites—such as Coinbase, Coin Café and Celery—that swap dollars for Bitcoins, there is often a wait time of up to four days for those who fund their bitcoins from bank transfers. The first time you try to pay with Bitcoins, you need to receive a text with the store's bitcoin address. This 34-digit string of alphanumeric code must be typed into your phone's payment app. You will also need to convert the price of the merchandise you wish to purchase from dollars to Bitcoins. Then, the Bitcoin operator at the store needs to receive a text confirming the transaction. The effort to start trading Bitcoins compares very poorly to the few hundreds of milliseconds it takes to swipe a credit card.

Bitcoin transactions offer anonymity, which is appreciated by customers making purchases of items and services that carry social stigmas. Some proponents of Bitcoins believe that the digital currency is safer than government-sanctioned currency in that the government will have a harder time confiscating it. When Cypriot President Nicos Anastasiades announced his plan in March of 2013 for confiscating 6.75% of the money held in every bank account in Cyprus, the price of Bitcoins surged, with particularly strong demand coming from Spain (as that country was believed to be next in line to catch the financial contagion sweeping Europe).[33]

Bitcoin's anonymity is also a point of concern for law enforcement and financial regulators as the virtual currency could facilitate money laundering and shields purchasers of illicit merchandise. It is my understanding that essentially all of the purchases of handguns produced from 3-D printers are facilitated with Bitcoins. Silk Road, an online forum where illicit goods and services are traded for Bitcoin, was temporarily shut down by the Federal Bureau of Investigations.

In addition to the elimination of expensive credit card fees, merchants are attracted to the irreversibility of bitcoin transactions as they are relieved of charge-backs due to fraud or customer returns. Bitcoins could expand the customer base for merchants whose customers are barred from paying via PayPal and traditional credit cards. PayPal blocks access from over 60 countries due to higher fraud rates as well as for political and regulatory reasons. Many credit card companies have similar restrictions.

Nevertheless, there are significant risks associated with maintaining money in the form of Bitcoins. Governments could regulate bitcoins out of business or users' confidence in that virtual currency could disappear in a flash. Also, unlike a U.S. bank failure, in which deposits are insured by the government, there may be little recourse for people whose money is locked up in shuttered bitcoin exchanges. This is not a theoretical concern: about a half a billion dollars in the digital currency went missing from vaults maintained by Mt. Gox, once the pre-eminent exchange for buying and selling bitcoins. Also, hackers stole 18,000 bitcoins, or $5 million in client funds, from Bitstamp, the world's second-largest Bitcoin exchange. Other exchanges that convert bitcoin to other currencies have collapsed or closed.

Quotations for bitcoins are extremely volatile (in part, due to bitcoin exchanges allowing the trading of bitcoins on margin), adding significant risk to bitcoin account-holders. In fact, many companies that accept

---

[33] The risk of confiscatory government policies is widespread and could be a driver for Bitcoin. According to Australia's Herald Sun, the Australian government seized a record $360 million from 'dormant' household bank accounts in 2013 alone. I received a similar letter from my bank, relating to an account I set up for my son, saying that unless I called the bank to reassert ownership of the assets, they would be seized due to a lack of activity in the account. Poland transferred to the state the bulk of assets owned by the country's private pension funds without offering any compensation. The U.S. Treasury Department intercepted $1.9 billion in tax refunds in 2013. The International Monetary Fund has advocated "mobilizing domestic revenue" which translates to "the direct confiscation of assets."

Bitcoins convert them into cash as soon as they can. For installment purchases or reoccurring charges (for subscriptions or monthly insurance premiums, for example), buyers and sellers undertake an exchange-rate risk which greatly reduces the appeal of using bitcoins.

The following are among the issues that should be considered before diving into bitcoin commerce:

- What are the risks that your Bitcoin account could be hacked and current balances diverted? Given that hackers have infiltrated credit card data maintained by mammoth retailers such as Home Depot, Target and Best Buy, what is to prevent them from infiltrating Bitcoin accounts? What are the risks that Bitcoin payments might be intercepted? If such breaches were to occur, what would be the account-holders' recourse? What would be the liabilities for the Bitcoin exchange operators? What recourse would Bitcoin exchanges have if Bitcoin value was stolen from them?

- What are the consequences of Bitcoin exchanges often being rejected when they attempt to open bank accounts? One reason that banks often refuse to accept deposits from Bitcoin operators is that the banks do not want to be responsible for bitcoin exchanges failing to receive money-transmitting licenses for every state. Fundamentally, it must be difficult for bankers to get motivated to accommodate clients whose mission is to replace them. Perhaps those sentiments would change if banks were allowed to count assets held in virtual currencies towards their capital requirements.

- Is the popularity of Bitcoins overstated? Are hip companies announcing their acceptance of Bitcoins as marketing ploys while really hoping that few customers will make payments with Bitcoins? For instance, in December of 2014, Microsoft teamed up with digital currency payment processor BitPay to allow customers to use Bitcoin when using their online Microsoft accounts for purchases of content in stores that house Xbox Music and Xbox Video. A closer review of the Microsoft announcement indicates that the software giant does not have high expectations for Bitcoin. The related announcement was merely posted on its blog and slotted into the FAQ list of billing and payment queries on its website. The service is U.S.-only at this point and there is a $1,000 limit to how much money can be added to an account daily. Microsoft executives described its Bitcoin initiative as "a toe-dip rather than aggressive guns blazing."

- There are tax consequences of using bitcoins to conduct commerce. At least in the United States, bitcoin buyers have to pay a tax based on the spread between what they paid in dollars for bitcoins and the dollar value attributed to the bitcoins when they spend them. Sellers are subject to a tax based on the dollar value of the Bitcoins they receive when they sell a good or service. Thus, buyers and sellers of bitcoin must track all of their bitcoin activities and report such transactions on their tax returns.

- Are bitcoins used to purchase legalized marijuana? If not, why not? Bitcoins offer the anonymity that many purchasers of marijuana crave and marijuana dispensaries are in dire need of alternative currencies.

Crowdfunding Operators

Crowdfunding, whereby dedicated platforms facilitate individuals making small investments into small companies, has been entombed in the netherworld of regulatory reflection since the Jumpstart Our Business Startups (JOBS) Act was signed into law in April of 2012. Regulations regarding how small businesses are allowed to raise funds from non-accredited investors were due from the Securities and Exchange Commission (SEC) by December of 2012. More than two years on, these rules have not been written.

Even when these rules are produced, I just cannot see this business model working. The protections that the SEC wants for individual investors will present excessive costs and liabilities for small business owners, especially in view of the relatively miniscule streams of money they stand to receive from non-accredited investors. Investors in small or emerging companies want to invest in people with whom they are familiar, or who are at least accessible. (I know a New York City venture capital firm that will only invest in companies within a 40 block radius of its office.) If the proprietor of a bicycle shop in Lexington, Kentucky cannot find investors in his region, does it really stand to reason that he will be able to secure investors in Lexington, Nebraska?

When the rules are written and crowdfunding gets off to the races, the following are among the issues I would consider before getting involved in crowdfunding:

- What regulations are in place to ensure that investors do not lose more money than they can afford?

- Will any amounts of money raised from investors on portals be directed to listed companies or will minimum amounts of money have to be raised before the company receives any capital?

- How will the expenses associated with listing on portals compare to those associated with raising capital via angels and venture capitalists?

- To what extent should listed companies expect to be compelled to communicate with investors?

- What will companies that list on portals have to provide in terms of financial reporting? In terms of registration with regulators?

- Who will have the obligation—the portals or the listed companies—to qualify investors? To ensure that investors are not exceeding, on a cumulative basis, the maximum allowable investments in small companies? Will the portals be required to conduct background checks on key people at the listed companies?

- What kinds of investor education materials will crowdfunding platforms be required to make available?

- To what extent will listed companies be required to disclose "related party" transactions?

- What obligations will companies have relative to disclosing their intended "use of proceeds"?

- Will crowdfunding portals be permitted to take equity interests in listed companies?

- How will investors achieve liquidity?

I am differentiating the crowdfunding platforms envisioned above from the likes of Kickstarter and Indiegogo. The crucial difference between the two varieties of crowdfunding platforms is that investors in the former will be shareholders and will expect returns on their investments. They will have the right to be kept abreast of their companies' developments. On the other hand, individuals contribute to a campaign, not too dissimilarly from the way they contribute to charitable causes (perhaps through Kiva, discussed below), on the likes of Kickstarter and Indiegogo. These contributors have no rights to the projects they support or to any return on their contributions.

Legacy Crowdfunding Platforms

Major crowdfunding companies, such as Kickstarter, Crowd Supply, Crowdfunder and Indiegogo, have enjoyed a great deal of success. For instance, Kickstarter has received more than $1 billion in pledges from more than 7.5 million people since it launched in April of 2009. In addition to providing a fund raising medium, these platforms help artists and entrepreneurs boost awareness of their talent, products and businesses.

The concerns about crowdfunding addressed below are germane to both permutations of crowdfunding platforms. First, a tremendous amount of work is required to have a successful crowdfunding raise. Founders must promote aggressively. Marketing material must be produced. Social media campaigns need to run full throttle. Inquiries require attentiveness. Inducements in the form of product samples and beta versions as well as free t-shirts and hats are often used to clinch contributions.

According to CNN, 84 percent of Kickstarter's top projects shipped their promised prototypes late, if at all. This is problematic because as crowdfunding becomes more commonplace, consumers are starting to treat it like a service, rather than a fundraising tool. They expect the same level of service from an early-stage venture as they do from Amazon or eBay. (Interestingly, according to Wharton Professor Ethan Mollick, there is a direct correlation between how much money a company raises over its goal and how late it delivers its merchandise to its backers.) All of this has led to infuriated supporters who still have access to the crowdfunding pages where they can freely express their outrage and may even organize legal action against non-performing project creators. Even when backers refrain from disparaging a campaign, when something is free consumers are less likely to provide the creator with important feed-back.

Analytical Consideration Will tax authorities consider the relationship between the crowdfunder and its contributors the same as that of a vendor and its customers for purposes of collecting sales taxes? If so, crowdfunders will be further burdened with administrative duties such as record keeping and the scheduling of tax remittances.

Despite all of these efforts, contributors can usually decrease or cancel their pledges at any time—except within the last 24 hours—during the campaign. Most successful crowdfunding campaigns raise less than $10,000 and 10% of projects have finished without receiving a single pledge.[34] Venture capitalists approached in the aftermath of a crowdfunding campaign will not be impressed with companies that failed to gain traction during their crowdfunding attempts.

At the conclusion of their campaigns, promoters relinquish between 4% and 9% of the funds raised to the platform operators. And creators that have not protected their intellectual property all over their world are exposed to knockoffs. For instance, Ostrich Pillow, a unique public napping pillow that looks like a plush helmet, raised $195,000 on Kickstarter. In the wake of its successful crowdfunding campaign, that company saw numerous blatant copycat pillows offered on various websites for a fraction of Ostrich Pillow's prices.

---

[34] A significant amount of the capital flowing through crowdfunding sites is going to celebrities, underscoring the fact that contributors wish to back known entities. For instance, Director Rob Thomas raised more than $5.7 million, Zach Braff's proposed film "Wish I Was Here" hit $3.1 million, and Shaquille O'Neil raised at least $450,000 when he launched a crowdfunding campaign.

Flash Sales Operators

Flash sales operators have generated hundreds of millions of dollars of revenues over the last several years. Flash sales occur when selected merchandise—which, in the case of the Gilt Groupe, consists of selling out-of-season designer apparel—is made available during brief spans of time. The idea of selling limited inventory during limited periods of time is to create a lot of excitement as well as fear, on the part of customers, of missing out. Thus, clothing designers can dispose of excessive inventory, blemished products and out-of-season merchandise through flash sales operators without damaging the designers' brand.

Despite the intriguing nature of flash sales sites such as those operated by Rue La La and One Kings Lane, the following are among my concerns with that business model:

- There may be legitimate reasons why such merchandise did not sell in the traditional channels. Trying to sell unpopular merchandise can be an uphill battle no matter the channel used.

- Requiring members or customers to shop during brief spans of time is anathema to the convenience that is supposed to be afforded by shopping on the Internet. In other words, people want to shop whenever they want, not during dedicated periods of time determined by distant etailers.

- The ease of comparing prices across the Internet makes it harder for the flash sales sites to provide compelling prices.

- Generous discounting is a mainstay of the fashion retail industry. Walk into a department store any day of the year and you will see signs for discounts of 50% off or even 70% off. How are flash sales sites to compete with this aggressive discounting especially when they do not have the scale to make the kinds of large volume purchases that off-price retailers such as T.J. Maxx can?

- The more efficient designers become in managing their production, inventory and sales through traditional channels, the more severe the lack of inventory will be for the flash sales operators.

- The competition brought about by the proliferation of flash sales sites has resulted in the removal of the aura of exclusivity that was initially conferred upon those shoppers fortunate enough to have been invited to shop on the sites. It has also resulted in flash sales shoppers becoming inundated with promotional emails. Flash sales sites have disappointed customers with their slow and expensive delivery service and reluctance to accept returns. Finally, some of the flash sales sites have begun offering private label merchandise which erodes the high class image that these sites wish to project as well as presents a brand dilution risk to the designers whose merchandise is sold through such sites.

Charitable Giving Business Models

There are two permutations of charitable giving business models that I will address. The first model— represented by companies such as Crowdrise—are relatively simple. These platforms enable contributors to route contributions, via the credit card they file with the site, to the charities that they select.

I find it difficult to see the compelling advantage of such platforms. Since it takes charities enormous amounts of effort to secure large donations (such as persistent outreach initiatives and holding carefully orchestrated events such as galas), it seems like these platforms will only receive small contributions. Even small contributions will be difficult to garner through such sites as most charities make it convenient to donate directly through their own sites. Contributors will be especially reluctant to donate through a platform that takes commissions of anywhere from 3% to 10% which is in addition to the 3% to 5% fees taken by the credit card companies.

Analytical Consideration Many philanthropists want to make sure that their targeted charities have modest overhead-to-endowment (or adminis-trative expense-to-endowment) ratios. That is, they do not want the adminis-tration of the charities to consume too high a percent of their contributions. Sounds like a reasonable issue to raise with targeted charities. However, the savvy philanthropist should ask two follow-up questions: First, to what extent is the charity's funding in the form of donations of used possessions (with ambiguous values) versus cash or shares of public companies (which carry much more readily and confidently ascertainable values)? Second, how does your charity value contributions that fall into the former bucket?

The issue that I am getting at is that a charity can make its overhead-to-en-dowment ratio appear more reasonable by inflating the value of illiquid contri-butions, the denominator in the equation. For instance, if a charity is collecting used clothing to send to Africa, it can disguise a high overhead-to-endowment ratio by valuing used T-shirts that it receives as donations at $100 each.

Kiva

Kiva is an online platform that facilitates micro-lending in 78 different countries. These loans are directed to supporting micro businesses that are largely located in emerging countries. (One way that Kiva has been able to facilitate more than $643 million in loans, at the time of this writing, is that Kiva allows people to join a variety of lending groups on its platform which compete with other lending groups in terms of making microloans. These lending groups can be dedicated to investing in different regions, different kinds of businesses or grouped by the profile of the lenders such as Christians or seniors.) No question about it—Kiva, and microlending in general—sounds like a wonderful idea to advance the plight of entrepreneurial people that find themselves in challenging surroundings.

How does Kiva actually deliver a microloan that you might make to an enterprising individual in Africa, Latin America, Eastern Europe or Southeast Asia? All loans originating through Kiva are sent to microfinance institutions (MFIs). It is these local institutions that administer the loans to people without access to traditional banking systems.

While it is difficult to find fault with the mission of Kiva, like every other business, there are causes for concern associated with Kiva's business model. For instance:

- While the profiles of borrowers posted on Kiva might seem worthy of a dose of financial assistance, they may not be ideal candidates to receive loans. They may have had little education (and therefore not understand the terms of the loan), have a history of unstable incomes and be confronted with greater risk of serious health issues. The lack of appropriate infrastructure in their countries and the instability of local governments adversely affects the ability of entrepreneurs to develop their businesses.

- Borrowers in developing countries are not immune to issues such as overborrowing that affect borrowers in developed countries. In fact, in recent years, nearly 60% of Bosnian borrowers had multiple loans, and almost 20% of these loans were more than thirty days delinquent. Of those with multiple loans, the average was 2.3 each. In situations such as these, many loans are not used to build businesses but to pay down existing loans. This is borne out by one of the Kiva groups, Late Loaning Lenders, investing solely in loans nearing expiration.

- The competition among Kiva's groups may inadvertently engender overlending in particular markets. If there is a surge in lending to sandal makers in Bangladesh, the sandal makers will flood the market for sandals and the prices will decline. Excessive lending erodes profits (by fueling competition) in developing markets just as much as it does in developed markets, causing loan repayment to become a more tenuous proposition. Banks that originate loans in Florida and Phoenix are not immune to growing irrationally quickly by offering ridiculous incentives. Neither are microfinance institutions in developing countries. For instance, SKS Microfinance, a MFI that was preparing to go public a few years ago tried to accelerate its growth by launching a massive drive to expand the number of loans it made. Prizes offered to field agents most successful in recruiting borrowers included televisions, home appliances, and bonuses geometrically higher than their annual pay.

- While there is often tension between a lender and a delinquent borrower, I have to believe that these tensions are at much greater risk of boiling over when the lender and borrower represent two distinct ethnicities. How aggressive would a Serb lender be in demanding repayment from a Croat? On the other hand, these ethnic issues may reduce loan originations as a Muslim Malaysian MFI representative might not want to facilitate loans to an ethnic Chinese Malaysian.

- Roughly half of Kiva's unpaid loans have resulted not from individual clients failing to repay, but from the partner MFI itself breaking down. The MFI may encounter adverse economic developments, be plagued with poor management, or experience external shocks such as a lack of electricity, rendering an already unreliable management information system dysfunctional. Quite often, MFIs are not the only game in town. Local black-market moneylenders do not appreciate it when a legitimate MFI rolls into town and starts offering more reasonable terms. In such situations, MFI loan officers face the real possibility of physical violence.

Before you whip out your credit card to shoot over a microloan to a deserving businessperson in a distant land, you might want to consider issues such as:

- How aggressively do the MFIs price loans to the borrowers?

- Do centralized credit bureaus exist in the destination countries so as to enable MFIs to communicate with each other regarding the creditworthiness of potential borrowers? Is there a mechanism whereby—upon the MFI detecting borrowers being overleveraged—loans can be rerouted to other eligible borrowers?

- What are the norms for debt collections in the borrower's country? What mechanisms exist for complaint resolution between the MFI and the borrower? Are threats common? Is there a risk of physical violence if the loan becomes delinquent?

- Is defaulting on a loan in a given culture the source of such shame that suicide is a real possibility for a defaulter?

- To what extent does the local government have regulations in place to govern micro-lending? Is the government sufficiently strong and corruption-free to enforce such regulations?

- How closely tailored are the loans to the needs of the borrowers? For instance, loans should be of varying durations depending on the industry addressed. Is seasonality accounted for? Do some loans include insurance that protects the entrepreneur in the event that he becomes sick or passes away?

- To what extent are the loans secured with collateral? Are critical personal assets such as one's home and motor scooter exempt from repossession? If loans are secured with assets owned by a group (of villagers) can they be repossessed if the loan goes into default?

- What is the degree of difficulty in a MFI returning the loan principal to the original lender? Are there required waiting periods for the repatriation of loan principal? Lenders to micro businesses in India must wait for at least three years before their original principal balances are returned.

- What steps are taken to ensure the privacy of client data?

Freemium Business Models

The freemium (the portmanteau for "free" and "premium") business model bifurcates customers into segments that are content with rudimentary products that they receive free of charge and another customer category that requires—and is willing to pay for—enhanced features.

Online file sharing companies such as Box and DropBox provide sound illustrations of the freemium business model. These companies provide full functionality of file storage and file sharing for free, but only up to a limited amount of bits of data stored. By the time the customer reaches this data storage threshold, they are likely very happy with the product and are inclined to pay to upgrade without too much cajoling. These premium customers also get hooked to the cloud's sticky features which make defections disruptive once one gets in the routine of collaborating with many of his business associates through an online file sharing platform.

Computer virus detection software is another service that benefits from employing the freemium business model. Companies such as Spyware Doctor allow non-paying users to detect computer viruses for free but if a virus is detected and the customer would like it removed, the customer would have to migrate to the premium group and pay for the removal.

Some providers of freemium services cover the cost of providing the free portion of their services by requiring those users to view advertisements. For instance, Spotify's free users have to listen to, or view, advertisements while its premium customers can listen to music on different platforms such as mobile without advertisements.

There are several merits of the freemium business model. Given the proliferation of competition in many industries and the complexity of various product offerings, no amount of advertising will effectively communicate a product's features. Marketing free access to a product to a wide cross-section of the population could be a good strategy if it is not known which segments of the market might be most interested in the product.

Thus, it might make more sense to provide the product gratis so that customers can experience it first-hand. Usually, app providers receive their free users' names and contact information which can be used for upselling to them later. Also, app providers can track their free users' interaction which allows the apps to pinpoint where user disengagement is occurring, which helps developers improve their apps.

> **Analytical Considerations** One impetus for app developers to offer the freemium model is that they can boast to their angel investors and venture capitalists about having attracted huge numbers of customers. I would ask promoters of the freemium model, "What is your history of converting free, or basic service, customers to premium paying users?"

App developers have devised a way to monetize their free users. In addition to charging advertisers to put ads in front of free app users, many apps generate in-app sales. These in-app sales are most common in freemium video games where they are also called free-to-play games. Free-to-play gamers are allowed to work their way through a large chunk (if not all) of a game at no charge. However, if they want to add more levels, skip long wait times until new games load, get more in-game weapons, or complete against other players in real time, they are required to pay a fee. Perhaps the best example of free-to-play games is *The Sims Social*, whose three million daily active users generated well over $50 million in revenue for Electronic Arts. I have seen statistics that indicate that in-app purchases account for 76% of Apple's App Store revenue.

Challenges and Concerns of the Freemium Model

There are several challenges and concerns associated with the freemium model. By definition, limitations must be placed on what the free users receive. If these limits are too low, people may be frustrated and not able to use the free portion of the offering. They may even vent their disappointments on social media sites. If the functionality available to free users is too generous, free users may never convert to premium customers.

Also, free users might be low quality leads who are unlikely to convert while still demanding the attention of the app provider. Even if little customer support is expended on the free customers, the app provider will still be confronted with higher data, bandwidth and hosting costs. Finally, the indiscriminate granting of free access to a product limits some of the marketing strategies that the business can pursue. For instance, there is a conflict in offering everyone access to a product while also offering free trials to premium services.

The One Dollar Effect should be taken into account by companies considering implementing a freemium model. It is easier to get customers paying one dollar a month to boost their fees to ten dollars a month than it is to get a free user to spend one dollar a month. The One Dollar Effect holds that if you can't derive one dollar per user per month, you probably will never be able to charge them anything because these customers view their relationship with the app provider as binary rather than the paying customers making an assessment of how much value they are getting for their money.

Finally, the freemium model is not appropriate when a business seeks to enforce a policy or to change behavior. For instance, if a sales manager wanted to require his sales team to aggregate all of their leads and log all of their sales calls with a salesforce management tool, using a program with limited capabilities—such as not allowing multiple people to see the same information—is not appropriate.

Massive Open Online Course (MOOCs) Operators

Success is not always a binary issue. Undoubtedly, Massive Open Online Course (MOOC) operators such as EduX and Coursera have had, and will continue to have, some success. Many of the best universities in the world—including Duke University, Yale University, Johns Hopkins University, University of Tokyo and Tel Aviv University—share selected courses through MOOCs. Coursera has generated over 22 million enrollments while EduX announced that it has more than three million users taking over 300 courses. Just as millions of people already learn a great deal from a multitude of very informative videos on YouTube, millions of people will learn a great deal from MOOCs in the years ahead. My company, the Business Development Academy, generates a nice stream of revenue by making many of its courses available via webinar to registrants all over the world.

While many people will not complete their chosen courses of study by way of distance learning, they will still learn a great deal from the lectures that they listen to via MOOCs. Such courses can be accessed without sitting for college entry examinations, completing lengthy applications or traveling. Mission-driven, just-in-time learning is valuable. A job candidate can turn to MOOCs the evening before an important interview to help formulate intelligent questions. Parents who need to brush up on algebra or European history so as to help their children with homework could find MOOCs helpful. So too, might lawyers or consultants who need to prepare for client meetings.

Market Analysis

There has been tremendous hype surrounding MOOCs. Some commentators expressed the belief that MOOCs will shake the very core of traditional education and even supplant many traditional universities. The notion that the addressable market for MOOCs is essentially boundless—prospects needing only a rudimentary understanding of English and access to a computer with an Internet connection—has been largely disproven. The big MOOC operators boast huge numbers of registrants, but registrants do not always become students and students do not always complete courses.

All politically correct pandering aside, a very small portion of the population has the intellectual capacity and perseverance to complete degrees offered by the likes of Harvard University or the Massachusetts Institute of Technology. Given that applications to top schools are almost completely composed of the most intelligent and ambitious young people in the world and that the rejection rates for New York University, Columbia University, the University of Chicago and the United States Naval Academy are notably above 90%, isn't it ridiculous to believe that essentially everyone is a prospective MOOC graduate?

In fact, most of those who enroll for MOOC courses already have college degrees as did 80% of the students enrolled in University of Michigan and University of Pennsylvania MOOCs in 2012-2013. Similar statistics hold for registrants from developing countries. Also, many distance learners fail. According to an experiment conducted at San Jose State University, in which credits towards degrees were to be issued, as many as 75% of the students failed their coursework, much worse of a showing than was the case of on-campus equivalents. Perhaps part of the reason for the dissonance between the quality of the instruction and failure rates is that world-renowned subject matter experts are accustomed to teaching the brightest students, and may not understand the motivations, academic difficulties and self-discipline of the average student. Of course, online learning makes it difficult for students to seek the assistance of the lecturers, teaching assistants and even other students.

Supplier Analysis

University courses constitute the content that MOOCs disseminate to their enrollees. While some of the most prestigious universities—such as Harvard, Princeton and the Massachusetts Institute of Technology—have signed up with MOOCs, their long-term dedication to the MOOC model is not guaranteed. These schools, and others, may just be experimenting with MOOCs.

Many senior university officials do not really understand why they are experimenting with MOOCs. Mr. E. Gordon Gee, former president of Ohio State, whose university was slated to offer a few courses from its College of Pharmacy, said he had some concerns about giving away content with no revenue stream in sight. "We're doing this in the hope and expectation that we'll be able to build a financial model, but I don't know what it is. But we can't be too far behind in an area that's growing and changing as fast as this one." Similarly, I read an interview with then Princeton University President Christopher Eisgruber in a local Princeton newspaper. It was clear that he had no idea why Princeton University was making (some of) its courses available for free via Coursera. Rather, Mr. Eisgruber made a series of vacuous statements such as, "We've jumped into the pool and we're learning how to swim."

The long-term success of an industry is questionable when its key suppliers do not know why they are doing business with companies in that industry. However, there is some legitimacy of universities taking an option on what could be a large opportunity. A company cannot identify the opportunities that await it until it enters the space. And MOOCs that generate a huge amount of traffic to their sites may find a means to monetize such traffic. (A corollary can be seen with LinkedIn which is making a lot of money from its professional recruitment tool. However, in its earlier days, LinkedIn did not know that the tremendous amount of data its users provide about themselves could be repurposed into a tool that expedites recruiters' ability to identify suitable candidates.)

Universities may be less sensitive to losing money than most enterprises because the paramount mission of universities is not to make money but rather to disseminate knowledge. Thus, embracing money losing MOOCs could still have appeal to universities. Nevertheless, MOOCs may be inimical to delivering excellence in education and this factor could retard the acceptance of MOOCs in the academic community. Taken to the extreme, there would be no need to have multiple professors lecturing on the same topic if the most accomplished professor agreed to make his lectures available to all through MOOCs. Thus, we could wind up with just one professor of Civil War History. This would not be accretive to scholarship because fecund scholarship requires that academicians share their research and spar with one another.

MOOCs claim to deliver efficiency to education. Indeed, some technologies allow professors to determine where students get stuck or lose track of lectures, thus enabling the professors to revise those parts of their lectures. I do not think such practices facilitate education. Such technologies shift too much of the onus of learning from the students to the instructor. I believe that students should apply themselves and take responsibility for their own learning (or at least take the initiative to tell the professor when they do not understand.) Further, the real generator of education is not the passive intake of crisp lectures but rather instilling in students the hunger to learn and the drive to study until subject mastery is achieved. Weaning students on edutainment should be opposed by serious educators.

Revenue Analysis

Aside from tuition, the following are among additional revenue sources that well-trafficked MOOCs might be able to tap into:

Recruiting Fees. MOOCs might be able to direct their better students to other universities in return for a recruiting fee. Similarly, MOOCs could migrate into professional recruitment, earning fees from companies that hire their students.

Certificates. MOOCs might be able to group similar courses together and charge students to receive a Certificate of Completion in a given niche discipline. However, an antilog to this strategy is provided by Smarterer. Smarterer scored individuals on some 500 digital, social, and technical skills including those associated with Excel, C++, InDesign, and WordPress. When skills were demonstrated, Smarterer issued its students digital badges which could be placed on the individuals' websites, indicating the test-taker's proficiency in the subject matter. As far as I can tell, Smarterer's "badges for proficiency" initiative has been dramatically deemphasized which portends poorly from MOOCs undertaking similar strategies.

Brokering Courses. MOOCs might be able to make money by brokering the licensing of courses from one university to another. For example, if the University of Delaware has a renowned professor of quantum mechanics but the University of Maryland has no professors in this discipline a MOOC could make money by arranging the licensing of the quantum mechanics course from the University of Delaware to the University of Maryland.

Sponsorships. MOOCs might be able to convince universities to sponsor running their courses through the MOOCs platform as doing so might be good marketing for the university.

Ancillary Services. Some MOOCs are considering charging for additional services such as providing and grading exams as well as providing tutoring services.

So, we see that it is possible that well-trafficked MOOCs can find monetization schemes. However, investors and business development professionals should place higher emphasis on what is probable versus what is possible. After all, anything is possible. Below are some of the questions and concerns that I would raise if a MOOC provider was soliciting investment from me:

- Professors spend decades researching their areas of expertise, drafting papers and polishing their lectures. Why would they agree to give their content away for free? To what extent are professors' lectures protected by copyright law? A similar question for the universities: why would they give away their core product, especially when doing so would introduce price pressure from students who are otherwise prepared to pay full freight to take live courses at the university?

- You claim to have a large number of registered users. How do you define a registered user? Can one be a registered user and not have paid any money to the MOOC? Can one be a registered user and not have completed any courses? Can one be a registered user and never have initiated any courses? What is the attrition rate of students who enroll for courses but fail to complete their courses? What is the difference between a MOOC's registered user and an Amazon customer who has never purchased anything from Amazon but has items in their Amazon shopping cart?

- These are important questions as most MOOCs have had course dropout rates exceeding 90%. These extremely high attrition rates do not surprise me because from my experience in executive education, when people do not pay for webinars, they do not value them or give them their full attention when they are running.

- What percent of a university's curriculum is most suitable for delivery via MOOC? I would think that courses that have a technical or methodical bent such as engineering and mathematics would be best suited for delivery online. In the humanities, commentary and grading are subjective, making it much more time-consuming to provide feedback to MOOC students in such disciplines. In the social sciences, a great deal of learning occurs when discussions are facilitated among the students rather than from the lecturer to the students. However, even in the hard sciences such as biology and engineering, MOOCs could inhibit critical thinking as there could be too much acceptance of information without challenge.

- MOOCs boast about attracting students from so many countries. Coursera has reported that its students hail from 196 countries. I would ask to see a breakdown of the locale of these students together with an analysis on what such students can afford to pay. At Coursera it was reported that the second and third largest contingents come from Brazil and India. As the majority of students from these countries are not likely to be able to afford the same tuition levels that North Americans and Europeans pay, MOOCs revenue opportunities from these constituencies would be limited.

- Would learning be disrupted if some students raced ahead of their classmates by listening to too many lectures at the beginning of the semester? Would teachers have to police such scenarios and restrain ambitious students?

MOOCS vs. Traditional Universities

If I was tasked with developing business for a MOOC, I would have to contend with the advantages that traditional universities offer students. Below are some related issues:

- Students spend the vast majority of their university years outside of the classroom. Thus, learning from their classmates outside of class and offline is extremely valuable. On the other hand, learning by MOOC is isolating.

- It is the selectivity of top universities that imbues their students with tremendous value. For example, being able to state that one was admitted at Harvard or attended Harvard (even for one day) will open many doors for the rest of one's life. The fact that you were able to make it through the highly discerning screening process becomes the most noticed part of your education. The fact that MOOCs are aggressive in soliciting students devalues whatever form of recognition MOOCs bestow upon their students.

- Top universities offer tremendous networking opportunities that often propel careers for decades to come. The friendships students forge at universities often remain intact for their entire lives and it is not uncommon for students to find their spouses during their university years.

- MOOCs are currently no match for universities in terms of providing career advice and placement services.

- Attending a live university provides students with experiences and memories that they will cherish their entire lives. Being accepted into a fraternity or sorority, working on campus, studying aboard for a semester, playing sports, and dating are all important parts of growing up and these phenomena cannot be experienced virtually.

- In many cases, when foreign students obtain an undergraduate degree at an American university, so doing will improve their odds of being able to work and live in the United States.

Hits Businesses

Some businesses and product launches are binary, they are either very successful or they are utter failures. Power laws are in effect in hits businesses, meaning that something like 10% of the product launches will be successful while 90% will be commercial failures. The probabilities of hits businesses, such as movies and video games, scoring two consecutive blockbuster hits are infinitesimally remote. King Digital Entertainment is struggling to find a replacement for its Candy Crush just as Zynga is facing difficulty in producing a new hit after Farmville. Many executives and investors avoid hits businesses because of their unpredictability.

Some companies in hits industries have been able to reduce the volatility of their financial results because they have grown to the point where they have large, diversified portfolios. Coty, the leader in producing celebrity branded perfumes is not reliant on marketing the fragrances associated with one or two superstars. Rather, Coty maintains the largest roster of celebrity brands, including Lady Gaga, Sarah Jessica Parker, Shania Twain, and David Beckham. Electronic Arts' financial results have become more predictable as it has become a larger company with a larger portfolio, as well as its leveraging off of its partners' brand equity through licensing agreements with the likes of the National Football League, Fédération Internationale de Football Association and Disney (for its Star Wars properties). Rovio has extended its Angry Birds brand into numerous areas by inking more than 200 licensing relationships.

> **Analytical Consideration** In assessing the revenue potential of digital games such as Candy Crush from King Digital Entertainment, one metric to apply is the percent of average monthly users that are paying customers.

The Movie Production Business

The movie business is unpredictable for two primary reasons. Audiences are fickle and the business model behind movie production is dysfunctional. Most movie studios are loose constellations of talented but pampered prima donnas (i.e., actors, directors, producers and others involved in making movies) who spend enormous amounts of time negotiating their contracts which often call for equity interests in their films as well as an exhaustive list of conveniences to be afforded during filming. No matter how much compensation they receive, the talent has no loyalty to the movie studio. These cast and crew members are overwhelmingly interested in using the current production as a springboard to advance their brands and careers. While a movie production team at a traditional movie studio may eventually reach a point of mutual respect, camaraderie, and effectiveness, the problem is that this crescendo of bonhomie is inversely related to the number of remaining shooting days.

Pixar Animation Studios demonstrates how hits business models can be rejiggered to be more predictable. Pixar eliminates the need for actors through its use of animation. At Pixar, the movie is the star, not specific members of the cast or the production team. In contrast to the traditional studios, Pixar is a tight-knit company of long-term collaborators who learn from one another and strive to improve with every production. At Pixar University, tremendous efforts are exerted to enhance the skills of everyone employed so that its professionals can direct their talents across the studio. More than 110 courses—which run the gamut from classes on painting, drawing, sculpting and creative writing—are offered and every employee is encouraged to devote up to four hours every week to their education.

Analytical Consideration Analysts should consider the extent to which movie production companies' earnings are attributable to refundable credits. Many states offer movie production companies refundable credits which reimburse companies for their investments, even if they do not owe any state taxes that year. Refundable credits, unlike transferable credits which decrease a state's tax revenues, can take money directly out of state coffers. In some cases, these credits can be sold to businesses outside of the movie industry. These incentives appear unsustainably generous and, therefore, I would not model in that a company would receive such credits long into the future.

The Logic of Casting Superstars

Notwithstanding the problems associated with featuring superstars in movies, there are legitimate reasons for movie studios to cast the most famous and expensive actors in their films. Casting a movie idol is analogous to the *Intel Inside* advertising campaign; the movie leverages off of the fame and following of the top actors from the outset. Superstars, especially those that attract teenage girls to movie theaters, since they tend to travel in cliques and often watch their favorite films multiple times, can deliver blockbuster opening weekend ticket sales. This is crucial because each weekend's winner is ensured a great deal of free publicity, due to the media's coverage of the most popular movie releases. Also, studios receive higher percentages of revenue, compared to the exhibitors, in the early weeks of a film's release.

Analytical Consideration Do not let anyone browbeat you for articulating supposedly contradictory analyses. Life is full of inconsistencies, exceptions, paradoxes and contradictions. You will be a better analyst or business development professional for accepting the complexities and nuances that are associated with business decisions. Doing so will force you to continue to monitor business model dynamics and industry developments which is much healthier than wallowing in the illusion that you have arrived at definitive conclusions. It is true that there are advantages associated with entirely replacing actors with animation and reality shows. It is also true that there is logic in casting the most expensive talent in movies. These are parallel realities, not contradictions.

Success in the first few weeks of a movie's release is determinative of its success in the aftermarkets. Since countries outside of the United States have fewer movie screens per capita, their exhibitors only want to show the films that have demonstrated the most box office success in the U.S. Movies that do not do well in theaters will find it very hard to generate revenue from DVDs and streaming and will have fewer product licensing opportunities.

Also, if studios refrain from casting the most popular actors, they risk demotivating their sales and marketing teams as well as diminished access to movie scripts from the best screenwriters. Finally, since the top actors receive a portion of their films' revenues, if their films bomb, the studios' risks are mitigated.

Music Streaming

Music streaming services such as Spotify and Pandora Media provide their members with access to enormous libraries of music streamed real time through the Internet. Streamed music relieves users of the complications of downloading, synching, storing and backing up of music files on a variety of devices, many of which are driven by non-compatible operating systems. Many music streaming companies allow their users to create several of their own channels, each of which streams a specific genre of music. Users are able to indicate their musical preferences by "Liking" or Disliking" songs (or by clicking on thumbs up or thumbs down icons) and these preferences are fed into streaming companies' algorithms, enhancing the targeting of their recommendations. Some streaming companies go a step further in trying to ensure that the right music is streamed to the right listener by pairing its algorithms with the work of experienced curators. Thus, such services provide their users with convenience at no cost or low cost.

Of course, there are shortcomings with streaming services. For instance, the audio quality can be poorer than downloads and physical media. Streamed music can be interrupted if Internet connections are dropped and expensive if the downloading of songs exceeds the data limitations stipulated in phone plans. Unless you pay for a premium service, you will probably have to listen to advertisements. Those who travel internationally may find that their music streaming service is not offered in other countries due to music licensing and advertising issues. Although Spotify allows its users to listen to the specific songs they choose without being connected to the Internet, most music streaming services restrict users' control in terms of the songs and the sequence in which they are streamed. There are even limits on how frequently listeners are allowed to skip songs. Further, as listeners do not own the music they download, their access to it ceases when their subscriptions terminate.

There are also critical concerns associated with the streaming services' business models. The issues of most potential lethality are that the libraries are excessively large and the streaming services' access to the most popular songs is in jeopardy. Xbox Music has 30 million songs in its library while Rdio, Spotify, Sony Music Unlimited, Beats Music and Google Play Music each host 20 million or more songs. One might think that these vast libraries are an attraction to listeners; they are actually a source of confusion and frustration to customers. While some of the streaming companies have developed as many of 400 channels to cater to the specific tastes of narrow selections of their customer bases, this still results in an average of 50,000 songs per channel for the companies that have 20 million songs in their libraries. Who can possibly have any interest in more than a small fraction of these pre-selected titles? The supposed virtues of serving long-tail customers have been erroneously eroticized. Rather, the entertainment business reflects power laws: most people want to listen to the most popular songs.[35] In any event, I am not surprised that some studies have concluded that more than 70% of registered accounts on streaming sites have been completely abandoned.

The second potentially fatal problem is that these sites are simply not generating enough revenue to pay the artists acceptable levels of royalties. Thus, a number of legends in the music industry (such as the Beatles) as well as popular performers such as Coldplay and Taylor Swift have decided not to distribute their music via streaming services. Some of the record labels that still have their music streamed through these sites are pressuring streaming companies to cease free-trial periods, become more aggressive in selling ads on their free services, obtain customers' credit card information sooner and redouble their efforts in terms of reducing subscriber churn rates.

Looking forward, it does not appear that streaming companies will generate enough revenue to entice the most popular performers to stream their hit songs. Of the active accounts that streaming companies have, most consist of non-paying listeners. Moreover, YouTube is causing significant damage to streaming companies as that Google-owned site hosts just about every hit song as well as millions of videos and interviews with the hottest

---

[35] According to a study by Echo Nest, four million songs on Spotify have not been listened to even once. Also, if there was such demand to listen to obscure songs, streaming companies would not have had to limit the number of times listeners can skip songs.

artists. While streaming sites enable listeners to buy the songs or albums being streamed, only a trickle of revenue is coming from such initiatives.

Analytical Consideration Music streaming companies have a variety of strategies for sourcing their songs. For instance, Spotify negotiates royalty rates with a multitude of artists, agents and record labels. Executing a different procurement strategy is Pandora Media, which obtains the rights to its library of music through the Copyright Royalty Board. Under such agreements, Pandora may play any song it wishes but must pay a per-song royalty set by the CRB.

One advantage of Pandora's procurement strategy is that it may deflect the animosity that many of the most successful artists have towards streaming companies. After all, Pandora is simply paying the royalty rates that a neutral board has determined to be equitable. On another note, one would think that since it is much more efficient to negotiate with one entity (in the case of Pandora) than to negotiate different agreements with hundreds of artists, agents and record labels (as does Spotify) that Pandora would have a much larger selection than Spotify. The reality is the reverse: as I write these pages, Spotify's music selection is roughly twenty times as vast as Pandora's. If I was considering investing in, or partnering with Pandora, I would definitely raise this issue.

Analytical Consideration SiriusXM, the satellite radio broadcaster, seems to have much less exposure to demands for higher royalty payments by performing artists than do the pure music streaming companies mentioned above. Half of Sirius's content is talk and much of that content is in the form of sports broadcasts. Using rough numbers, Sirius's royalty expenses and revenue sharing obligations have amounted to about 20% of its subscription revenues while Pandora's royalty costs have approximated 60% of its total revenues. However, this is not a true comparison because Sirius spends additional money on acquiring and producing its content, the costs of which do not come under its royalty or revenue sharing model. Making a related adjustment would have yielded Sirius a royalty-to-revenue ratio of roughly 30%, still much lower than Pandora's royalty-to-revenue ratio.

The following are among the questions that can be posed to music streaming company executives:

- How user friendly is the user interface? What is the incidence of your streaming crashing or timing out? How much bandwidth is consumed during streaming sessions?

- How easy or difficult is your selection to navigate? How many steps or clicks does a user have to make to find a song he wants to listen to?

- How many users and devices are supported for any given subscription? How many devices can stream the same music simultaneously? Are revenues being lost due to multiple family members sharing accounts?

- How many stations can users set up? How many stations can be stored for off-line play? How many attributes does the service take into account when selecting the next song? What are the credentials of the curators?

- For the non-paying customers that are required to listen to commercials, what is the ratio of advertisements to songs? Are the ads targeted to users, so at least the ads carry some relevance?

- Given that royalty remittances are such a point of contention between music streaming services and artists, how frequently are remittances distributed? What assurances can you give me that your accounting processes are robust enough to navigate the intricacies of the recording industry? (In many cases, songs are written by multiple authors and are not always registered properly.) Do the recording studios or performers have the right to audit your royalty accounting records? If so, what is the history of such audits concluding that artists have been underpaid?

- How extensive are the linkages with your streaming services and social media? Are these linkages lubricants to accretive social interaction or are they invasive?

- How is your company faring in terms of auto original equipment manufacturing installations? Success here could mean that growth in subscriber counts becomes less important since auto OEM installations should help streaming companies boost total listening hours.

e-Book Subscription Services

e-book subscription services such as Oyster and Scribd are the literary corollaries to music streaming services such as Rdio and Deezer and movie streaming services such as Netflix. For monthly membership fees of roughly $10, readers can access and read as many books as they like. These services recommend books to their readers based on their completed questionnaires or based on what others are reading.

These services face numerous obstacles. First, pricing compared to music and movie streaming services is an issue because people cannot consume as many books, compared to music and movies, per month. While the whole family can enjoy a streamed movie together, there is no practical analogy to this with e-books. Not only do e-book subscription services compete against libraries that lend their books free of charge (and can procure just about any book through inter-library loans) but they also face the Las Vegas Conundrum in that Amazon's lending library allows Kindle device owners to borrow one book a month from a collection of 500,000 books.

> **Gedankenexperiment** Let's say that you would like to determine the extent to which people are reading books from electronic readers. Maybe you are at a café or airport lounge. As you are getting your coffee, you notice that some ten people are reading from Kindles or Nooks. All of a sudden, there is an Internet outage. How many of those ten people are still reading from their dedicated e-readers? If only two are, then eighty percent of people using e-readers are doing so to access the Internet, not to read books.

Second, not only are potential royalty payments to publishers and authors scant and difficult to calculate, but such payments are not even triggered until a reader reads a large chunk of a book (maybe 20%). The problematic economics associated with e-books repel some major book publishers—such as Hachette, Macmillan and Penguin Random House—from making their titles available. Even those publishers that place their titles with e-book companies make exceptions for their newest and most popular books. Other books that contain a lot of visual elements, such as cookbooks and medical textbooks, present formatting issues that make reading e-books less effective.

Another concern with e-books is that once a reader cancels his subscription, access to the books he downloaded expires. There are privacy concerns because someone will always know what subscribers are reading. These concerns are accentuated in cases where e-book service providers pressure their readers to sync their e-book reading activities to their Facebook profiles.

The following are among the questions that can be posed to e-book service providers:

- Can readers change text sizes? Can they take notes? Can they sync up the reading of books with friends and chat about them through your service? Can they easily purchase printed and digital books through your service?

- On which platforms does your service operate? On desktops and smart phones? On dedicated e-readers and tablets? Which browsers are needed? Will it function on the Android and Apple platforms?

- How many books can be stored on such devices? How many devices can each reader use to access the books he has downloaded? Does your service allow readers to sync from one device to another? For instance, Kindle Unlimited allows users to sync their reading with audio versions of the same book. This service enables users to read a book at a coffee shop and then switch to the audio version on their drive home.

- Do the books consume memory on the selected devices? If so, how much memory does the typical book consume? How does reading books on such devices impact battery life?

The Sharing Economy

Owners of assets such as cars, boats and homes find that the sharing economy enables them to monetize their idle assets by allowing responsible people to use them for brief spans of time. On the other side of sharing transactions, renters who get used to paying inexpensive rents or are amenable to reciprocating, may come to the conclusion that it is not necessary to own similar assets.

In the sharing economy you will find people willing to rent spare rooms in their homes for short periods of time and to let strangers drive their cars. Through its matchmaking services for adults willing and able to co-parent, Family by Design enables the sharing of families. DogVacay. com facilitates the sharing of pets by matching pet-owners with pet sitters. Fon enables people to share some of their home Wi-Fi networks in exchange for receiving free Wi-Fi from any one of its 14 million Fon Spots. NeighborGoods allows its members to share everything from clothing to lawn care equipment and from power tools to sports equipment. PlugShare provides a database and maps of homeowners who welcome electric vehicle owners to charge their cars in hosts' garages. MamaBake is designed for women to cook and bake together and then divide up the prepared foods so that each bakers' family will have a variety of dishes to taste. Finally, Boatbound matches boat owners looking to make extra money with those who wish to take an occasional trip to sea but have neither boats nor the skills to handle a boat.

Nevertheless, there are a few issues to keep in mind before becoming too enamored with the sharing trend. First, it seems to me that the sharing economy is economically sensitive. Sure, when incomes are depressed, it makes lots of sense to charge strangers to stay in your house or to use your car. However, when the economy is robust such sharing may not be worth the hassle to either the asset owner or the renter.

Second, there are real risks to your physical well-being associated with allowing complete strangers to sleep in your house, ride in your car with you and to prepare your meals. All of the permutations of the sharing economy rely on a tremendous degree of trust. When you host someone in your house through Airbnb, you are at their mercy. When you turn your car into a car-sharing service with the help of Lyft, you are picking up strangers in cars that do not have security cameras or windows between the front and back seats as do commissioned taxis. (In fact, Lyft actually encourages passengers to sit up front with drivers so as to facilitate a better conversation.) When you eat food prepared by a stranger (thanks to Feastly) in a kitchen that has never been inspected, you can only hope that you will not get food poisoning. Of less but still of great consequence is that you are trusting strangers with your most valuable possessions such as your house (when using Airbnb or Roomorama), car (through RelayRides) and pets (through Rover).

It is true that substantial efforts are made to reduce these risks. Due to the popularity of social media, asset owners can take a quick gander at their prospective customers' Facebook, Twitter or LinkedIn profiles. They can get a sense as to the character and trustworthiness of potential customers by reviewing one's educational and work histories, posts and tweets, and friends and contacts. Companies such as Lyft and Airbnb require their riders and guests to be rated by previous drivers and homeowners. RelayRides initially enabled drivers to retrieve cars by swiping their membership cards through a reader that was installed on all of the participating owners' cars.

These readers were retired and now renters and owners make the handoff of the vehicle in person. All of TaskRabbit's prospective "rabbits" are interviewed and have their backgrounds screened before being logged into that database. In other cases, prospective customers must register with a credit card so that the owner is guaranteed of payment. Airbnb has established a customer service hotline that is always available. Many sharing sites provide generous insurance coverage to asset owners. Nevertheless, there are still risks with allowing strangers into your home and car.

Home Sharing

There are quite a few benefits of staying in someone's home. Since the home room rates are generally less expensive than those of hotels, you can take longer vacations. Not only are the room rates lower, but you will avoid the high costs of food in hotel districts as well as tips and maybe Internet charges. You are likely to find that homeowners are more accommodating in terms of check-in and check-out times. Frequent visitors might be allowed to store a few sets of clothes as well.

Home sharing is much better suited than hotels in enabling guests to experience different communities and cultures. There isn't much to distinguish four and five star hotels in Bangkok, Bangalore, Athens, or Santiago. They all have nice rooms and gym facilities, taxis at the ready, and friendly, English-speaking staffs. When you arrive at the breakfast hall you will see a well-appointed buffet and fellow guests that much more resemble you than the locals. However, when you stay in a neighborhood with a local, you get a much more authentic experience and have the opportunity to learn about the local scene from your host.

The revenues that homeowners derive from letting out their rooms is not just a matter of extra spending money. For those that actively market and manage their spare rooms, home sharing may mean that they can afford to purchase larger homes, build up home equity faster and pay off their mortgages sooner. The chart below illustrates that a home owner who rents out an extra 400-square-foot room for an average of 12 nights a month at an average nightly rental rate of $50 can generate $600 per month. This revenue enables the homeowner to cover a higher mortgage with $132 a month to spare. If this money if used to increase the monthly mortgage payments, 3.1 years of mortgage commitments will be extinguished.

	No Homesharing	Homesharing
Desired Square Footage	2,200	2,200
Affordable Square Footage	1,800	2,200
Cost of House (2200 sq. ft.)		$600,000
Cost of House (1800 sq. ft.)	$491,000	
Down Payment (%)	20%	20%
Amount Financed	$392,800	$480,000
Mortgage, Term	5%	5%
Mortgage, Interest Rate	30	30
Monthly Mortgage Payment	$2,108.64	$2,576.74
Size of Rentable Room	0 sq. ft.	400 sq. ft.
Average Number of Days Room Rented per Month	0	12
Average Room Rate	$0	$50
Rental Revenue	$0	$600
Rental Revenue after Excess Mortgage Coverage		$132
Reduction in Years of Mortgage Payments		3.1

The advantages of home sharing are definitely resonating with home owners and travelers. More than 25 million guests have found accommodations through Airbnb in more than 34,000 cities in over 190 countries. Cities benefit from hosting these travelers in terms of their patronage of local businesses and concurrent sales tax remittances. In some cases, cities are reliant on the home sharing concept to accommodate surges in visitors. For instance, Omaha's hotels cannot accommodate the annual pilgrimage that Berkshire Hathaway's shareholders make.

Nevertheless, let's consider the challenges that confront companies such as Airbnb and BedyCasa going forward. Travelers—especially those traveling for business reasons—may not get the same peace of mind when booking through a home sharing site that they get from booking through a reputable hotel chain. Those traveling on tight schedules or those who find travel exhausting want the comfort of knowing that when they finally arrive at their hotels, there will not be any unexpected drama. At least as per my experience, some drama can be expected when road-weary travelers arrive at vacated private homes at two in the morning.

One of my few encounters with an apartment sharing company was extremely disappointing. I booked a room through a service similar to Airbnb because all of the hotels in Chicago were full when I needed to be there. The apartment owner seemed legitimate and the building was in a nice part of Chicago. However, a few days before I was to arrive in Chicago, the owner emailed me saying that her personal situation just changed and that I could no longer use the apartment. Business and mature travelers appreciate having predictable experiences at their hotels. They also look forward to some degree of pampering—whether that be maid service, wake-up calls or help hailing taxis.

Hotels and their unionized employees are threatened by the Airbnb business model. So too are the government entities whose tourist taxes are threatened by home sharing. The reaction on the part of some city and state governments is to assess tourist taxes from renters. When home sharing companies agree to implement such taxes they are no longer threatened with related sanctions but the gap in prices for home rental rooms and hotel rooms narrows.

New York City and New York State have been very much opposed to the Airbnb business model. Such authorities have subpoenaed Airbnb on the grounds that short-term rentals orchestrated by Airbnb violate coop agreements and state hotel laws. Since hefty fines for short-term rental violations in New York City are levied against building owners (as opposed to guests or hosts who are the parties contracting the short-term rentals), building owners can be expected to oppose the Airbnb business model. In fact, some building owners hire investigators and install cameras in their buildings in attempts to dissuade their tenants from engaging in short-term rentals.

Neighbors and community leaders have legitimate concerns about home sharing. A procession of transient lodgers does present a security risk. These fleeting visitors may not be considerate to the neighbors in terms of noise, parking protocols and sanitation practices. While the homeowner may not be present during these visits, the neighbors are. And as far as I can tell, neighbors cannot rate home sharing guests. Also, some community leaders are concerned that home sharing could lead to speculative investment in buy-to-rent properties, which could create a housing bubble and squeeze local home buyers out of the market.

How can you determine if the potential of a new business model is limited to the size of the market that it most closely resembles or if the new business model's potential exceeds the size of the industry most threatened by it? In other words, is the potential market for home sharing operators like Airbnb limited to the amount of revenues collected by the hotel industry? One way to answer this question is to review pricing trends in the legacy business. If hotel room rates are declining in lockstep with the ascendency of home sharing bookings, then, yes, the potential of home sharing operators might be limited to the hotel industry's revenues. But if home sharing bookings are soaring and hotel room rates are stable or rising, then it is likely that home sharing platforms are opening up new markets and its potential exceeds the revenues generated by the hotel industry.

The following are among the questions that you might wish to ask if you are considering becoming involved with home sharing companies:

- What is the trend in companies reimbursing employees when they stay in private homes? Do employers face liabilities if they pay for home sharing and their employees are injured or assaulted in in such unlicensed facilities? Are employers concerned that they may be taken advantage of, in that, employees will inflate their expense reports and funnel money to friends and family? If employers allow some of their employees to lodge at private homes, would the employers lose their leverage in negotiating volume discounts with established hotel chains?

- Does the home sharing platform operator have sufficient insurance to cover injuries sustained by renters and damage caused by them? If renting out one's apartment or house is in violation of his lease or relevant law, can his insurance carrier refuse to cover any damage or theft caused by short-term renters?

- How do the home sharing companies' cancellation policies compare to those of the hotels?

- Are the search tools on hotel booking sites such as Hotels.com becoming more efficient in returning results for inexpensive rooms?

- To what extent are micro hotels and hostels proliferating? To what extent are micro hotels and hostels becoming more attractive than staying at private homes?

- It is my understanding that state authorities will pursue multi-unit rental owners most aggressively. Thus, what is the distribution of unit owners by numbers of units owned on your site? For instance, if owners that rent out three or more properties account for 30% of the total number of units listed on your site, I would be much more concerned than if the percentage was 3%.

Time Sharing Offices

I have wondered whether the time sharing of offices could be a viable business model. Just as homeowners benefit from generating revenue through renting out extra rooms, so too could office tenants. The terms of such arrangements should be simple because visitors would not need telephone lines and could use the office's existing WiFi network. While a good bit of work can be done in coffee shops, they have their limitations. You can't put forth your utmost concentration, do not want to conduct critical calls in public and probably feel a little guilty about cheating the proprietor out of business by squatting for extended hours. Also, some coffee shops are limiting access to seating and their WiFi networks.

Nevertheless, the time sharing of offices may violate tenants' leases and insurance policies. The security regimen to enter large buildings in business districts adds a layer of unwanted nuisance. Temporary users of the office could invite their clients and business associates for meetings, causing the tenant to lose control. These arrangements may not be necessary as travelers can work in most hotel rooms just as easily as they can from an office. Also, when travelers go to a different city they often meet several clients at their offices, greatly diminishing the appeal of going to yet another office.

On a separate but related note, there has been a great deal of excitement about WeWork and its $5 billion valuation. WeWork provides shared office space and is popular with young entrepreneurs. A key selling point to potential tenants is the idea sharing, collaboration and sense of community fostered by WeWork's open environment. WeWork tries to accelerate the success trajectory of its tenants by bringing in professionals—such as ad agency executives—willing to share their advice. WeWork also hosts demo days where its tenants can deliver informal product or roadshow pitches.

While all of this sounds well and good, a few concerns about WeWork include:

- Do the tenants have money to pay their rent? Some tenants are surely well-funded thanks to angel investors and venture capitalists. But at the beginning of every month, landlords need to collect rent from all of their tenants. Long-term tenants are preferable to itinerant ones. But the vast majority of start-ups end in failure and I would imagine that those that succeed, outgrow shared spaces. While the vibe among the tenants, who spend so much time chatting to one another, is reported to be very positive now, how will that change once some tenants are evicted?

- Sometimes businesses have to get work done. You do need quiet and solitude to think, interview candidates, write reports and development financial models. I was involved in several Internet start-ups in the late 1990s and early 2000s, and I can tell you that work environments populated predominately with twenty-somethings can get very boisterous. Even some twenty-somethings find it very unprofessional and disrespectful to blast music or bring one's dogs to the office. In such settings, it would be hard to attract tenants whose age is even one standard deviation away from the mean.

- For the first several years of its existence, WeWork was a highly secretive company. Its investors were sworn to silence. Fair enough. Secrecy is often needed to protect ideas from being usurped by competitors. Given WeWork's background, isn't it inconsistent to promote a business model that nourishes the unrestrained sharing of ideas? As if it isn't bad enough to have your concept misappropriated, patents can be invalidated if there are disputes about who conceived various ideas that are incorporated into patent claims. These inventorship disputes rise in proportion to the amount of idea sharing.

- The WeWork model will compete with incubators and accelerators. While it does not appear that WeWork requires equity from its corporate tenants, those tenants neither receive small cash infusions nor do they benefit from the haloes of the incubators' brands.

- There is a mismatch in the duration of WeWork's revenues and rental obligations. That company is locking itself into long-term leases in a period of record-high rents while charging rents for very short spans of time. A softening of demand on the part of tenants would imperil WeWork's cash flow.

- It has been reported that one of WeWork's co-founders, Adam Neumann, served in the Israeli navy for five years. (I certainly commend that. I only went through basic training.) However, service in navies requires living in very tight quarters for long periods of time. I would imagine one could go a little stir-crazy. Thus, a question that I would have is, does Mr. Neumann put an excessively high value on open spaces, given his experience living in confined surroundings?

If I were to consider collaborating with, or investing in, WeWork, I would conduct an analog/antilog analysis with Loosecubes as a comparable. Loosecubes had a vision similar to that of WeWork—and raised over $9 million from highly successful ventures capital firms such as Battery Ventures, Accel Partners and New Enterprise Associates—but shut down in late 2012.

During the Internet euphoria, companies in a wide array of industries went out of their way to associate their firms with the Internet. For instance, some ditch digging companies cast themselves as fiber-optic installation providers who played a crucial role in building out the Internet's infrastructure. Haven't companies like Regus, that enable the sharing of office space, been around for quite some time? Just asking.

Car Sharing Services

There are two permutations of car sharing services. The first permutation of car sharing services consists of car owners allowing other people to drive their cars at prearranged times. Companies such as RelayRides and Getaround connect car owners with renters, screen the renters in terms of major driving violations, secure payments and make remittances to car owners after deducting their fees. These facilitators usually do not inspect the road-worthiness of the cars rented. These quick-rent services allow car owners to boost the utilization rates of their vehicles, which otherwise stands at 8% in the U.S., Canada and Western Europe.

One of the most lethal challenges that the rapid car rental companies face relates to insurance. Some insurers have stated that they reserve the right to decline to renew policies if they find out that customers put their vehicles in car-sharing pools. While the temporary car rental service companies have provided $1 million insurance policies to their car owners over the last several years, this coverage has proven inadequate when accidents have injured multiple victims, thereby exposing vehicle owners to tremendous liabilities.

A New York state law holds that anyone driving a vehicle must be considered under a car owner's personal insurance. New York officials cited this law when they held that RelayRides was engaging in false advertising when that company told customers they would be protected by RelayRide's insurance policy if any accidents were to occur. The result of this deviation from prevailing law was that RelayRides exited from the New York market entirely. However, three states—California, Oregon and Washington—passed laws that prevent insurance companies from canceling owners' policies if they rent their vehicle on a short-term basis.

On-Demand Taxis

The second permutation of car sharing is the on-demand taxi business model. These companies provide livery/taxi service whereby prospective passengers use smart phone applications to arrange pickups at their stated locations. Companies in this space include Uber, Lyft, Hailo and Sidecar.

Driver Issues

Taxi apps offer advantages for drivers because they reduce the time drivers spend searching for fares, have a lower incidence of deadheading (for example, traveling back into city centers after making a drop in the hinterlands) and can achieve greater utilization of their cars, insurance coverage and fuel. However, in the current extremely competitive environment, the fare cuts and commissions collected by the taxi app operators make driving less lucrative. While taxi app companies do not prohibit tipping, some of them do not encourage the ritual.

Of more angst to drivers are the customer ratings systems imposed by the app companies.[36] While most drivers do not have a problem with the notion of being rated, they are concerned that they will receive poor marks for circumstances beyond their control. Customers can give even the most earnest drivers bad ratings for any reason such as bumpy rides over pothole strewn roads, traffic congestion and passengers underestimating how much time they need to reach their destinations. Miscommunication between passengers and drivers can occur because passengers cannot speak the local language, are drunk, or fall asleep and cannot direct the driver to their remote destinations. Perhaps some passengers just do not like the ethnic group to which some drivers appear to belong. Circumstances such as these are clearly the fault of passengers who may rate drivers poorly nonetheless.

Drivers with low ratings can be expelled from on-demand taxi services. This unfairness is compounded to the extent that drivers make large investments in their cars, insurance and fuel. Making drivers, who basically invested in a franchise, vulnerable to expulsion from a system because of unfair ratings seems to me to be a potential source of dissention or even litigation.

Another concern associated with the taxi app business model is that drivers only have 15 seconds to respond to notices of pick up opportunities. Drivers that fail to respond in such tight windows lose the business. Repeat failures to make timely responses can result in temporary suspensions. This pressure, and related distractions associated with interacting with handsets, is applied simultaneously with all of the challenges of navigating traffic in a variety of weather conditions. Foremost, this is a driving hazard that imperils everyone in the vicinity. It also ties in with the ratings systems because drivers are only rated on the rides they complete. Drivers who claim rides but abandon the customer if it looks like the pickup will be delayed have no ratings risk. Paradoxically, no ratings results in the worst customer service as passengers end up stranded.

---

[36] I have often thought about why taxi drivers are so unfairly disrespected. Maybe part of the reason is due to their lack of audience. When complaints about waiters in restaurants need to be made, diners typically use tact and a soft voice. When it comes time to leave a tip in a restaurant, there is an audience so patrons behave themselves. When a passenger of a taxi has a complaint or when it comes time to give a tip to a cab driver, there is no audience. Unfortunately, some passengers feel this gives them license to berate drivers as they will not bear any social costs. Maybe another reason for passengers' discourteous treatment of cab drivers is their anonymity. Chances are you will never see a given taxi driver again but people tend to frequent the same restaurants repeatedly.

Passenger Issues

Those tech savvy enough to use taxi apps benefit from the convenience. Passengers can order cabs through their phones while waiting in cafés or pre-order taxis for designated times the following day. Thus, they will not have to bother standing in the rain or heat trying to hail cabs. They will not risk getting into fights with other passengers who claim to have flagged the same cabs. While no ratings systems are perfect, they do provide passengers with the peace of mind that they are stepping into cars with safe and courteous drivers.[37] The on-demand transportation companies are more innovative than regulated taxi companies in providing services—such as discounts for frequent passengers, free rides in return for referrals, and discounting fares when groups of passengers head in the same general direction—that save customers money.

Taxi commissioners rightfully claim that the proliferation of on-demand transportation companies results in many stranded people meandering on city streets. This can be more than inconvenient; it can be downright dangerous if one is left alone in an unfamiliar neighborhood at night. Not everyone has a smart phone and not everyone wants to bother with activating apps. Not every passenger even speaks the local language. The downside of these taxi apps became apparent to me during one of my trips to Singapore. After spending the whole day in client meetings, I wanted to return to my hotel without any drama. Reminiscing of times of old, I naively thought that one can just hail a cab. Boy was I wrong! As everyone had already ordered cabs through their smart phones, there were no cabs available for hours. After a sleepless night induced by jetlag, a full day of hard work, and exposure to Singapore's high humidity, I was in a state of unadulterated agony. In this situation, should I really have been expected to start fumbling around with activating some cockamamie metrosexual app, create an account (and pray that my not having local texting service would not impede my ability to create an account), enter my credit card information (and hope that my American credit card would be accepted by a Singaporean app), and, only then order a taxi?

---

[37] Interestingly, Kenneth Arrow won the Nobel Memorial Prize in Economics in 1972 for proving that attempts to develop a perfect voting scheme are fruitless.

Regulatory Issues

Taxi drivers from San Francisco to Milan to China have staged massive protests against pre-order taxi operators. Drivers of regular taxis believe that new car service operators present a threat to their livelihoods and have unfair advantages in trying to do so in that they are skirting regulations. Taxi drivers are joined by taxi commissioners in their strident opposition to on-demand taxi services. There are legitimate concerns that passenger safety could be compromised when taxi app drivers are not rigorously vetted. Regulators want to make sure that taxi app drivers are subjected to the same screening regimens as medallion drivers which includes finger-printing, random drug tests, criminal background checks (in some cases, reaching back ten years), and physical tests (to demonstrate that drivers have the stamina necessary to drive for extended periods of time). Other points of driver evaluation include referencing criminal databases and sex offender registries as well as the monitoring of motor vehicle records.

Taxi commissioners have argued that passengers of taxi app companies lack convenient means to report errant drivers to regulators in the way there are hotlines for passengers of medallion taxis to report their complaints. Further, regulators want to ensure that taxi fares will be consistent and predictable which is contrary to some taxi app companies charging premium prices during hours of elevated demand.

In view of these concerns, and in light of traditional taxi drivers' significant investments in their medallions and automobiles, taxi commissioners have taken to battle the pre-order transportation companies on multiple fronts. For example, taxi app company Uber was forced to eliminate "Cab" from its name. Regulatory opposition to taxi app operators is rampant. Only a few illustrative data points will be provided here. They include:

- The California Public Utilities Commission issued $20,000 fines against Lyft, SideCar and Uber for "operating as passenger carriers without evidence of public liability and property damage insurance coverage" and "engaging employee-drivers without evidence of workers' compensation insurance".

- New York's black car and livery lobby sued Uber (unsuccessfully) claiming that the app would discriminate against the elderly who lack smartphones as well as six other causes of action.

- In Chicago, Uber was ordered to "cease and desist" in regards to its practice of adding 20% tips to fares.

- The Washington D.C. Taxicab Commission pushed for legislation that would have required sedan services—like the ones used by Uber—to charge at least five times more than traditional taxicabs.

- The French government said it would temporarily freeze registration of new car-service vehicles used by companies like Uber after traditional taxi drivers said Uber represented unfair competition. Penalties for operating without proper licensure in France are severe and can include two years in prison and a €300,000 fine.

- The process of licensing drivers in India is prolonged and arduous: once a fleet taxi driver has his commercial license, he undergoes a police verification process which can take three months.

- The local Seoul, South Korea government approved the equivalent of a $900 bounty for those who inform local authorities of illegal taxi services such as those run by the large taxi app companies.

- Police in Cape Town, South Africa have taken to setting up checkpoints to review the credentials of drivers. As a result, Uber's drivers lacking taxi licenses have had their cars impounded.

Business Model Portability Analysis

The two largest U.S.-based on-demand transportation companies, Lyft and Uber, are based in San Francisco, the perfect launching pad for that business model. To the extent that other cities' characteristics' deviate from those of San Francisco, the portability of progressive taxi services becomes less certain.

San Francisco resembles a custom built stage for casting unregulated livery services in the most favorable light. San Francisco has a very young and tech savvy population which generally ranks environmental stewardship above auto ownership. In other words, San Francisco boasts the ideal demographic for embracing taxi apps. The prohibitive expenses associated with parking and auto insurance renders on-demand taxi services a valuable proposition while San Francisco's hilly terrain discourages walking and bicycle riding.

Many large cities have centralized all of their public transportation offerings under one management authority, such as New York City's Metropolitan Transportation Authority. In contrast, San Francisco probably has the world's most balkanized transportation system with six or seven distinct bodies. The result of these transportation agencies having largely failed—in terms of syncing the schedules of various modes and lines of transportation as well as granting riders discounts on integrated journeys—is that end-to-end travel in San Francisco is uncoordinated. On top of that, at 8.1 miles per hour, San Francisco's light rail system, which feeds in the metro service, has the infamous distinction of being the slowest in the U.S. The problems associated with the halting tempo of parts of San Francisco's disjointed transportation network are compounded by the fact that hundreds of thousands of San Francisco's commuters are required to work on East Coast time. Those required to arrive at their offices extremely early in the morning—many of those whose jobs are tied to the opening of the New York Stock Exchange have to arrive at their desks no later than 5:30 am local time—are very receptive to alternative transportation solutions.

Interestingly, BlaBlaCar from France is another car sharing service that is enjoying success. It seems that some of BlaBlaCar's success is attributable to Europe's aging transportation infrastructure as well as the high incidence of strikes paralyzing transit in countries such as France.

Separately, there are two interesting business line extension possibilities available to on-demand transportation service providers. First, these companies are well-suited to resolve the pain experienced by parents who struggle to chauffeur their children to their extra-curricular activities. Thus, it seems to me that there is potential for companies such as Boost and Shuddle to ferry children from one activity to another. However, I would imagine that such service is only suitable for children old enough to be unaccompanied by an adult while engaging in their activities as it would be excessively expensive to pay the driver to remain with the child throughout the duration of their activities.

The second potential line extension for on-demand transportation providers is package delivery. If unregulated taxi companies delivered packages for Internet commerce companies such as Amazon, the former would be better able to utilize their vehicles and leverage their drivers' time while the latter would be relieved of building out their own fleets of delivery vehicles.

Further Analytical Queries

The following are among the questions that could be posed to executives of taxi app companies:

- Does your company pay the fines that its drivers incur? To what extent are fines issued to taxi app companies such as yours punitive?

- To what extent will local traffic authorities collaborate with software developers to produce competing taxi apps? I understand this is happening in Shanghai.

- What is your company doing to reduce the capital investments required of its drivers? Are you negotiating volume discounts on auto sales for your drivers? Is your company subsidizing automobile acquisition costs for its drivers? Is your company active in negotiating favorable auto financing terms for its drivers? Are you providing your drivers with handsets or navigation devices? At what point in your assisting drivers with issues such as these cause the drivers' status to shift from independent contractors to employees? When drivers' relationships to the company are so defined, what are the implications for managing your drivers? How will expenses for compensating drivers be affected?

- To the extent that your company assists drivers in activities such as those queried above, is your company creating a Catch-22 situation for itself and its drivers? For instance, if your company assists a driver in obtaining a vehicle at favorable prices and with favorable financing, can your company expel that driver from your network if his driving record is unsatisfactory? It would seem that if the answer is "no," then your company would knowingly retain an unsafe driver. If the answer is "yes," your company could be accused of burdening him with significant financial obligations while also barring him from the means to honor such obligations.

- What is your company's exposure with respect to many new car warranties stating that using new vehicles for livery services voids the warranties?

- What is your company's position with respect to picking up and dropping off passengers at airports?

- In certain developing markets, such as Russia, it is common for private citizens to use their cars as gypsy cabs when times are tough. As companies such as Uber and Lyft search for international markets, are gypsy cabs expeditors of growth or sources of competition?

Driverless Cars

Driverless cars, should they become a reality, could have a tremendous impact on pre-order taxi services. The impact could be extremely accretive to the earnings of these companies as expensive drivers could be eliminated. The impact of driverless cars could also prove to be catastrophic for on-demand taxi companies as they themselves could be eliminated. Nevertheless, two of the major obstacles to driverless cars displacing drivable cars are their vulnerability to hacking and political resistance as nearly three percent of the U.S. workforce—about 3.6 million people—earns its living by driving taxis, ambulances, buses, delivery trucks and other vehicles.

Municipal Bike Sharing

Municipally sanctioned bicycle sharing is a readily observable phenomenon on the streets of New York City and London and in locales as disparate as Sao Paulo, Minneapolis, Mexico City, Taipei and Paris. Riders typically use credit cards or membership keys to unlock bikes from docking stations. When riders approach their destinations, they return the bikes to the closest docking stations. Popular uses include sightseeing, commuting, running errands, exercise and even barhopping.

Bike operators that are allowed to advertise on municipal bikes stand to receive an additional revenue stream. Also, there is the prospect that the bike sharing operators can monetize the reduction in carbon emissions that they enable. For instance, CityRyde in Philadelphia calculates the emissions saved by each ride and converts those emissions savings into offsets that it can then sell on the voluntary carbon market. However, my understanding is that such revenue is currently in the neighborhood of 1¢ per mile. Given that most bicycle commuters do not ride many miles, revenues received through selling offsets on the carbon market are just not a significant revenue generator.

Despite the growing armadas of bicycle fleets, as far as I can determine, only a few of the bike sharing operators are making any money. Aside from New York City where Citicorp sponsors Citi Bike, almost every municipality has been forced to subsidize its shared bike service. For instance, from 2009 to 2013, Montreal guaranteed loans of $108 million to keep its shared bike operator afloat. Toronto's city council canceled its community bike program. The prospect of continued municipal bailouts of bike sharing operators is not palatable to many politicians: less wealthy people who live on the periphery of large cities would have to contribute to such bailouts which would only benefit wealthier city dwellers.

It seems to me that if the bike sharing business model is failing everywhere it is attempted, that is all anyone interested in investing in this space needs to know. Nevertheless, below is a discussion of some of the challenges that operators of municipal bicycle fleets face.

Municipal bicycling is not suitable for all cities. Some parts of the world—such as Scandinavia and the Benelux countries—are already saturated with bicycles. In other parts of the world, such as India and Africa, the roads are in such disrepair and so rife with homicidal driving behavior that bike sharing programs would have little chance of success. Cities that have hilly terrain, such as San Francisco and Rome, are less likely to generate to sufficient demand. Very humid cities—such as Singapore and Miami—are not-well suited to bike sharing programs because bike riders there perspire profusely even when riding short distances. Bike sharing programs are unlikely to work where there is a high occurrence of thefts or vandalism of bicycles, which are additional reasons that bike sharing has not been successful in Rome.

Cities that have extremely high levels of vehicle ownership—as measured by registered vehicles per 1,000 inhabitants—are unlikely to persuade enough vehicle owners to switch to riding bicycles to make a noticeable shift in commuters' behavior. The broader sharing economy intersects with municipal bike sharing in that companies such as Liquid (formerly known as Spinlister) provide rental bikes from many neighborhoods. This raises another question: If bike shop owners see that there is growing demand for bike rentals, what is to stop them from becoming more aggressive in promoting their rental programs? Also, wouldn't those most likely to ride bicycles most frequently buy bikes instead of renting them?

The following are among the questions I would ask if I were researching a municipal bike operator's chances of success of moving into a new city:

- What is your exposure to paying the city for lost parking revenue? Cities that rely on metered parking fees and parking tickets to fund municipal operations are concerned that bike racks compete for metered parking spaces. It is my understanding that Alta Bicycles, the operator of Citi Bike in New York City, is contractually required to pay for lost parking revenue.

- To what extent are you required to rebalance your portfolio of bicycles each day or throughout the day? Rebalancing is the expensive process of moving some of the parked bikes from full bike racks to bike racks that are largely empty. Why is rebalancing sometimes necessary? Well, commuters like to ride municipal bikes to work. Thus, bike racks in the neighborhoods quickly become depleted early in the morning causing the bike racks in the business districts to reach capacity shortly thereafter. People wishing to ride bikes to work but who can't find any bikes remaining at docking stations become frustrated. So too do those who can't dock their bikes when they arrive at work. This scenario is anathema to most people preferring predictable routines in the morning as opposed to the drama of not knowing how they will arrive at the office.

- What are your expectations with respect to the frequency of bicycles being in disrepair or bike docks malfunctioning? What are your contractual obligations with respect to making related inspections and repairs? Is your company required to keep the docking stations free of litter and leaves?

- What is the ratio of annual dues to daily or weekly passes? Daily passes are much more profitable because daily users may pay $9.95 while annual pass holders pay $95 a year.

- Are there sufficient bike lanes in the city to make the bicycle usage safe and efficient?

- To what extent will the city in which you operate allow bicyclists to take their rental bikes on to public transportation such as buses, trains, subways and ferries?

- Are sharing bike riders required to carry insurance? Would an accident between a car driver and a bicyclist result in the driver having to pay no matter how reckless the bicyclist behaved?

- How many potential rental riders would be dissuaded by not being able to adjust the seat and handlebars?

- To what extent do employers offer their employees shower facilities in the new city?

Freelance Platform Operators

Through their websites, freelance platform operators such as Elance, Freelancer and Guru.com connect people that have work that needs to get done with people looking for short-term assignments. Freelance sites typically make commissions on the fees paid to the freelancers. Some freelance operators derive revenue by charging their clients fees to list jobs.

There is merit in the premise behind such business models: these sites remove the bureaucracy and associated legal liabilities with hiring full-time employees. Paying people through freelance platforms can be accomplished with the ease of swiping a credit card which compares very favorably to having to pay a payroll provider to navigate multi-tiered, byzantine employment laws. If the employer is dissatisfied with a freelancer's performance, termination can be immediate and is virtually risk-free.

Further, some freelance sites offer a slew of related services. For instance, TaskRabbit is charging extra fees for allowing employers to browse candidate profiles and reviews by previous employers as well as to chat online with prospects. That company can file W2 tax forms and provides workers' compensation and unemployment insurance. TaskRabbit also launched a portal to offer its independent contractors discounts on health care, cell phones and other tools they need to perform their tasks.

However, as mentioned earlier in this book, there is a natural inclination on the part of players on both sides of brokered transactions to circumvent the platform operator so as to avoid paying commissions. Also, network effects are in operation here. For each category of positions and projects, there is only room for one or two dominant freelance platform operators because there needs to be a deep well of available projects and a deep well of candidates to complete such projects. Since a large number of projects are crucial for attracting a large number of candidates, it will be difficult to assess monthly listing fees because these fees will discourage the listing of projects.

Despite the general appeal of freelance sites, the following are among the concerns associated with them:

- There may be a large disparity between the number of projects listed and projects completed. The number of projects completed is the important number as this is what triggers commissions.

- The best candidates often do not like to participate in auctions as they find the price competition to be demeaning. Further, it is natural for freelancers to become discouraged when they pitch their services for several jobs and are not only not selected, but receive no response from the client. Thus, many of the freelancers listed on such sites may be inactive. To address these issues, TaskRabbit is shifting from an auction model to automated algorithms that match workers with people requesting household services.

- The auction, price-based nature of freelance sites militates towards reduced payment levels for advisors and thus lower commission levels for the freelance site operators. For instance, Fivr was posting jobs for an average fee of $5. However, some sites are taking steps to counter price-based competition. Elance discourages people from lowballing, so if bidders go 30% below the client's stated budget, they are blocked. Elance tracks how often freelancers use pricing as a strategy to win work. If they do it too frequently, they get penalized over time on the Elance reputation system.

- The higher the value of the listed project, the more difficult these projects are to define. Very nuanced projects are extremely difficult to scope without having some conversations or meetings. Of course, language barriers can exacerbate communications problems. These issues give rise to disputes. Thus, we should ask about the incidence of disputes as well as the dispute resolution mechanisms maintained by freelance platform operators.

- Freelance sites may face more competition from review/referral sites such as Angie's List as these sites are becoming more active in collecting fees for services that result from these sites' reviews.

Payback on Debt Analysis

Freelance platform operators must generate significant volumes of commissionable projects in order to cover their operating costs as well as meet creditors' covenants. Let us suppose that a freelance platform operator borrowed $15 million to launch its operations. The terms for the loan are 8% annual interest and the duration of the loan is 10 years. Just to pay the interest on such loans, the site operator would have to generate revenues of $1.2 million annually. To pay the interest and principal, the site operator would have to generate free cash flow in excess of $2.2 million. In this abbreviated analysis, operational costs like wages are not taken into consideration.

Let's further assume that the freelance site operator has an average project size of $1,000 and for the projects that are completed without disputes, the commission rate is 8.75%. Given these assumptions, the freelance operator would need more than 25,000 projects to close every year, or more than 2,000 projects per month. Of course, this exercise assumes that the company is financed with relatively inexpensive bank debt. More likely, such a company would be financed with venture capital and the return expectations would be much higher.

Hypothetical Freelance Operator	
Loan Amount	$15,000,000
Annual Interest Rate	8%
Loan Term (years)	10
Average Project Size	$1,000
Commission Rate	8.75%
Commissions per Project	$87.50
Annual Payments	
Interest Payments	$1,200,000
Principal and Interest	$2,235,442
Repayment Requirements	
Number of Projects Needed (per year)	25,548
Number of Projects Needed (per month)	2,129

Questions to Ask When assessing one particular freelance platform operator over another, the following are among the questions that can be posed:

- What processes does your site have in place to assess the legitimacy of its project listings before they are posted? Does your site administer tests to freelancers, or by other means conduct verification, to ensure that the freelancers possess the skills they claim they have?

- How many skills classifications does your site feature? How has your site's search engine been optimized to help clients and freelances find one another? Does your site have a recommendation engine to direct clients to qualified freelancers and vice-versa? If the client needs a team of freelancers to work on a large project, how would your site address such needs?

- What tools—such as video conferencing, instant messaging and document sharing—does your site make available to facilitate collaboration between freelancers and clients?

- What assurances can your site make to clients in terms of their proprietary information not being misappropriated?

- At what point in time is the site operator's commission triggered? When an agreement between the client and site operator is reached? When funds are remitted? Is the freelancer still required to pay a commission if an agreement is in place and monies have been received by the site operator, but then the project is suddenly cancelled before any work has been done?

- How are the monies in freelancers' accounts managed? Are these funds a source of working capital for the freelance site operator? Does the freelancer receive any interest on such monies? Are freelancers required to maintain minimum levels of cash in their accounts, perhaps as a form of escrow in case there are problems collecting commissionable fees from clients? Are freelancers' accounts frozen if there is a dispute with a client or if the client has not remitted payment? If so, and there is a dispute, is the entire balance of the freelancers' account frozen or only to the extent of the dispute?

Cloud Storage

While there is no definitive definition of cloud storage, it is generally accepted that cloud storage entails storing data in virtual servers over the Internet. Like other forms of utility computing, cloud storage provides the means to dynamically modulate capacity and capabilities without investing in new infrastructure, training new personnel, or licensing new software. The subscription payment plans associated with cloud storage enable users to avoid upfront costs associated with buying servers and other networking equipment while only paying for the computing capacity that the company needs. The ability to dial up computing capacity when companies are scaling up operations or to dial down capacity when users are downsizing means that cloud storage clients have minimal stranded costs.

While there is a great deal of excitement surrounding cloud storage, the following are among the concerns that clients and investors should be aware of when reviewing cloud storage providers:

- Will small companies be able to fully utilize cloud storage? Some small companies may not have sufficiently robust bandwidth which is needed for broad upload capability. This concern could be exacerbated when one wishes to get information on an array of mobile devices.

- To what extent will enterprises be able to eliminate onsite information technology staff if they transfer to cloud storage? In some cases, even when an enterprise uses cloud storage, onsite information technology support will be needed as IT professionals will need to know where the data resides on the cloud. They may also be called upon to decrypt information on the cloud.

- What are the risks that customers will determine that they are overpaying for cloud computing and therefore demand price or capacity concessions? A closer examination of cloud computing services rendered may reveal that clients are receiving more computing power than they need—for instance, servers assigned to the client are more powerful than necessary—or that computer tasks are left running unsupervised by the client.

- How secure are clouds? How much security software and other software will be needed to run local machines on the cloud? Are all of the files stored on the cloud automatically encrypted? Does the cloud host guarantee that no viruses or malware will be streamed from the cloud to its customers' computers? If so, how broadly or narrowly does the cloud host define such terms (e.g. "viruses" or "malware"). To what extent can customers (or third parties) conduct security audits or at least review cloud hosts' security policies? Are cloud hosts invulnerable to power outages? Natural disasters? Hackers? Bankruptcy?

- Will sufficient privacy protections be put in place? Will the cloud hosting company mine its customers' data for its own marketing purposes? Will they sell clients' data to third-party advertisers? At the time of my writing this section, cloud companies state that customers should have no expectation of privacy or that the cloud companies will protect clients' trade secrets. For this reason, some companies such as Ford Motor Company and the law firm Nixon Peabody do not allow their employees to use cloud services.

- To what extent will customers be trapped in the cloud due to restrictions on transferring their data to other cloud providers?

- Many large companies have gone to great expense to customize their companies' enterprise resource planning (ERP) systems to run in their corporate data centers. Such customization is not just a matter of convenience or competitive advantage for companies. Rather, such efforts have been expended in order to remain compliant with critical prevailing regulations such as Sarbanes Oxley or the Affordable Care Act. How readily will these companies migrate to the cloud?

- Given that many companies forbid placing their proprietary information on clouds and in view of a great deal of highly valued corporate information residing on ERP systems, how likely is it that companies will want to have some of their data in corporate data centers and other data on the cloud? This concern may be compounded by the fact that some servers that constitute the cloud may be in different countries where espionage and the misappropriation of trade secrets are at an elevated risk. Thus, analysts should be careful about projecting high levels of wallet share and organic growth within existing client bases.

- What is the risk of having the monthly charges for cloud storage placed on corporate credit cards? One concern is that the true cost of cloud storage may be hidden outside of corporate budgets. Another issue is that when the holder of the corporate credit card tied to a cloud account leaves the company, the company's subscription to the cloud may be jeopardized.

- What are the cloud provider's policies with respect to data retention for legally required purposes, such as litigation e-discovery or preservation of evidence upon law enforcement request? If a subpoena needs to be served to a cloud provider that operates server farms in a multitude of countries, where should the subpoena be served? How long will cloud providers hold on to data after a contract ends? Are longer retention periods more or less desirable than shorter retention periods?

- Can large corporate customers dictate the technology that is used to store their data? To what extent can customers configure their cloud environment?

- How much of a large company's existing IT infrastructure would have to be replaced in order to make the system compatible on the cloud?

- How is the customer experience affected by conflicting architectures among the cloud storage companies? For instance, some companies such as Dropbox embrace open architecture while Apple's iCloud is a closed ecosystem. Does the cloud storage service provider facilitate retrieving data onto smartphones and tablets?

- How stable is pricing in the cloud business? Investors should be concerned about price wars. For instance, in March 2014, Amazon,

Google, and Microsoft announced price cuts in the 30% to 80% range. According to Amazon, that was the 42nd price reduction for the Amazon Web Services division. On the other hand, of concern to customers might be the risk of aggressive price hikes when the cloud services companies realize that their customers are locked in.

- How will the Aero ruling impact cloud storage companies? It is my understanding that this ruling means that cloud companies could be liable for copyright infringement if they enable the unauthorized rebroadcasting of (video) content from their servers. Dropbox had to adjust its Terms of Service to comply with the Digital Millennium Copyright Act, which establishes a notification-and-takedown system for addressing claims of copyright infringement.

- Countries around the world, from Brazil to Russia, have indicated that they may require companies domiciled in their jurisdictions to have their data stored on servers within their borders. If such policies are enforced, how will cloud storage companies ensure privacy? What operational difficulties might arise?

Gamification

Before we broach gamification, let's consider how peer-pressure—or at least the desire not to rank poorly within one's community—affects behavior. Paul Green was disappointed with the lack of motivation of his students to practice their musical instruments. Then he came up with the idea of getting some of his students to start playing together in a rock band's rehearsal space. Paul Green's students were embarrassed to play badly in front of each other. He found that peer pressure caused his students to rehearse more often, which improved their performance. Their progress persuaded him to open his own for-profit School of Rock music studio so that all of his students could rehearse with each other and then put on live performances for parents and friends.

Okay. Now back to the subject at hand. Gamification. Gamification is the use of contests by companies and other organizations to elicit the customer and employee behavior that the game sponsor seeks. Players are typically rewarded the more they participate as defined by website visits, posting of comments, or purchases of products. Such actions are often acknowledged by awarding points, badges, and elevated levels on leaderboards but the primary driver of behavior is the social acceptance and recognition that is conferred upon participants. Perhaps the best way to understand gamification is by example, three of which are provided below:

- Nike, of course, wants to sell more running shoes. One way to do that is to encourage people to run more miles with the result being that their shoes will need to be replaced at a faster clip. Gamification has proven to be a catalyst for running more miles. The Nike+ initiative facilitates the tracking, sharing and comparing of running sessions on an individual as well as group basis. The way this works is that Nike+ training shoes come with embedded sensors which capture movement and performance information. Nike's proprietary algorithms use this information to calculate statistics such as how far the wearer has run. These statistics are then synced directly to the Nike+ Training app on mobile devices using Bluetooth technology. Now that runners can log their miles they can push themselves and fellow group members to run more miles.

- Re-Mission 2 is a game designed to help children fight cancer. It can be played on both computers and smartphones. Each free Re-Mission 2 game depicts different ways of fighting or treating cancer. For example, "Nanobot's Revenge" lets players protect lungs and blood vessels from tumor-building baddies by shooting them with Radiation Beams while "Nano Dropbot" involves dropping Chemo Bombs on cancer cells while rescuing healthy tissue. Studies have found that patients who play games designed to fight disease such as Re-Mission are more likely to comply with treatment, including taking medications regularly and understanding how their own behaviors could impact their treatment.

- Cold Stone Creamery, the chain of ice cream parlors, uses a game it developed called Stone City to help new employees learn about portion control, waste, and overall profitability. Rather than its employees considering the dishing out of a slightly excessive scoop of ice cream as a small, one-time event, the game shows the implications of that scoop if it were replicated across the entire enterprise. Suddenly, employees understand that a ten-cent mistake could mean a ten-thousand dollar expense for the chain.

- The Israeli government initiated a program whereby that country's supporters would be elevated in virtual military rank in accordance with their efforts to defend Israel in the media. For instance, someone who only "Liked" a positive article about Israel on Facebook might be designated a private while the author of the article might be designated a colonel.

Companies such as Badgeville, Bunchball, Gamify, and Igloo Software that build gamification platforms are well-positioned to provide their clients with the tools to increase workforce productivity as well as generate more customer engagement.

▌Smart Homes

The promise of smart homes is that most electronics in the home will be preset and controllable from computers or smart phones. When you open up the garage door, your front door will unlock and your kitchen lights will turn on. When your alarm clock rings, your coffee pot will begin percolating. If your son forgets his house keys, you will be able to unlock the door but will prevent the television from turning on until 6:00 pm, giving him time to complete his homework.

Does this sound like the wave of the future or an unnecessary annoyance?

Sure, technology enthusiasts will welcome the opportunity to gadgetize their homes. Many other home owners will surely embrace dedicated services such as video monitoring so that they can keep an eye on their contractors and observe the babysitter's treatment of their children. Owners of two homes may find it worthwhile to invest in video monitors or leak detection and alerting systems which could act as valuable safeguards on maintaining a second home.

Before investing in any provider of smart home technology, I would be interested to hear such providers' responses to the following concerns:

- For most people, their homes serve as their refuge from the constant bombardment of technology. Home is the place where people most want to tune out, zone out and take a time out. Smart Homes render living at home more complicated. Instead of just turning a light on or off, Smart Homes could require us to boot up computers, activate apps, enter passwords and type in commands.

- Setting up a smart home is costly in terms of money and time. The majority of homeowners will not relish the efforts required to synchronize and manage their homes. They will especially not have patience when the inevitable technological glitches rear their heads. They will not want to acquaint themselves with switches, dimmers, keypads, wiring, junction boxes, and surge protectors. If these components were not intimidating enough, they would have to address the interoperability of components based on different technologies such as Insteon, Wi-Fi, Bluetooth, ZigBee, Z-Wave and earlier proprietary technologies. Homeowners will have to make sure they are not overloading their house's electrical capacity. Many homeowners may come to the conclusion that the complexity of managing every light switch and gadget in the home will outweigh any conveniences Smart Homes (even when they are functioning as advertised) may provide.

- The roll-out of Smart Homes is hindered by the issue of veto power. All family members want the flexibility to turn lights on or off, adjust the volume on television sets and remove food from the refrigerator at their convenience. When performing these basic functions, they do not want to have to go through the trouble of overriding a centrally controlled house that was programmed by one family member.

- Do people really want to become vulnerable to hackers, the inability to control their homes, or invasions of their privacy? Your house could begin going haywire if you forgot your password to your computer or if your phone fell into the wrong hands. Just think of the damage that hackers could inflict if they infiltrated your smart home. They could unlock your doors, disrupt power to your refrigerator, ratchet up the heat, take inappropriate pictures of your family members, and make it impossible for you to turn off your stove.

- To the extent Smart Home data is stored, will it be subject to subpoena if charges of law breaking are made? AT&T alone already reportedly receives 700 such requests every day. Such requests are also being made in the context of civil disputes such as divorce.

- I do not know all of Google's intentions with its acquisition of Nest Labs. However, it is within the realm of possibility that very large technology companies will learn what you eat, what you watch on television, how long you shower on average and what time you go to bed. At a minimum, this would be an invasion of privacy and could result in you receiving unrelenting targeted advertisements. For instance, if you remove the last carton of Dannon yogurt from your refrigerator, you could receive an advertisement from Yoplait yogurt asking you to give its brand a try. Ads could start showing up all over your house such as on digital clocks and on refrigerator panels. In fact, Google has already declared to the Securities and Exchange Commission that it plans to deliver ads to thermostats and other connected devices.

Vehicle-to-Vehicle Crash Avoidance Systems

This seems to be an apropos place to say a few words about vehicle-to-vehicle crash avoidance systems because some of the related concerns parallel those of smart homes. First, auto owners do not want all of their activities (such as driving destinations and speeds) digitized and reported to repositories, especially as some of this information could be collected by the police, insurance agencies or marketing companies. Second, these systems cannot escape the lethal risks of viruses and cyber-assault. Third, auto makers want to avoid getting sued if passengers riding in a vehicle equipped with crash-avoidance technology nonetheless suffer injuries in a collision. Fourth, dedicated vehicle-to-vehicle crash avoidance systems may be less necessary as smartphone applications like Waze are already providing much of the functionality promised by vehicle-to-vehicle communications. Finally, automakers may be wary of such systems as they do not want to cede—to Internet or telecom companies—their already tenuous relationships with customers.

Electric Vehicles

There is certainly a great deal of excitement over electric vehicles. Many consumers are attracted to the generous government incentives available for electric vehicle purchases as well as the reduced ownership costs. Instead of fueling up with expensive gasoline, electric vehicle owners can recharge their autos by plugging into the much-less-costly electric grid. Fully-electric vehicles do not use oil to lubricate their engines, thereby eliminating the need for oil changes. Because of fewer moving parts in electric vehicles, engine maintenance costs are lower than owning a vehicle powered by an internal combustion engine. Since brakes will not wear out as quickly, replacing brake pads in electric vehicles will be less frequent.

Electric vehicles offer quiet and smooth rides and, due to high torque, electric vehicles enable rapid acceleration. At least in terms of actual driving, electric vehicles cause less pollution than vehicles powered with internal combustion engines as the former have no tailpipes from which exhaust can be emitted. Further, electric vehicles are becoming increasingly mainstream as they are available in an ever wider array of price points and performance ranges.

Challenges for Electric Vehicles

Of course, there are obstacles to electric vehicles taking market share from gasoline powered vehicles. One of these challenges is the high upfront costs of electric vehicles, government subsidies notwithstanding. Another is range anxiety, which is the tension that knowing that you can only drive a limited distance before recharging. Since recharging stations are not as readily available as gas stations and since recharging takes notably longer than injecting gas into a car, long-distance trips are not practical. While electric vehicles' limited (but increasing) driving ranges are sufficient for large swaths of the population, range anxiety is more acute when there is inclement weather, when traveling to remote or dangerous destinations, and if the passengers are children or elderly people. Also, when assessing the entire supply chain involved with producing electric vehicles, the environmental impact of electric vehicles versus internal combustion vehicles becomes more difficult to determine.

The following are among the questions that could be posed when trying to assess the prospects for electric car manufacturers such as Tesla Motors:

- On average, how large are the income tax credits that states/countries provide for electric-car purchases? Are these subsidies so large that they are at risk of being politically unsupportable, and therefore, phased out?

- How expensive is local electricity? What is the off-peak rate, during which time much recharging will occur? The less expensive off-peak electricity is, the more quickly electric vehicles will be adapted.

- How expensive is gasoline and how quickly are regular cars increasing their fuel efficiency? The less expensive gasoline is and greater fuel efficiency offered by regular cars, the less compelling electric vehicles become.

- What percent of anticipated buyers of electric vehicles will park their cars in garages of homes they own? Landlords will not welcome the higher electricity bills triggered by tenants recharging their cars. Further, property managers are likely to put up some resistance to the charging of electric vehicles on their premises due to both higher electric bills and the risks of power surges. While most western electric vehicle owners own homes, the same is not true in promising markets such as China. Even wealthy city dwellers in large western cities, who own apartments, often park their cars on the streets. Where are they supposed to recharge their electric vehicles?

- Are local companies big supporters of electric vehicles? If so, employee purchasing groups might be able to organize the purchase of electric vehicles at volume discounts through their companies. Are employers assigning preferred parking spaces to electric cars? To what extent are employers facilitating the recharging of electric cars? This is an important issue as cars parked at work remain idle for many off-peak hours each day, which are ideal times for recharging. However, the Icarus Paradox might be at play here. Electric vehicles have become so popular in Orange County, California that public charging stations there are overwhelmed to such an extent that tickets are being issued to owners of cars that recharge for more than two consecutive hours.

- What are the trends in electric vehicles' selling prices, costs of producing batteries, driving ranges and refueling times?

- Will any new taxes be placed on electric vehicles that parallel gasoline taxes? If not, how will the nation's roads be maintained if electric vehicles displace regular vehicles?

- What are the risks of electric vehicle batteries igniting? What disclosures must manufacturers of electric vehicles make in this regard? What implications does this issue have for the owners' insurance premiums and coverage? What is the trend in fire departments having policies of not extinguishing electric vehicle fires, but instead just preventing collateral damage?

- What is a reasonable expectation for the longevity of an electric vehicle, in terms of miles driven and years on the road? What is a reasonable expectation for the longevity of batteries in electric vehicles, in terms of miles driven and years on the road? If the battery wears out before the car, isn't it prohibitively expensive to replace the battery?

- What percent of electric vehicle owners purchase another electric vehicle when they retire their cars? What percent return to driving internal combustion engine vehicles?

- Is it true that the standards for certifying electric vehicles for use on public roads are lower than for internal combustion engine cars? Is it true that electric vehicles are given exemptions in terms of crash safety requirements? If so, why are the standards lower for electric vehicles? What would be the ramifications if electric vehicles had to meet the elevated standards of regular cars?

- To what extent could electric cars impede public transportation? For instance, electric cars have access to bus lanes, which bus drivers find to be a source of interference. At what point will such preferred access be rescinded?

- To what extent are auto garages equipped to service and repair electric vehicles? If electric vehicles cannot be serviced at auto shops, they will have to be taken to dealerships where service costs are typically higher.

- How well does battery power scale in terms of the size of the vehicle that it powers? Would batteries be suitable in SUVs? Aren't medium and heavy-duty fleets repelled from buying electric vehicles because battery costs are absolutely prohibitive on larger vehicles?

- Will electric vehicles be more or less compelling than regular cars to pre-order taxi services such as Uber, Hailo and Lyft?

- Will electric vehicles be more or less compelling than regular cars to pioneers in car sharing services such as Relay Rides, Getaround and Community CarShare?

- Will electric vehicles be more or less compelling than regular cars to developers, such as Google, of driverless cars?

Tesla Motors

Tesla Motors is the purest play on electric vehicles. However, producing electric vehicles is fraught with challenges. Even Warren Buffett has experienced significant difficulties with Berkshire Hathaway's investment in BYD, a Chinese manufacturer of electric vehicles. The following are among the questions that can be posed to Tesla's management:

- What percent of the purchase price of Tesla's cars are subsidized by government entities?

- To what extent are Tesla's revenues in the form of pollution credits that it sells to other auto makers? Won't these revenues decline as the larger auto makers become more aggressive in producing electric vehicles?

- As discussed earlier in this book, Tesla has had difficulties establishing company-owned sales outlets in a variety of states. Thus, I would inquire about Tesla's distribution strategy.

- How heavy are Tesla's batteries? Do Tesla's batteries degrade the longer they are in use after a charge? Do the batteries become lighter as they dissipate? How much space do they require?

- What disposability issues exist with respect to the batteries? How toxic are the batteries?

- In connection with its customer guarantees, has Tesla accrued sufficient reserves to fund the replacement of batteries in its cars ten years post sale?

- What is Tesla's exposure to its guaranteeing residual values on its cars that are leased to customers? If these guarantees are high—which is likely since generous guarantees make its cars more affordable—Tesla could be compelled to pay its customers the difference between its guaranteed prices and the market prices when such leases expire.

> **Analytical Consideration** The issue of valence is important in considering Tesla's customers' satisfaction. Ratings of new owners are misleading as they are almost invariably delighted with their cars. But these ratings are not what prospective car buyers are concerned about. Rather, they want to know how satisfied car owners are three to six years into owning their vehicles. Since Tesla's cars are so new, these higher valence ratings are not available so no one knows how satisfied new electric vehicle owners will be after the new car smell wears off.

Drones

Drones were legalized in Japan, Australia and Mexico several decades ago. Today, drones are being used in a wide array of applications, even in the United States where they are largely illegal. The Germans use drones to deliver medication and drones are suitable for delivering emergency supplies during snowstorms, tornadoes and floods. The Chinese use drones to transport cakes and, by mounting infrared cameras, to monitor and collect data on industrial polluters. Companies such as Precision Hawk, Snaproll Media and SZ DJI Technology use drones to film movies, inspect homes and monitor crops. The chase in the 2012 James Bond film "Skyfall" used drones to capture 007 racing across the rooftops of Istanbul. Drones can be used to pursue a car that flees an accident and to spot cattle that have escaped from a ranch. Drones are being used for vanity purposes: Those who snap pictures of themselves from drones produce "dronies".

Drones are not only used for commercial, civil works and humanitarian purposes. Drones could be harnessed by those wishing to spy on spouses suspected of infidelity. During the 2014 World Cup, French players complained that a drone-borne camera spied on their training sessions. As the price of drone service plunges, drones could be used for carpet-bombing junk mail (in the form of newspapers) throughout a neighborhood.

Drones are becoming the preferred method of assassinating suspected terrorists. One advantage that drones have over jets in such missions is that they are able to hover over a target for days at a time. Hundreds of thousands of gallons of jet fuel would be burned if a procession of jets had to maintain positions in the skies for such extended periods of time. Drones are also more versatile than jets as drone operators can easily make mid-flight changes to a drone-fired missile's trajectory. Further, drones are easy to maintain as they are essentially powered by high-performance snowmobile engines.

The following are among the questions that could be posed to executives in the drone industry in an attempt to ascertain the potential of drones:

- What kind of licensing will be required of drone operators? What level of training will be necessary to secure such licensing? Will drone operators have to obtain pilot's licenses? If so, how many hours of flying manned aircraft will be required to operate drones? How frequently will recertification be required? What kinds of insurance will companies have to take for their drone operators? Will drone operators have to undergo frequent alcohol testing? What will be the allowed ratio of operators to drones? Will drones be required to remain within sight of the operator? How will such regulations vary depending on whether the use of the drones is for recreational or commercial purposes?

- Will the operation of drones be limited to certain hours of the day or to daytime hours? Will drones be limited to a certain number of vertical feet?

- What precautions are being adopted by the drone industry to minimize the incidence of flyaways (which occur when people lose control of their drones, often due to wind currents, software glitches, bad Global Positioning System data and lost connections to controllers)? What precautions are in place so that the drone will not wander into restricted air space such as airports or flight paths or violate no-trespassing ordinances with respect to private property?

- Will people on the ground be afraid of drones and oppose drones flying in their airspace?

- What is the level of difficulty for individuals to weaponize drones?

- In the military, what is the level of status, prestige and respect that is accorded to drone operators? Are they considered to be inferior to fighter pilots or are they held in high esteem because they are controlling cutting-edge technologies?

- Is the newness and fear of drones a liability? If there is a mishap with drones, will entire fleets, or models, of drones be grounded? It seems to me that if a drone collided with an airplane or injured a pedestrian, there would be a significant risk of many drones being grounded. Such reaction would be disproportionate to the practice with respect to errant delivery trucks. When a delivery truck causes an accident, there is no risk of the delivery company's entire fleet of trucks being grounded. Even vehicles subject to recall can still be driven. In any event, to the extent such risks exist, the value proposition of relying on fleets of drones diminishes.

Drone Deliveries

Drone deliveries could be a perfectly fine solution for industrial zones. When one factory is in need of a part from a supplier a few miles away, a drone delivery could be highly efficient. These areas often have congested roads and most of the logistical issues (see below) associated with residential deliveries are absent.

However, retail deliveries could be much more problematic. For instance, Amazon's warehouse strategy has been to put its fulfillment centers close enough to make standard delivery quick and cheap, but also far enough away so that the millions of square feet of land required for the warehouses is also inexpensive. Building distribution centers in dense urban areas to make drone delivery feasible would be a massive cost that would be anathema to Amazon's business strategy.

The following questions are among those that can be directed to those drone operators that pursue delivery services:

- What assurances are there that drones will not crash into children, animals, or doors? Should the propellers collide with children or animals, how damaging could the injuries be? Could drones cause decapitation?

- Will drones avoid power lines and light posts? Will drones have enough precision to reach a specific doormat? Even if the precision was sufficient, would drones really be able to deliver packages to apartment dwellers? How would signatures be obtained from doormen? Would it really be safe to leave packages in front of residential buildings in large cities?

- How many drone deliveries would be needed to replicate the delivery capacity of one UPS truck? Would this number of drones flying over residences look like an air armada? To what extent could drones conserve gas consumption compared to delivery trucks?

- How much community opposition will result from the sound annoyances associated with drones?

- To what extent will drone deliveries be impacted by inclement weather? How will rain or clouds impede the operation of drones? How will delivery companies contend with customers dissatisfied with weather-delayed deliveries?

- What is the carrying capacity of delivery drones in terms of weight? In terms of dimensions of the shipping boxes?

- What is the radius of delivery drones?

- What is the battery life of drones? How often will the batteries need to be recharged? How will this be efficiently accomplished?

- Will some people try to shoot drones out of the sky?

3-D Printers

It would be a mistake to extrapolate what a press release claims three-dimensional (3-D) printers accomplished one time in a laboratory versus what 3-D printing can be expected to produce at home or in a manufacturing setting. The former is not representative of the latter. In academia, for instance, success can be defined as producing a one-off result such as creating an artificial human organ by way of 3-D printing. Research centers are staffed with highly educated engineers who have a wealth of expertise in a range of related disciplines. These research centers are equipped with state-of-the-art testing equipment and are optimized for achieving breakthroughs.

Replicating such feats at home or in many manufacturing settings is just not realistic. Home hobbyists that are bedazzled with 3-D printing or the factory workers in developing countries have dramatically less skill in engineering than do researchers in academic settings. While the printing of any challenging end product can be heralded as success in a laboratory, regulators, manufacturing foremen and customers have much higher expectations. For example, a factory that produces medical devices must meet highly specific criteria to fit within the confines of approved medical devices. There is no room for defects or deviation from standards. Factories must be able to manufacture highly-uniform devices on a high-throughput basis and grapple with issues such as disposal of potentially harmful by-products that are outside of the purview of laboratory researchers.

Because the failure rate of 3-D printing is as high as 70%, such printing is more suitable for developing prototypes as opposed to producing en mass. Even at Ford Motors—which has embraced 3-D printing—printers cannot yet produce finished parts in large enough volumes to install in cars and light trucks. However, when a rough prototype is needed to review the viability of an idea, 3-D printing often compares favorably to injection molding. Also, 3-D printing could be compelling for products that have extremely long shelf-lives since retaining many parts for so long would be extremely expensive.

For the consumer market, 3-D printers are akin to having an infinite dollar store on your desk. A lot of what 3-D printers are now producing are trinkets which could be just fine for companies like The Lego Group. Lego's customers would be well-served by having the ability to print out specific Lego pieces when they need them. Customers would be spared having to purchase entire new Lego sets just to obtain the few pieces they might need and Lego could make additional revenue without incurring any additional production or shipping costs.

The following are among the questions that you might wish to ask before committing to the 3-D printer space:

- Will the quality of 3-D printed products really meet customers' expectations? In the case of clothing, will it be soft and comfortable enough to remain in contact with the skin for prolonged periods of time? Will the garments last long enough to justify the trouble of producing them via 3-D printing?

- How precise are 3-D printers? It is my understanding that most consumer 3-D printers operate in the Cartesian plane which means that printing occurs horizontally and vertically, increasing the printing error rate as well as extending printing times. Can 3-D printing truly meet exacting standards which require precision to a few thousandths of an inch?

- What are the size limitations of the printed products?

- What quantities of raw materials are consumed when printing 3-D? How expensive are the materials? To what extent can different materials be used in the same printer? What is the level of difficulty in procuring such materials? Will the materials be disproportionately expensive compared to 3-D printers in much the same way that printer toner is to office printers? How rigid are the materials that you are required to use?

- When printing out a piece of paper on a traditional printer, the costs of correcting an error are almost zero. However, when mistakes are made while printing 3-D, will the materials be recyclable or inexpensive enough to dispose of?

- For many applications, a variety of durable materials would be needed in order to create and test parts under realistic conditions. For example, car parts would have to withstand the stress of an operating engine. To what extent would this cause material costs to rise?

- What kinds of smells are emitted by the 3-D printing process? What are the toxicity risks associated with 3-D printing? What are the airborne particle emissions levels of producing plastic products with desktop 3-D printing? (Many 3D printers have spaces where bacteria can easily grow if they aren't cleaned properly.) What are the risks that these potentially unhealthy products will be placed in mouths? (For instance, children often put trinkets in their mouths and other products such as plastic eating utensils are designed to be placed in mouths.) What will be the required protocol for disposing of residual plastic used in producing 3-D printed items?

- How noisy is the printing process?

- What steps are 3-D printing manufacturers taking to ensure that their machines are not used for infringing the patent rights of others? What consequences could they (and the users of 3-D printers) face for failing to police infringement induced by their printers?

- Who has liability if products produced with 3-D printers fail to meet regulatory standards, are faulty or result in product liability claims? If a 3-D printed product does not win regulatory approval or if it exhibits manufacturing deficiencies, is the manufacturer of the 3-D printer at risk of having to make a refund? If the wheels fall off of a skateboard printed via 3-D, is the manufacturer of the 3-D printer liable for related injuries?

- How long does it take to produce a product? What is the typical user's value of time? Does it make sense for someone who bills $500 an hour (and can afford to buy a 3-D printer) to spend two hours to make a pair of dice that retail for $1.00?

- How limited is the range of materials that can be used in 3-D printing? How much material do you need to produce the product? How much do spools of material cost? What is the loss rate of such material?

- What is the rate of jamming?

- Which parts of 3-D printers are most likely to need to be replaced? What is the expected level of difficulty in detecting which parts need to be replaced? What is the expected frequency of the replacement of parts? How expensive are replacement parts? What level of skill is required to replace the parts?

- What kinds of maintenance regimens are required to keep 3-D printers in good condition? Does failure to undertake recommended maintenance regiments void any related warranties?

- What kinds of warranties are available in connection with the purchase of 3-D printers?

- How much electricity is used to print? How do these costs compare to injection molding?

3-D Movies

When 3-D movies began to be promoted in earnest several years ago, the-ater-owners believed that they had an elixir on their hands. It was expected that 3-D movies would attract hordes of patrons to theaters as 3-D would offer moviegoers a media far more preferable—than, for example, computer screens and video streaming—for viewing films. Theater-owners were also supportive of 3-D technology because they were allowed to retain all of the premiums charged on sales of 3-D tickets.

Well, 3-D movies have fizzled. Rather than running towards 3-D mov-ies, patrons are running away from them. Over the past several years, fewer and fewer movies have been released in the 3-D format and a consistently declining percentage of box office revenue is due to 3-D ticket sales. The stock prices of 3-D plays such as Real D and Dolby Laboratories have un-derwhelmed over the past five years.

Let's conduct a post-mortem analysis of 3-D movies so that we can understand where the exhibitors miscalculated.

Expense One easily observable problem with 3-D movies is their greater expense for patrons. Charging another couple of dollars can add up when taking a family to a movie. Not only might a family pay another $10 to $15 to watch a 3-D movie, but only a fraction of the run time is in the 3-D format. For instance, Justin Bieber's Never Say Never Again actually only featured 30 minutes of his concert in the 3-D format.

It has also been expensive for movie theater operators to convert their screens to accommodate 3-D movies. 3-D systems are digital, so first the theater owner must convert from 35mm projectors to digital projectors. Even theaters that can accommodate 3-D cannot exhibit films that have been shot in 2D and subsequently converted to the 3-D format very well. Such films have fading color quality, blurry and dark images, and are generally out of focus which annoys moviegoers. In addition, because 3-D glasses act like sunglasses on a picture (they lower the brightness), theater operators often instruct their projectionists to generate brighter images which incurs higher energy costs as projectors consume a lot of energy.

Chicken and Egg Problem Some movies cost hundreds of millions of dollars to produce and promote. Thus, studios insist on big opening releases for their pictures. This often means hitting more than 4,000 screens when the film premiers. The problem is that only a small fraction of screens can accommodate 3-D. Another problem with the paucity of 3-D screens is that the theater operators cannot afford to allow any one picture to linger too long because there may be other 3-D pictures that are waiting to debut on these screens. Thus, the 3-D films that are exhibited may be removed from the screens faster—while they still have potential to sell more tickets—to make room for the next 3-D movies.

Health Implications An additional problem is that some people feel unwell when watching 3-D movies as related complaints of headaches, eye strain and even nausea are fairly common. Pediatricians typically do not recommend allowing children under eight years of age to regularly use 3-D glasses as their eye muscles are still developing.

Social Implications One reason people choose to watch movies in theaters rather than from the comfort of their homes is to enjoy the shared effect of being with a room full of moviegoers. However, placing dark glasses over your eyes results in feeling isolated. Further, quite a few moviegoers wear glasses. Thus, having them wear 3-D glasses over their regular glasses is uncomfortable and awkward.

Robocall Blockers

Every month, the Federal Trade Commission (FTC) receives 200,000 complaints about illegal robocalls, making it the most common problem reported to the FTC. It is highly reassuring—but by no means a guaranty of commercial success—when a product is developed in response to widely publicized problems.

One company that rose to meet the challenge posed by annoying robocalls is Nomorobo. Nomorobo is a cloud-based technology solution for people who have Internet-based VoIP phone service. Nomorobo uses a service called "simultaneous ring" that is provided by most VoIP phone companies. This feature allows customers to have numerous phone lines ring at the same time. All of Nomorobo's customers' calls are also routed to Nomorobo's computers. The company uses caller ID and call frequency information to screen those calls. When Nomorobo decides a call is a robocall, it hangs up after the first ring. If the system is not sure, it presents the caller with an audio CAPTCHA to verify whether it's legitimate. For instance, Nomorobo might ask the caller to answer a simple addition question by keying in the response. Only if the calculation is correct does the call go through.

Some other robocall solutions providers are developing 'blacklists' (confirmed robocaller phone numbers) and 'whitelists' (numbers associated with acceptable incoming calls). I think the idea of blacklists and whitelists has limitations. Some people do not object to certain robocalls. I appreciate blacklistable robocalls, to an extent, from politicians and causes that I support because they remind me to vote or make a contribution that I intended to make but have not yet fulfilled. Whitelists are also problematic. If a long-lost high school friend wanted to call you, the whitelist would stand in the way.

The following are among the questions and issues that we could raise with Nomorobo's management:

- Does your service work on telephone service from cable companies? From traditional phone companies? From Google Talk? Can it block robocalls coming into my cell phone? If not, are there any (interoperability) obstacles to Nomorobo integrating its service with blocking apps—such as PrivacyStar, mrnumber and Blacklist Plus—that are available for Android devices.

- Is it true that your service does not require customers to purchase any dedicated hardware? If not, how expensive is the hardware? Where can I find it? What is the level of difficulty of installing it?

- What is the incidence of robocalls directed at your customers going through? What is the incidence of legitimate calls being blocked? Are there liability issues with wrongfully blocking legitimate calls? For instance, if a doctor's office calls to schedule a surgery and that call is blocked, are there risks for the call blocker?

- What is your revenue model? Do you charge customers based on calls screened? Calls blocked? Per month? How does your revenue model differ when serving residential customers versus business customers?

- How influential is the call center business (and the telephone equipment companies that supply call centers)? What efforts are these industries taking to defeat your technology?

- I understand that there are some movements afoot to encourage the crowdsourcing of robocall numbers included in blacklists. How serious of a threat is this to Nomorobo?

- Is it true that the FCC requires traditional phone companies to complete all calls and specifically prohibits them from blocking any calls? If so, doesn't the regulation significantly reduce your addressable market?

- Many politicians use robocalling during their campaigns. Is there really an appetite on their part to curb robocalling?

- It seems that the two-pronged attack—both technologically and legally—against spam emailing was an effective strategy. Legislation such as the CANSPAM Act deserves a lot of credit for reducing spam. This is evidenced by many email marketing platforms actively policing their customers' behavior to ensure that CANSPAM is not violated. Thus, if the penalties associated with robocalling become more prohibitive, wouldn't there be less need for technical solutions such as those provided by Nomorobo?

- Will an antivirus system or corporate firewall block Nomorobo?

Safety Devices

Sometimes, even the best intentioned products do not meet commercial success.

One technology designed to save innocent lives that has run into vociferous opposition has been personalized firearms. Such weapons would prevent children from accidentally shooting themselves and would also make it impossible for an assailant to shoot an officer with that officer's gun.

To address these issues, smart guns are designed only to fire if the gun recognizes that the rightful owner's finger is on the trigger. This recognition can be accomplished through biometrics or, as with the Colt Z40, if the gun has an embedded microchip that receives a signal from a corresponding chip in a wristband worn by an authorized user. The concern on the part of gun rights activists is that the government could remotely deactivate digital weapons.

It is hard to think of a better intentioned technology than one designed to ensure that young children will not die of hyperthermia when they are abandoned in the back seats of cars. Many of the purported technical solutions to children dying in hot cars are designed to function by electronically alerting parents or guardians when weight shifts in car seats after the vehicle's engine has shut off. Some related products beep, others activate key chains, while Cars-N-Kids activates a smartphone app.

A few years ago, the National Highway Traffic Safety Administration (NHTSA) conducted extensive testing of such devices. The researchers found several limitations in these products, including inconsistencies in arming sensitivity, variations in warning signal distance, potential interference from other electronic devices, children inadvertently disarming the device by slumping over or sleeping out of position, and limitations in the products' susceptibility to misuse or other common scenarios, such as an apple juice spill. Also, the sensor might not sync correctly with the receiver or batteries can run out without warning.

In addition to the examples of malfunctions above, I would question parents' ability to properly install these devices. Many parents do not install car seats correctly. I would imagine that quite a few parents would want to avoid a terrible tax on their conscious if they relied on a technology that they failed to correctly install and a tragedy were to occur. If I were assessing manufacturers of child abandonment prevention devices, I would ask how much testing they have conducted and what their experiences with false positives and false negative signals have been. Finally, I would want to make sure that companies that manufacture, market and sell such safety devices are covered in terms of product liability insurance.

Analysis of Selected Traditional Business Models

Restaurant Analysis

The restaurant business is fraught with risk and challenges. It has been said that the only way to make a small fortune in the restaurant business is to start with a large fortune. The following are among the challenges to the casual dining/upscale restaurant business:

High upfront capital expenditure requirements. Wedgewood china and Lenox glassware are very expensive. So too are the costs of installing a state-of-the-art kitchen and procuring linen tablecloths. Investments in the restaurant can run into millions of dollars.

High ongoing fixed and variable costs. Of course the biggest recurring fixed cost is rent which can include a portion of the restaurant's revenues. The recurring variable costs are for food, payroll and employee benefits, laundry, electricity, insurance and other typical business costs.

Capacity constraints. The higher caliber the restaurant is, the slower the tables turn over. This is not a problem if the patrons spend lavishly. However, some patrons that make reservations at fine dining establishments do not show up. Other customers dither and, in the case of coffee shops and casual dining establishments, some customers basically usurp restaurants for their own offices. Even if suitable adjacent real estate is available and funds can be raised, expanding an upscale restaurant runs the risk of it losing its aura of exclusivity and charm. Highly service-oriented restaurants may find it difficult to hire enough wait staff with sufficient decorum. However, lower and mid-tier restaurants can expand their capacity through take-out orders, deliveries and catering.

Vulnerability to cyclicality. When the economy deteriorates or corporations slash their travel and entertainment budgets, restaurants can experience long periods of anemic demand. However, upscale restaurants must still buy fresh food every day (which represents expensive and perishable inventory costs), maintain their premises, and incur all of the other operating costs.

Low barriers to entry and tremendous competition. Since it is prohibitively expensive for landlords to remove a fully-equipped kitchen from their premises, landlords seek out new restaurant operators to replace preceding restaurant operators. Thus, restaurant capacity is rarely eliminated. Millions of people believe that since they are good cooks, they can open a restaurant. Capital is usually readily available for starting a new restaurant since owning a restaurant provides a lot bragging rights to wealthy people. Television programs such as America's Test Kitchen and Hell's Kitchen further glorify the restaurant business and thus ensure a never-ending procession of aspiring restaurant operators.

High fragility. If an apparel manufacturer makes a defective shirt, a loose thread may be visible. If a mistake is made in the kitchen, a patron could get sick. Even one bad review from Zagats or the New York Times can be highly problematic for an upscale restaurant. If a pet store, massage parlor, astrologer or health clinic opens up next to the restaurant, droves of clientele could be dissuaded from patronizing the restaurant. Oftentimes, restaurants employ people who are going through transitionary periods in their lives and these personal problems can result in high rates of tardiness and absenteeism. Their personal issues may surface when they are on duty and can be aggravated by the alcohol and fire that is ever-present at restaurants.

> **Analytical Consideration** One of my favorite questions to ask when trying to determine the ability of a restaurant to maintain high standards of table service relates to how tips are garnered. The advantage of a wait staff team sharing all of the tips received each night is that the waiters are much more likely to be attentive to patrons sitting at other waiters' tables. This leads to efficiencies for the restaurant and more satisfied patrons.

Analysis of Gyms

The business models of gyms have several compelling facets. First, they require very little capital to open and operate. Because they are viewed as an amenity to residential and office buildings, landlords are willing to greatly reduce, or entirely waive, rents charged to gyms. Another reason that gyms are attractive to landlords is that they can utilize whatever space landlords have available. For instance, while a closet-sized room may not be of much use to a retailer, a gym can make use of it by placing a stationary bicycle there. The dedicated group exercise rooms that gyms have are very versatile and are used for programs as diverse as exercising and birthday parties for young children. Most of the equipment in gyms can be financed or rented, electricity can be generated from the aerobic machines and the trainers are independent contractors who do not receive remuneration from the gyms, but rather are paid directly by their clients. In fact, personal trainers share the fees they collect with the gym or pay the gym a monthly fee.

Another attractive feature of this business model is that there is a great deal of capacity in terms of selling memberships. Many people become dues-paying members of gyms but find they cannot exercise as frequently as they hoped. Nevertheless, every rose has its thorns. The other side of the low capital intensity coin is that there are very low barriers to entry for gyms. The resulting oversupply of gyms forces operators to market more aggressively to recruit new members. Since there are essentially no advantages in belonging to more than one gym in the same vicinity, the inundation of gyms in a community results in reduced membership fees for all gyms.

Airlines Analysis

What is obviousness is not always correct. What is observed is not always reality. What? Allow me to digress for a moment.

In the days leading up to Christopher Columbus's maiden voyage to the Americas, telescopes were not very powerful. When peering into one it must have been obvious that the earth was flat because every time a ship reached the point where the sky intersected with the ocean, the ship fell out of sight. A few centuries later, in 1894, Percival Lowell (for whom the Lowell Observatory is named) peered into his telescope. Lowell believed the blue lines he observed on Mars were artificial canals and thus evidence of life on that planet. It turns out that the aperture on Lowell's telescope was so small that it functioned as an ophthalmoscope, the device that doctors shine into to their patients' eyes. Thus, when Lowell looked into his telescope, what he saw was the blood vessels at the back of his eyes, not canals on Mars.

What does this have to do with the airline industry? Well, in my first book, I disparaged the structure of the airline industry and the related business models. I quoted Warren Buffett when he said, "Don't invest in airlines. It's the worst business of any size in the world, with huge fixed costs and lots of overcapacity." I argued that simply reviewing a few facets of the airline industry would cause investors to come to the conclusion that that industry's business model is obviously flawed.

The following are among the traditional problems that plagued the airline operators:

Fixed costs. Commercial airlines have long carried high fixed costs in terms of acquiring and maintaining aircraft, complying with regulations, paying landing fees to airports, and paying just about the entire workforce union wages while contending with less than pliable work rules.

Overcapacity. Before China and the Arab Gulf countries became major purchasers of aircraft, there was severe overcapacity in terms of seat-miles flown. This chronic overcapacity was fueled by a steady stream of business moguls looking for a fix for their addiction to vanity. The fact that many airlines were state-backed meant they were less sensitive to profitability and more concerned about bulking up their fleets for reasons of national pride. Rather than bankruptcy filings removing weak airline operators from the industry, airlines that reorganized under bankruptcy laws actually weakened the stronger operators. Reorganization allowed the struggling airlines to reduce their prices since they typically won labor concessions and were relieved of much of their interest payment burdens due to the removal of debt from their balance sheets.

Inventory. The airline industry had long been beset by its deleterious inventory dynamics. In anticipation of labor stoppages, boycotts or manufacturing bottlenecks, most industries can stockpile inventory. However, this luxury is not afforded to the airline industry; once an airplane has left the ground, the airline can never sell those empty seats to customers.

Diseconomies of Scale. Most companies become increasingly efficient as they grow in size. The airlines seemed to have successfully evaded this principle. The more routes an airline services, the more variability there is in the fleet. The more variability in a fleet, the more mechanics are needed to service the planes. The larger an airline's footprint becomes, the more difficult it is to arrange cost-effective staffing. Now that most meals (as well as blankets and pillows) have been eliminated from domestic routes, there is not much room to negotiate concessions on supplies.

Proximity to Disgruntled Employees. The airline industry, compared to every other industry, probably has the highest percentage of its staff come in face-to-face contact with customers. Thus, it becomes very apparent to— and unpleasant for—customers when airline employees are dissatisfied.

The Airline Industry Has Lifted Off

Times have changed and the airline industry has turned the corner. The airline industry exemplifies how smart management can overcompensate for a terrible industry structure. The airline industry proves that business model validation is an iterative process. Business development professionals and investors cannot just analyze the structure of an industry and believe that no changes will be visited upon that sector.

Now, the airline industry has recovered thanks to consolidation, which has yielded the airlines more bargaining power, and reduced capacity (in part due to less availability of pilots which is partially attributable to mandatory retirement ages and the minimum number of flight hours soaring from 250 to 1,500 for most commercial pilots). The airline industry is also benefitting from more passengers per flight (in part due to greater seat density), stronger pricing (due to analytics), and the imposition of a barrage of ancillary fees.

Selected Company-Specific Business Model Analysis

▌Segway

The Segway—the upright transportation machine that you see shopping mall guards riding—is another example of how success is not binary. True, Segway did not live up to the fever pitch hype surrounding its launch way back in 2001. In the run-up to its launch, not only were the benefits of Segway marketed as revolutionary but there was a tremendous amount of hype surrounding its backers–Steve Jobs, Jeff Bezos and inventor Dean Kamen. Sales from Segways are still far below the initial stratospheric expectations.

Nevertheless, Segway has carved out niches for itself in areas such as security, the operating of warehouses and for moving people around during organized tours. Segway has attracted security personnel (such as shopping mall and airport security personnel) because Segways are easy to mount, to dismount and to turn around quickly. Also, standing on Segways enables security personnel to see better and elevates their presence as they are seen more readily.

Here are some questions that may be (or could have been) asked in trying to determine the traction that Segways may achieve:

- Where are users supposed to ride Segways? On the road? On the sidewalk? Our cities are designed for pedestrians and speedy vehicles and since Segway was neither it had no proper infrastructure to support it. The Segway ran afoul of regulations in many countries where it was banned from sidewalks and roads because it did not fit any existing categories.

- Where can users park their Segways?

- How well do Segways handle steps, curbs and cobbled roads?

- How do you charge it? How often do Segways need to be charged? How far can Segways be ridden on one charge?

- At an initial price of $5,000 who would be able to afford it?

- Is a license needed to operate a Segway? Is insurance necessary to ride or own a Segway?

- Can Segways be ridden in the rain or snow?

- What are the relative advantages and disadvantages of the Segway over products such as RocketSkates which are essentially pairs of battery-powered, motorized roller skates?

The Importance of Iteration This presents a nice opportunity to mention the importance of iteration in business models. It would be arrogant for anyone to believe that their business model is without reproach or will be the optimal business model despite any changes that might affect their industry or the economy overall in the years ahead. Segway wanted maximum secrecy before its launch in order to build up excitement for the product. While there is merit in this marketing strategy, customer feedback would have been invaluable. (As an aside, companies that hold their proprietary know-how in the form of trade secrets may have a higher "lack of iteration risk" than companies that patent their inventions since the former strategy is consistent with maintaining secrecy.)

GoPro

GoPro manufacturers, markets and sells some of the most versatile cameras in the world. Many of these cameras are helmet-mounted and are used by extreme sports enthusiasts to memorialize their adventures and achievements. The GoPro business model is not terribly unique. Thus, the series of considerations to be applied to GoPro and similar companies such as Giroptic are more related to product analysis.

The following are some factors to consider when assessing the prospects for GoPro and its ilk:

- What is the size and weight of the cameras? How difficult are the cameras to set up? Are the cameras waterproof?

- How do your camera's prices compare with competing cameras, given the functionality offered? What is the ratio of accessory sales—in terms of units and dollars—relative to camera sales?

- What is the resolution of the pictures taken? How does the wide-angle functionality compare to that of the competition? Do the cameras automatically adjust for low-light situations? What is the stability of the cameras? How well is audio integrated into the cameras? Do the cameras feature wind-noise reduction technology so that the audio will be clearer during high-speed activities? Is WiFi built into the cameras? Can any software in the cameras be updated remotely?

- What is the frame rate? The more frames per second, the better motion will be shown in the picture.

- At what intervals (measured in seconds) do the cameras provide automatic photo capture? How many full-resolution frames per second are captured when holding down the shutter button?

- What is the level of ease or difficulty of manipulating and uploading content captured by the cameras? How many connectivity options exist in terms of downloading pictures and videos to computers? How easily can pictures and videos be shared via email, text, Facebook, Instagram, and other social media sites and applications?

- How does the battery life of GoPro cameras compare to that of the competition? How does the battery charging time of GoPro cameras compare to that of the competition? How many hours of video can be recorded per charge?

- What is the risk that such cameras will be consumed by other electronic hardware such as smart phones or possibly other variations of wearable cameras?

- How can GoPro monetize the content captured with its cameras? Does it have rights to the content that its customers capture? In addition to video that could be streamed on the likes of traditional broadcasting networks, ESPN, YouTube or Netflix, could such content be licensed to video game makers?

- How feasible would it be for GoPro to migrate into the drone industry?

SodaStream

SodaStream manufactures beverage carbonation systems which enable consumers to easily transform ordinary tap water into carbonated soft drinks and sparkling water. The company's products offer convenience by eliminating the need to carry bottles home from the supermarket, to store bottles at home or to regularly dispose of empty bottles.

SodaStream had a long run of being a very successful company: its products are available at more than 60,000 retail stores in 45 countries. Each year SodaStream provides 1.5 billion liters of homemade soda to millions of homes worldwide.

The fact that SodaStream users frequently make repeat purchases of syrups, carbonators and bottles is akin to the razor-razorblade business model. Not only does such replenishment offer SodaStream substantial recurring revenue, but it may enable SodaStream to capture prime shelf space at retailers as they too benefit from the repeat traffic that SodaStream generates.

Analysts are not supposed to be enamored with a company's past success. Rather, they are supposed to be critical thinkers and to try to determine what the odds are that the company will remain successful going forward. Thus, if I were to consider investing in SodaStream, I would ask the following questions:

- To what extent do people buy SodaStream for themselves as opposed to gifts for others? If much of the revenue is a result of sales for gift-giving purposes I would be concerned. This would indicate that people are not really embracing SodaStream but that it is a suitable wedding or housewarming present.

- What is the reorder rate for carbonators? If the reorder rate was low, that would indicate that people are not using SodaStream very often.

- How adverse are people to lugging carbon dioxide canisters? Green Mountain avoids the necessity of ordering, lugging and installing new carbon dioxide canisters.

- Do vast segments of the addressable customer base really want to put in the work required to enjoy a soft drink? Popping open a can of cola or pouring a glass of soda really only takes about five seconds which is hard to beat in terms of convenience. How many people really want to spend a few minutes preparing a drink when the alternative only takes a few seconds? I would want to know how often and how the machines are cleaned. After every use? Or at the end of each day of use? Or after 10 uses? I would want to know the exact cleaning regimen. What products need to be purchased to clean the machines? How expensive are they? How easily can they be obtained? How long is the cleaning process? Can all of the parts be placed in the dishwasher or are there some parts that must be cleaned by hand?

- Is SodaStream even trying to sell its beverage solution in markets other than the take-home market? If not, then the company is ceding these markets. If yes, can high throughput in terms of pouring drinks really be accomplished with SodaStream's products? Could McDonald's or a sports stadium really meet demand with SodaStream?

- It is very difficult for generic sodas to capture retailers' shelf space. In fact, generic soda represents less than 2% of all soda sales. How does SodaStream anticipate surmounting such challenges?

- To what extent is the consumers' experience with SodaStream a function of the variation in the quality of residential tap water? This is an important question for two reasons. First, every day, somewhere in the US there are problems with tap water delivered to homes. These kinds of problems are probably much more pronounced in most of the rest of the world. These kinds of issues negatively affect the taste and enjoyment of SodaStream products. The second major problem associated with variability of the quality of tap water is that it will be difficult to sign a major licensing agreement with a major brand. Companies like Coca-Cola are extremely concerned about their users' experience and the impact of such experiences on their brands' equity.

- What percent of syrups are sugary and unhealthy versus low-calorie, natural, and unsweetened? To what extent is SodaStream vulnerable to the imposition of fat taxes that are levied on other purveyors of soft drinks and snack foods?

- How much shelf space does SodaStream require and how much discretionary shelf space do potential customers have in their kitchens? How many households are essentially precluded from using a SodaStream product because of an absence of shelf space? I might take this line of questioning even further by asking SodaStream if they have commissioned any anthropological studies. Such studies would entail an anthropologist visiting numerous customers in their homes and observing all of their interactions with SodaStream. It would be interesting to know to what extent different customer segments—single people living alone, single people living together, married couples without children, married couples with children, retirees living together—engage with SodaStream. If it was revealed that certain of these segments substantially never use SodaStream and there were logical reasons for their refrain, I would remove such households from the addressable market.

- What is SodaStream's exposure to the anti-Israel Boycott, Divest and Sanction movement (BDS)? Anti-Israel forces oppose SodaStream having a major production plant in the Jewish town of Ma'aleh Adumim. I would ask, "Is the BDS movement just a noisy sideshow or does it have the ability to cause financial problems for SodaStream?" BDS operatives have picketed retailers in Canada, the UK and elsewhere when such retailers refused to remove SodaStream from their shelves. What percent of SodaStream's brand conversations through social media are related to BDS?

- Now that competitor Green Mountain Coffee Roasters, the maker of the single-serve coffee maker, has signed a 10-year partnership to sell Coca-Cola through Green Mountain, how much market share is left for SodaStream? To what extent will other coffee machines be able to produce carbonated beverages?

- How versatile is SodaStream? Can it brew soup? Can it be used for preparing energy drinks? Can it facilitate the production of hot beverages such as coffee and medicated teas? Even if SodaStream could be used to make coffee, how would freshness of the coffee be preserved? Unlike bottled or canned soda which can sit on shelves or in refrigerators for weeks while retaining its taste and carbonation, coffee needs to be freshly brewed in order to taste good.

- How sensitive is SodaStream in terms of being able to block non-approved uses? For instance, can it prevent the preparation of alcoholic drinks?

Analytical Consideration SodaStream has reported that its products have penetrated 25% of Swedish households while their household penetration rate in the United States is 1%. Thus, it may be tempting to model the potential market in the United States at 25 times its current level. While households in Sweden are probably not too dissimilar to those in the United States, Swedes may be more cautious than Americans about allowing bottles to pile up in landfills. So maybe you would think that the adjusted market opportunity for selling SodaStream products in the United States is 20 times its current level.

But does any American really think that 20% of the households would buy SodaStream machines? I can't imagine that happening. I have researched to a limited extent the disparity in adoption rates in SodaStream machines in Sweden and do not understand why the Swedes purportedly buy so many machines. Whatever the reason, Sweden seems like an outlier to me (especially in light of Sweden's anti-Israeli tendencies) and I would not extrapolate reported Swedish adoption rates onto other countries. If I were to research Sweden's alleged obsession with SodaStream machines, I would ask questions such as:

- Are Swedish households really buying so many SodaStream machines or are Swedish restaurants and offices the source of so much demand?
- Are so many end customers residing in Sweden or is Sweden a point of distribution throughout the region, thus inflating sales in Sweden?
- Is pricing comparable in Sweden with prices in peer countries?
- Is there any inventory build-up occurring in Sweden?

I would put the burden of proof on the company to explain the reasons for such strong demand in Sweden.

Keurig Green Mountain

As Keurig Green Mountain shares some parallels with SodaStream, a few words regarding the potential of Keurig's coffee makers are in order. At the time of this writing it is my understanding that Keurig machines are used in about 18 million U.S. households. The company estimates that 90 million American homes use coffee markers of some kind. However, the real addressable market must be much smaller than 72 million American households. A very large number of these households must be people who never or rarely drink coffee while many other households are content with having basic kettles. There must be a very large constituency of coffee drinkers who do not want to invest in sophisticated coffee makers which require ascending any learning curves. Thus, much of the so-called replacement market is not really ripe for embracing sophisticated coffee makers from the likes of Keurig.

Other questions related to assessing the potential of Keurig could include:

- What is the risk of boiling-temperature water spraying out, potentially burning users?

- How many types of coffee can be prepared? Regular American coffee? Lattes? Cappuccinos?

- How many servings can be prepared with one pod?

- Are the pods light enough to order online and ship through the mail?

- What else can the machines do? Can they prepare soups or cold beverages?

Final Analytical Considerations

Analogs and Antilogs

So, how do you validate a business model? One way is to subject the business model to both analogs (which consists of comparing similar features of your business against a comparable business) and antilogs (which consists of contrasting features of your business against a comparable business).

Analog Analysis

Most investors and business executives believe that they have validated their business model when they find one successful analog. If the baseline business is successful and somewhat comparable, it is tempting to emphasize the points of comparability and project that such commonality is sufficient to ensure the success of your business. However, more diligent decision makers will challenge the relevance of analogs as well as subject their business models to the scrutiny of antilogs.

The analogs you peg your business's projected trajectory to should be of similar time and place to your business. Earlier in this book, I discussed the business models of flash sales sites such as those run by the Gilt Groupe and One Kings Lane. Let's suppose that you are considering building your own flash sales site because you are impressed with the apparent success of the existing flash sellers. You identified successful analogs, or so you think. Should you proceed? Not necessarily. Gilt Groupe launched in 2007 and several of its peers launched shortly thereafter. During that period of time the economy was in shambles, there was scant competition and tremendous excess supply of designer apparel. Also, one of the pioneering flash sales operators that others try to emulate is Vente-Privée, based in France. Well, in France, "sales" events are heavily regulated and occur only twice per year. So to recap, your perceived analogs may not carry much precedential value given that they are distant in terms of time and geography.

Even when your business model is highly correlated to successful analogs, the fact that some companies are already successful in a given category reduces the chances of new companies becoming successful in that space. In the case of the flash sales sites, the existing companies have attracted both the high end customers (who most likely do not want to be bothered with shopping at multiple flash sites) and top-tiered designers (who do not want their brands tarnished which would happen if flash sales sites compete by slashing prices too aggressively).

Antilog Analysis

Let's say that you are considering backing an entrepreneur who wants to rapidly expand his fledgling chain of hot chocolate cafes. This entrepreneur is using Starbucks as his analog. His analysis is thorough as it runs the gamut from real estate strategy, customer profiles, price points, supply chain issues, employee training, marketing and more. After reading this entrepreneur's report, you may be prepared to invest in his chain of hot chocolate cafes. While the analog analysis is necessary, it is not sufficient. The analog analysis should be accompanied by antilog analysis, which in this example, would compare the hot chocolate shops with chains of cafés that failed. Taking a second look at the hot chocolate chain could cause you to come to the conclusion that the entrepreneur's shops and expansion strategy more closely resemble the hot beverage chains that failed.

Decision makers should consider the frequency at which companies with a winning concept elect not to promote that concept. Let's say that you are a business development executive employed by Dangote Cement, the leading cement producer in Nigeria. You want to expand your company's revenues. You conduct some research into best marketing practices that some of the world's most successful cement companies have undertaken to grow their revenues. During the course of this research, you learn that one of the initiatives that Monterey, Mexico-based Cemex took earlier in its history was to market cement to newlyweds. Cemex realized that most newly-married Mexican couples could not afford to move out of their parents' homes, but still craved privacy. Millions of Mexicans solved this dilemma by building additional rooms onto their parents' houses.

So, if you were a manager at Dangote, and you were looking for marketing angles and revenue expansion opportunities, you might try to emulate Cemex's success by redirecting part of Dangote's marketing budget to wedding planners and bridal stores. So far, this seems reasonable given the resemblance of the financial position and living preferences of recently betrothed Mexican couples to Nigerian newlyweds.

However, before you redirect your marketing budget to wedding planners and bridal magazines, consider just one more thing. Why haven't cement companies in other developing countries pursued cement sales to newly-married couples? Surely, many executives at cement companies are aware of Cemex's success in this regard. When I wrote a patent valuation report for a large Thai cement company, I brought the Cemex-bridal issue to that firm's attention but those executives did not show any interest in pursuing a similar strategy.[38] Cemex itself has been a serial acquiror of cement operators in developing countries. In many of its related press releases, Cemex stated that it will boost the acquirees' operations by sharing its managerial acumen. However, as far as I can tell, Cemex has not marketed its cement to newlyweds in other countries.

The point is that it is an error to use as an analog a strategy that was once successful but never replicated elsewhere. There is a stronger argument for the Dangote cement executive to refrain from marketing cement to newly-married couples than to pursue such a strategy.

---

[38] During the lunches and dinners that my hosts treated me to, several of the twenty-something executives at the Thai cement company mentioned in passing that they lived with their parents. My thinking was that if these successful people reside with their parents, such living arrangements must be common in Thailand.

Parting Thoughts on Making Business and Investment Decisions

I would like to leave you with a few parting thoughts as you go about making your business and investment decisions. First, as mentioned at the outset of this book, be aggressive in your due diligence and line of questioning when undertaking your research and when conducting interviews. Never be afraid to ask questions that could be criticized as being too elementary. These questions often prompt the most revealing insights.

The Use of Probabilities

Realize that the business and investment decisions that you make are not definitive and irreversible. Rather, decision making is iterative. It is highly constructive to cast your decisions in terms of probabilities and confidence levels because doing so will reinforce the fact that you are not omniscient and cannot predict the future with great accuracy. For instance, you should force yourself to complete the following sentences:

- I believe there is a xx% chance that I am making the right business decision.

- I believe there is a xx% chance that I will make a xx% return on this investment decision.

- I am xx% confident in the decision that I am making.

Qualifying your decisions with probabilities will give you the flexibility to modify your assessments and projections when new information becomes available. It will also enable you to save face when you need to modify your business plan or to unwind an investment position.

Assessing New Information

When new information becomes available relative to your business and investment decisions, do not consider it in a binary fashion. Let's say that you owned shares of Apple Computer in the beginning of 2011 for a variety of reasons. You believed that Apple's current and future hardware products would prove to be very popular, that Apple had developed a very lucrative retail strategy, that its apps store and iTunes initiatives would be extremely profitable, that it built an unassailable patent portfolio and had great management. Then, you learn of Steve Jobs's passing in October of 2011. How would your investment thesis have changed?

Many people view such important news and developments as either being transformative or immaterial. They are likely to state that they are going to sell all of their Apple shares because Steve Jobs was such a major factor in Apple's success. Or, they report that they will not sell any Apple shares based on the belief that the many thousands of talented people at Apple will be able to continue developing terrific products. In other words, many people make the mistake of reviewing critical data points with a binary lens. It is better to modify your business decisions and to rebalance your portfolio in proportion with the release of new data points. For instance, you might have set decision tripwires back in the beginning of 2011. Such decision tripwires could have been that if Steve Jobs were to pass away, you would reduce your position in Apple by 25% or that if Apple won its patent litigation against Samsung, you would increase your stake in Apple by 5%.

Decision Tripwires

I alluded to the notion of decision tripwires above, but allow me to expand on that idea. Before making an important decision, you usually have quite a few doubts and concerns. However, two minutes after you make the decision, you typically have almost complete confidence that you made the right choice. I had this experience when considering which of two houses would be better for my family. Before I pulled the trigger on one of the houses, I could list lots of pros and cons for each house. I thought, on balance, either of the houses would be just as suitable as the other. However, just moments after making an offer for one of the houses, I was absolutely sure that I made an excellent decision. This doesn't seem logical, does it? No new information about either house surfaced in those few intervening moments.

So, what's the point? The point is that after we make bold decisions, our confidence in those decisions is irrationally elevated. Thus, in addition to reminding ourselves that we could be wrong by attaching probabilities to our decisions, we need to set up decision tripwires that will automatically cause us to assume more or less exposure to our business and investment initiatives when new information becomes available.

Let's say that you work for a cigarette manufacturer. You decided not to produce electronic cigarettes. This decision was based on your belief that electronic cigarettes are just a passing fad. However, since the market for e-cigarettes is embryonic, you are not sure that your assessment will prove to be correct. Thus, you set decision tripwires, whereby if the following conditions are met, your company will begin producing one million electronic cigarettes a month:

- When electronic cigarettes capture 5% of the domestic market.

- When the price differential between regular and electronic cigarettes is more than 35%.

- When smoking ordinances become more lenient towards electronic cigarettes.

- When the American Medical Association declares that e-cigarettes are of much less concern than regular cigarettes.

Alternatively, suppose you are developing an application for smartphones that will help drivers locate parking spaces in congested cities. Knowing that you do not have the resources to fight City Hall, your decision tripwire might be to retreat from your parking app initiative when three out of the following five events occur in a targeted city:

- The minimum incentive that you need to pay drivers to report available parking spaces exceeds $5.

- The city implements "congestion pricing," requiring all drivers entering designated areas to pay the same flat fee.

- The city rents more than 15% of its parking spaces to peer-to-peer car-sharing services such as RelayRides.

- The city installs smart parking meters that are designed to keep more parking spots vacant by charging higher rates during times of peak demand.

- The city installs sensors in parking spaces which alert drivers with smartphones of available parking.

Conclusion

Conclusion

Well, we are now at the end of my book. I hope you learned something from reading these pages. I don't expect that you will agree with everything I wrote. That's fine because my objective was to provide you with new insights and dimensionality that you can apply to your review of investment and business decisions. I hope the mental gymnastics that I put you through will help make you an even better business executive and investor.

This book should not be considered a definitive treatise but rather the foundation for building a more in-depth analytical process. I would welcome the opportunity to continue the discussion. The best ways to accomplish that would be for you to join one of the courses that I run on the topic of the Valuation of Emerging Companies or training for the Devil's Advocate Auditor designation. I would also be pleased to carry on the discussion at your company. Just drop us a line at <u>info@bdacademy.com</u> if interested.

A Note About Sources

One of the most rewarding aspects of my work is the constant learning that I derive from it. Without exaggeration, I have learned something interesting every single day of the past 25 years of my career about both mainstream and disruptive industries. As most of my client engagements are covered by non-disclosure agreements, I am prohibited from disclosing such companies as specific sources.

Many of the issues written about in these pages were the product of discussions that were part of the courses which I currently teach through The Business Development Academy and have taught at The New York Institute of Finance. The conferences that I developed in partnership with The New York Society of Security Analysts and with The Wall Street Transcript provided me with unparalleled learning experiences. There have been thousands of very bright participants in these courses and programs and I am indebted for the insightful comments and illuminating perspectives that so many participants have brought to bear.

I have read some 1,000 'serious' books over the past 20 years and have learned something of interest from the vast majority of them. Having so many kernels of knowledge twirling around in my head from so many contributors over so many years makes it difficult to attribute specific comments to specific people. (I would like to think that some of the ideas presented in this book have their genesis in that same head.)

Anyway, I have created a Recommended Reading List which is available on our Devil's Advocate Auditor site at www.devilsadvocateauditor. com. There, you will see a few hundred of the books that I believe are worthy of your attention. I broke the books into subject categories, provided some general ranking within each category and made comments relative to the books' readability.

▊ In Appreciation to My Readers

Buyers of this book are entitled to receive a $100 discount on any program run through the Business Development Academy, Certified Emerging Company Analyst, Certified Patent Valuation Analyst, Devil's Advocate Auditor, and Institute for Strategic Negotiations. In addition, a $250 discount may be applied to the reports or consultations commissioned through Business Model Validation, Devil's Advocate Auditor, Negotiating Battle™, Negotiating Confidant, Patent Fairness Opinions, or Trade Secret Valuation. Also, covered are consultations to investment firms. No other offers apply. One discount per reader. Offer subject to expiration on January 1, 2019. To take advantage of this offer, contact info@bdacademy.com.

Acknowledgements

I would like to thank my father, Dr. Lawrence Wanetick, for reviewing my manuscript and for making so many helpful edits. (Dad, thank you for giving me so much invaluable advice and guidance throughout my life.) I greatly appreciate my good friend, Jonathan Brown, taking the time to review my manuscript and providing me with keen insights. (Jonathan, I look forward to figuring out what other businesses we can pursue together.) Laura Cier deserves a great deal of credit for reviewing the manuscript several times and for catching so many of my typographical and grammatical mistakes.

This book is the culmination of many years of hard work and it would never have seen the light of day without the assistance of so many exceptionally intelligent, talented and kind professionals. They deserve much more recognition than I can give them here. But I would be remiss if I neglected to note their role in my pursuits.

Professional Team

I would like to extend my appreciation to John Goldschmidt, Emmett Collazo and Thomas Kent for providing me with outstanding legal representation and advice. I must thank Michael Strebel for being a fantastic accountant. Jacob Azulay, Stephanie Sposito, and Lisa Lannoy, I owe you a world of gratitude for looking after my real estate interests. Bela Thakkar thank you doing such a great job of managing the accounting and administrative responsibilities at the office. I would like to thank Nitin Thakkar and Bryan Bruder for managing our information technology at the office. Barry Brinster has provided me with much more than great website development; he is a trusted strategic advisor.

Worldwide Marketing Partners

Many thanks are due to partners of the Business Development Academy who work so hard in marketing our courses throughout the world. To this end, I wish to express my sincere appreciation to Barbara McManus and Judith Black at Management Forum for their representation of my courses in the United Kingdom and throughout Europe; Gary Tay and Allen Yeo of Patnova for their representation of my courses in Singapore and Southeast Asia; Jeffrey Teh and Wendy Fung at Innoxcell for their representation of my courses in China, Hong Kong and Taiwan; Naoya Yoshikawa, Soji Suzuki and Shima Wakako for their representation of my courses in Japan; Renad Al-Noubani and Majd Kaddash of the Licensing Executive Society in Jordan for their representation of my courses in the Arab Gulf; Ajay Batra PhD. of the World Intellectual Property Rights Bank for representing my courses in India; Carlos Alvarez and Francisco Velasco of Knowledge Innovation Management for their representation of my courses in Spain and Latin America; Beth Jones and Melissa Marris of Patent Resources Group for their representation of some of my courses in the United States; and, to Deborah Fyfe of IA Seminars for representing my Valuation of Emerging Companies course in various locations around the world.

I would also like to thank Lindsay Bringardner and David Wallman for marketing my patent valuation work through Lexis-Nexis. I am indebted to Larry Plonsker and David Schwartz for publishing several of my articles in Les Nouvelles and Technology Transfer Tactics, respectively.

Facilities Sponsors

Many of my friends have made their lovely offices available for running my courses. The following have been very generous and gracious hosts: Michael O'Shea, Sanford Warren, David Newman, R. Mark Halligan, David Barbash, Kara Cenar, Mark Zyla, Adrian Samuels, Michael Crichton, Piper Redmond, Nicholas Florio, Nader A. Mousavi, Mark Radcliffe, Steven Rizzi, Antoniette Konski, Kevin Spivak, Mark Wicker, Ira Levy, Joel Cohen, Bas Berghuis van Woortman, Maarten Schut, Camilla Kiorboe, Sos Pihl-Poulsen, Matthew Cassie, Jeff Talcott, C. Marc Benoît, Charles-André Caron, Alan Grimaldi, Ronald S. Borod, Jacob Reinbolt, Donald Rudnick, David Bailey, Matt Ritter, Ehud Hausman, Bernie Vogel, Richard

Woodbridge, Li Tao, and Sa'ar Plinner. You have all been of immense help to me.

Lecturers

I am indebted to all of the esteemed professionals who have run courses for the various designations that are offered by the Business Development Academy.

Certified Emerging Company Analyst

Some of the professionals that delivered exceptionally informative webinars made available through the Certified Emerging Company Analyst designation include: Kevin R. Yeanoplos, Frank Tobe, Terry Wohlers, Rod Burkert, Brian A. Ostrow, Mohanjit Jolly, Robert LeBoyer, Anat Segal, Frank Graziano, David Croslin, Theresa Zeidler-Shonat, David Anderson, Dr. Stanley Jay Feldman, John Barrett, William A. Johnston, PJ Patel, Scott M. DeMarco, Andrew E. Goldstein, Neil J. Beaton, Stephen Nagler, David Feldman, David Gitlin, Bart Greenberg, Gregory B. Sneddon, Lloyd George, Peter R. Spirgel, and Dean M. Spear.

Devil's Advocate Auditor

Some of the professionals who made insightful comments during webinars recorded for the Devil's Advocate Auditor designation include: James G. Steiker, F. Eric Fryar, Mark F. Radcliffe, Dennis Cagan, Steven M. Haas, and Peter G. Spanberger, Ph.D.

Certified Patent Valuation Analysts

I would like to thank Paul Hickman, Eric Bensen, Lynda Calderone and Joel Bootzin for delivering exceptional webinars for—and remaining pillars of—the Certified Patent Valuation Analyst designation. The Certified Patent Valuation Analyst designation has been extremely fortunate to have attracted many of the world's leading authorities on patent issues to contribute their time in preparing and delivering world-class webinars. These professionals include: Ron Lurie, Ron Epperson, Matthew Blackburn, Kristie Prinz, Charles R. Macedo, Dale S. Lazar, Timothy Lohse, Thomas L.

Irving, Amanda K. Murphy, Donna M. Meuth, Blaine M. Hackman Ph.D., Chris Sommers, Giulio Corraggio, Patrick Jewik, Mercedes Meyer, PhD., Robert E. Krebs, James B. Altman, Aaron Rabinowitz, Arthur Mitchell, Seiji Niwa, Michael L. Kiklis, Gregory A. Castanias, William Sloan Coats, Peter J. Toren, J. Eric Sumner, Michael R. Annis, S. Gregory Boyd, Thomas J. Scott Jr., Michael W. Caldwell, C R Jacob, John Boyd, Steven P. Fricke, C. Andrew Keisner, Andrew Rosener, Joren De Wachter, Kris Johansen, Ph.D., William J. Cotreau, Martin Lindsay, Margaret Savory, Christopher V. Carani, David Healey, Steven Rizzi, Matthew A. Karlyn, Charles A. Weiss, Larry Schroepfer, Neil Wilkof, John W. Goldschmidt, Jr., Eric Lund, David Case, Dr. Tobias Hahn, Dr. Keith F. Sellers, Paul Hunt, Gill Eapen, Dr. Stanley Jay Feldman, Tyler Maddry, Jeffrey L. Harvey, Michael A. O'Shea, Jake M. Holdreith, Janal M. Kalis, Kevin R. Spivak, P. Branko Pejic, Dr. Sarah Rouse, Emma Wheatley, Ira Jay Levy, Fernando Torres, Robert F. Reilly, Kevin M. Zanni, Erik Verbraeken, Nader A. Mousavi, Kris Williamson, David A. Kelly, Joshua M. Kalb, James G. McEwen, Sidney P. Blum, Stephen G. Harsy PhD., Emily Bauer, Emmett S. Collazo, Christopher Geehan, Ednaldo Silva PhD, Daniel Broderick, Dr. Laurie Kellogg, Kelly Merkel, Paul Rossler, Raymond Van Dyke, James E. Richardson, David L. Newman, J. Derek Mason, Anne L. St. Martin, Ph.D., Cheryl Perkins, Patrick Clusman, Christopher L. Holt, David Clonts, Johannes van Melle, Paolo Foà, Katie McConnell, P. Anthony Sammi, Sha Liu Lecallier, Colin Lamond, Dr. Helen Waugh, Dean D. Gordon, Dr. Jonas Heitto and Robert D. Katz.

Institute for Strategic Negotiations

I learned more than I can describe when working with the following elite negotiators in connection with running programs through the Institute of Strategic Negotiations: Andrew Sherman, Dan Harris, David I. Albin, Charles J. Morton, Jr., Eric Marcks, John McNally, Edwin E. Smith, C. Edward Dobbs, Rosemary Coates, Arthur Mitchell, Ayako Kawano, Kenneth A. MacKay, Richard C. Schoenstein, Michael S. Diamont, James C. Chapman, Carter Klein, Mark F. Miller, Thadford A. Felton, Barry M. Block, Jeffrey A. Carr, Kenneth A. Gerasimovich, Vincent R. Martorana, Christopher G. Dorman, Kevin M. Johnson, Scott Hutton, Dimitris Papakanellou, Tony Canzoneri, D.C. Toedt III, Robert Mihail, Paul Burmeister, Danny Guggenheim, Chad Buelow, Benoit J.P. Flammang,

Rachid Belbachir, Stephanie O'Rourke, Valery Gorokhov, Larry Woodard, Ricardo Resendiz, Frank Vollrath, Timothy R. Croll, Marc Fosse, Jay Zeinfeld, Paul Hartzell, Thomas Earl Patton, Robert C. Long, Stephen C. Jones, David J. Taylor, Rodney L. Benson, Sharie A. Brown, Susan C. Alker, Charles F. McCormick, Heather Stone, Edward Rosenfeld, Dr. Paul Papayoanou, Roger Thorne, Martin H. Abo, Dan Bailey, Jude Kearney, Douglas Kaplan, Savio Chan, and Stuart I. Teicher.

Select Attendees

I have had the good fortune to run courses with thousands of exceptionally intelligent and successful people. (Among the attendees were MIT physicists, NASA rocket engineers, world-renowned venture capitalists, serial entrepreneurs and prolific inventors.) While there are too many past attendees that meet that description to acknowledge here, they made an impact on me that will never be forgotten. I not only learned a great deal from their intellect but continue to derive inspiration from it. A few exceptionally noteworthy individuals that I would like to point out are: Dr. Sinai Yarus, Christopher Martinez, Shlomo Armony, Nicholas Kim, Lampros Fatsis, David Zimmerman, Murray Vince, Michael Patterson, Kishore Sreenivasan, Elias Greenbaum, Joyce Tan, Mauro Villanueva Monzon, Jasmine Kway, Alfred Tan, Lori-Ann Johnson, Konstantinos Diakoumakos, Par Hjalmarsson, Stephen Zavell, Andrew Young, Tim Myers, Michael Tyerech, and Mark Dickson.

Other Critical Associates

Most of my friends have yielded far more value to me—in terms or insight, advice, and introductions—than I have been able to reciprocate. Thus, I must express my appreciation to Ajay Varma, Bruce Berman, Don Boreman, Colleen Henderson, Grace Parke Fremlin, David Jarczyk, Richard Egli, Charles Pershing, Eric Kirsch, Alain Kaiser, Andrew Kaplan, Joseph Choi, David Schuster, Bruce Lehman, Navin Agarwal, Michelle Hermelee, Dick Bransford, Eric Garland, Steve Bortnick, Brian Boyer, Jeffrey Cozzo, Taina Saksa, Joseph O'Shea, Beth Stewart, Michael Gorman, Dorron Mottes, Eefje Vandamme, Dr. Marcin Peksyk, and Lisa Desjardins.

My sincere apologies to the many that I failed to mention.

Index

Company Names

Twitter 16, 52–53, 65, 134–135, 189, 216, 258

Z

Names of People

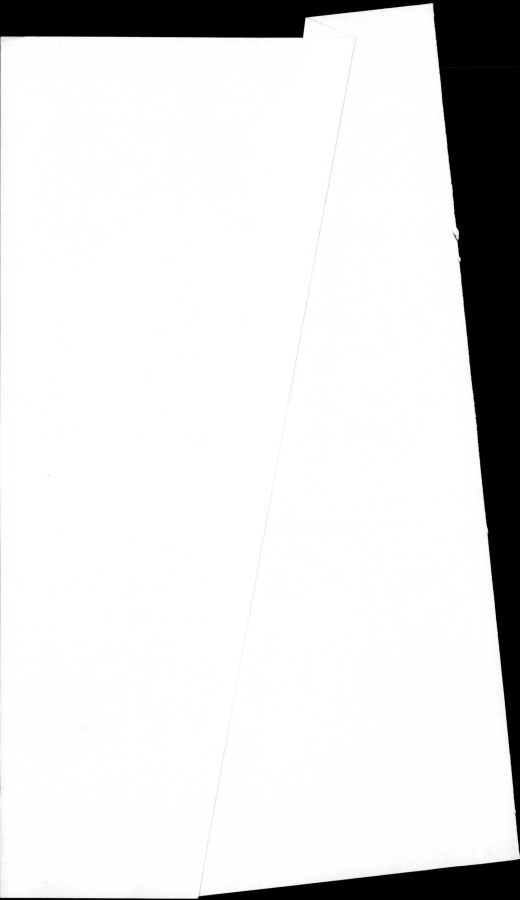